The Putlitz Dossier

WOLFGANG ZU PUTLITZ

THE

PUTLITZ DOSSIER

London

ALLAN WINGATE

First Published by
ALLAN WINGATE (Publishers) LTD.
12 Beauchamp Place, London, S.W. 3.

Copyright 1957

Made and Printed in the Netherlands by
N.V. Drukkerij Levisson, The Hague

First Impression March 1957

PREFACE

THE PUBLICATION OF this book in London means a lot to me, because I hope that it may restore some old ties which had seemed irreparably broken. I know that a number of my British friends failed to appreciate, or even resented, my motives in returning to my home in Eastern Germany, and perhaps my book will serve to dispel their misgivings and allow them to understand me a little better. I want them to know that I remember their friendship and help in my difficulties during the war years and after with deep gratitude. I cannot mention them all, but I would like at least to name Lord and Lady Vansittart, Sir Colville Barclay, Colonel Graham Christie, Mr. and Mrs. "Paul X" and Mr. Anthony Blunt, whose kindness and understanding I will never forget.

WOLFGANG ZU PUTLITZ

East Berlin, August 1956.

CHAPTER ONE

AN ICY WIND swept through the grey December dusk that seeped over the Stahnsdorf Goods Station and seemed to penetrate into one's bones. Shivering on the platform, I watched the shadowy figures of my men unloading their equipment from the train. I was not quite nineteen years old and a lieutenant in the Third Uhlans of the Guard. The year was 1918.

Only two weeks ago my soldiers and I had been in the north of Finland, waiting and wondering whether the long-overdue troopships would ever arrive to take us home to Germany, or whether we were to be left forgotten amidst the snow and ice of a foreign land. The ships had arrived at Helsinki at last and had brought us back to Stettin. Now, at least, we were in Germany again and tomorrow, God willing, would be back in our old barracks in Potsdam.

It was over two years since most of us had set eyes on our own country, and during the last ghastly months of the war we had been isolated and without news. One hope had been uppermost in our minds, and that was to get home as quickly as possible and, by a miracle, before Christmas.

All around me on the dimly lit platform the grey, ghostly figures of my men seethed and struggled with their kit and machine-guns, and heaved the heavy iron field kitchens down from the trucks. Then, quite suddenly, as I stood slapping my half-frozen hands against my sides, I felt two arms about my neck and a warm kiss on my cheek. In the gathering darkness I could only just make out the shoulder tabs of a private. As they were red and not yellow, I knew that their wearer did not

1

belong to my battalion. Then, with a cry, I recognised my brother.

"Gebhard!"

I had last seen him two years ago shortly before I had left for the front, when I had visited my old school, the Knight's Academy at Brandenburg. Then he had been a fifteen-year-old fifth—former in short trousers; now he was an officer cadet in the Fuerstenwalde Uhlans. He explained excitedly how he had managed to find out that my regiment was arriving at Stahnsdorf and for the past two days had been awaiting me.

"You can spend to-night with me in my billet. At least it'll be better than sleeping in some damned cold shed," he laughed. "You can have my featherbed and I'll sleep on the sofa. I don't care if it is too short for me. After all, you deserve a comfortable bed more than I do."

Though I was dog-tired, I slept little that night, for Gebhard and I had much to talk about. How were Father and Mother? How was my sister? Had the Soldier's Council requisitioned our house? I peppered him with questions.

"I don't think anything has changed much," he reassured me. "At any rate, I've got my discharge papers in my pocket and I'm off home to-morrow morning—or is it this morning?" he added with a laugh.

Dawn was breaking when I put the question to him which I knew had to be asked.

"Gebhard, what are we going to do now?"

He looked at me quizzically. "Why, start to learn farming, of course," he said simply. "I suppose father will apprentice us to some estate or other for a couple of years. But what makes you ask?" I realised that so far as he was concerned our future presented no problem at all. He considered it in the natural course of events that we should both become farmers. Yet, for some strange reason, ever since I was a child I had dreaded the idea, secretly hoping that I might find some way of escaping from this traditional duty as heir to my father's estates. I

2

realised now that while my years in the army as a fighting soldier had been wretched enough, at least they offered a means of escape from the inevitable.

"I don't believe I shall ever be a farmer, Gebhard," I stammered.

"What rot!" he laughed. "Don't tell me that you're still barking up that tree?"

It was useless to argue with him, for although we were brothers, our temperaments were utterly different.

But before we finally fell asleep, my brother regarded me seriously and said: "Look here, Wolf, I don't suppose father will die before I've become a full-blown farmer, so if you insist on going your own way, when the time comes I will look after your estates for you."

As so often before, I found myself thinking: "How would you ever cope with life without Gebhard?"

The following morning I marched once more with my regiment to the Potsdam Barracks. As I did so, I could not help remembering how we had set out on that day in 1914, riding proudly on our horses, pennants aflutter, wearing our shining blue ulankas with their smart yellow facings: "The Guards whom the Kaiser loves, who die but never surrender!" Now we were battle-stained and shabby in our field-grey and shapeless steel helmets, as we slouched along horseless in our infantry boots.

"Three lilies, three lilies I plant on my grave, tra-la-la!" we sang.

"How piddling!" commented Prince zu Solms-Baruth, a tall Captain of Horse.

Yet the regiment retained a certain military order, for its old iron discipline had not yet crumbled. The majority of the men were sturdy peasants and, although we already had our Soldiers' Councils, these consisted only of corporals and lance-corporals of long and trusted service.

On the parade-ground outside the Potsdam Palace a large

crowd had gathered to greet their returning Uhlans. But as I looked up at the windows of the palace rising above me in the grey winter mist, I thought of our Imperial Kaiser who had once so proudly taken our glittering parades, now dejectedly sipping coffee by his fireside at Doorn. I had little time for such reflections, however, for soon our old commanding officer, General von Tschirschky und Boegendorf, former A.D.C. to His Imperial Majesty, had us marching once again in goosestep. He stood there, that claret-loving old soldier, moustaches bristling but tears coursing down his weathered cheeks.

When the parade was over, we marched in the gathering twilight to the familiar yellow barracks in the Jaegerallee, there to spend the last poignant days of our military careers.

The following afternoon, while we were preparing for demobilization, we suddenly received orders to fall in on the barrack square in full battle kit. Cursing our luck, we marched to the local railway station where a train stood waiting for us. It took us by the familiar Wannsee-Zehlendorf line to the Potsdam Station in Berlin. The latter's vast entrance hall, usually seething with people, was now dark and deserted. In the strange silence I remember that some trigger-happy soldier let off his rifle, shattering a pane in the glass roof, so that the splinters fell about us as we stood waiting and wondering where we were going. Then the old General's stentorian voice gave us the order to march to the Reichs Chancellery in the Wilhelmstrasse. The latter, when we arrived there, was as dark as the grave, and outside the Chancellery only two lampposts shed a feeble light. For what seemed an age we stood before the great gates stamping our feet against the bitter cold. Then, once again, we hear Tschirschky's voice: "Officers and Soldiers' Councils to the front—March!"

I could see the General standing under one of the lampposts with a fat little man with a pointed beard, wearing a black civilian overcoat and a wideawake hat. Tschirschky talked to him excitedly and almost in a whisper so that I could catch little of their conversation. But I did hear him say: "Now, Herr Evers, you must say something really inspiring to these men."

It was then that I recognised the little man as the Commissar of the People, later to become Reichs Chancellor, Friedrich Ebert. It was possible that the old General really did not know the Commissar's name at that time, but I am inclined to believe that he mispronounced it purposely to stress the gulf that lay between an A.D.C. of His Imperial Majesty and commander of a regiment, and a mere politician.

Ebert, half hidden in the darkness, then addressed us. "Whenever the Fatherland has needed them, the Guards have always been readly in the front line," he shouted. "To-day, perhaps for the last time, you are called to your final and most important duty; one that will write the name of your regiment in letters of gold in the annals of German history. It depends on you whether Germany will perish in these critical days or survive to rise gloriously once more. Never has the German people appealed in vain to the patriotism and courage of its Guards. It is in your hands to help forge a new future for your country which will bestow upon us all peace, liberty and justice, and will unite us as brothers!"

The little man's oratory moved us deeply and filled us with a determination to do whatever he ordered. We listened in silence as he told us that what he called a band of lawless rowdies were set upon spreading chaos and tyranny throughout the country. To crush these elements was our sacred duty. Some of them, a group of Spartacist sailors, had already barricaded themselves in the Imperial Palace.

We were so moved by Ebert's speech that even we officers— most of us counts and barons—determined to prove our spirit of comradeship. For the first time in our lives, as we marched off, each of us seized a couple of heavy ammunition boxes and dragged them after us along the Unter den Linden.

I remember that I was marching next to fat Lieutenant von Kriegsheim, who was clad in a heavy fur coat, the sweat

5

pouring down his face. He was a tremendous roué and a patron of the fashionable bar of the Hotel Bristol. As we passed the dignified porter standing outside the latter, poor Kriegsheim hung his head in embarrassment.

We spent that night sleeping beside our troops in an empty room in the University building which was already crowded with soldiers sleeping or dozing with their rifles beside them.

In the pale light of dawn the following morning we marched off to take up our positions. I myself was in charge of two machine guns mounted behind columns of the cathedral portico, immediately opposite Gate V of the Imperial Palace. In the half light I saw the balcony from which, on August 1st, 1914, Kaiser William II once spoke rather similar words to those of Ebert; "From now on I know only Germans......"

Some early morning beer wagons rumbled slowly past, but when their drivers spotted us they whipped up their great horses and went clattering over the Spree Bridge. Peering ahead of me, I noticed a group of men talking earnestly together at the gate, and among other officers spotted Kriegsheim. Apparently they had been asking the sailors behind the barricade to surrender. Then, suddenly, they turned and ran helter-skelter towards our lines and, as they did so, artillery in the Lustgarten opened fire upon the Palace. A shell sent half the huge Imperial coat-of-arms crashing down exactly on the spot where the little party had been standing a few moments before. Seconds later, my lefthand gunner, Kasperczok, got a shell splinter in his leg, and started to yell with pain. The firing went on for several hours until, at about ten o'clock in the morning, I saw a white flag flutter over the Palace. Shortly afterwards, the gates opened and we marched triumphantly into the courtyard.

We were at once surrounded by sailors surrendering their arms to us. What next, we wondered, as we stacked their rifles? We were as hungry as wolves for we had had no breakfast, and were overjoyed to hear from the sailors that they had found vast quantities of biscuits and chocolate in one of the rooms, which had apparently been stored there at the Empress's orders. In no time at all, victors and vanquished alike were gorging themselves happily and laughing and joking together. But this state of affairs was interrupted suddenly by a shouted order for us to take up firing positions at the windows. Since this order only concerned us soldiers, the sailors suggested we ignored it, but, nevertheless, we dashed to the long windows. The sight below appalled us. A vast crowd like a sinister dark wave rolled towards us across the snowcovered ground from the Lustgarten. Apparently thousands upon thousands of Berliners had overwhelmed our outposts on the Insel Bruecke and were now sweeping up to the Palace. As I stood horrified at my window I could hear their threatening shouts: "Murderers! Bloodhounds! Kill them! Kill them!"

We broke into terrified little groups, whispering among ourselves. What were we to do? In that surging mass advancing upon us many of us had relations or friends. How could we possibly shoot them down? How could we turn our rifles and machine guns on our own kith and kin? We waited trembling, white faced, as the crowd battered down the gates. Some of us then dashed down to the courtyard and were almost overwhelmed by the seething onrush of people. I found myself, with a dozen or so of my men, surrounded by an excited, gesticulating mob. As we stood there in the snow, a little man with a mass of dishevelled hair, clad in a pair of hussar's breeches, a sailor's cap and a civilian overcoat, clambered on to a window ledge, from which he started to harangue the crowd. They cheered his every word. Suddenly, his wild, fanatical eyes lighted on me, and spotted my silver epaulettes.

"Bastards like you are only fit to be hung as tinsel on a Christmas tree," he yelled. "You wait! Your turn will come soon!"

I stood rooted to the spot with horror. Then a hand seized me by the shoulder and, turning, I saw the jolly face of one of the sailors with whom, only a few minutes before, I had been

7

laughing and sharing the Kaiser's chocolate. He was a youngster of about my own age.

"Mate," he whispered, "clear out or you're for it. I wouldn't like to see you conked. You're not such a bad bloke."

"But how?" I whispered, "how?"

"Wait here. Stay where you are," he said, and forced his way back through the crowd.

In a few seconds he returned with some of his friends who seized me and my soldiers, shouting: "Off with them to Kassel!" The mad orator on his window-sill probably thought that the lot of us would either be thrown into prison or would have our throats cut as the sailors manhandled us away. Only after we had passed through the great gates, which a few hours ago we had entered so triumphantly, did I breathe freely again.

I remember that one of my soldiers, Mohrmann, cut his knee badly falling headlong over the shattered remains of the Imperial Eagle still lying in the street. Two of us half carried, half dragged him through the screaming crowd.

"Chuck the swine in the river!" they yelled "Hang them on a lamp-post! Kill them!"

The sailor who had saved me did his best to calm them. "The poor devils haven't had time to be trained politically," he reasoned. "They're only just back from the front. They don't know what's happened."

It seemed hours before the first train for Potsdam pulled into the Boerse Station, and while we waited the young sailor did his best to convert us. But by then I was far too exhausted to grasp what he was talking about and it was not until long afterwards that I realised the full significance of the ghastly situation from which I had escaped.

As the train pulled out and I waved goodbye to my sailor, I remembered too late that I had forgotten to ask him either for his name or address.

That same evening, safe and unhurt, I sat at the great mess table in our barracks in the Jaegerallee with the other officers of my regiment. There was fat Kriegsheim cursing because he had lost his fur coat, and Count Schimmelmann almost in tears because his epaulettes had been ripped off. But, apart from such trifling incidents, nothing serious had happened to any of us, although most of us had horror stories to tell. There were rumours of officers being thrown into the Spree, having their fingers cut off, being trampled underfoot by the mob or brutally murdered. But I cannot remember that any of these stories were substantiated. Since I was the youngest present and no-one took me seriously, I ventured to express my doubts. From that evening onwards I was nicknamed "Red Puttchen".

CHAPTER TWO

I ARRIVED BACK at Laaske on Christmas Eve and for the first time for two years the whole family were together again. The Christmas tree stood in the long yellow garden-room, its tinsel-hung branches winking with the lights of a hundred candles that were reflected in the tall glass doors leading to the conservatory. From the walls looked down the family portraits; elegant ladies in their lace caps and frills and austere generals resplendent in their bemedalled uniforms. The sound of my mother playing the piano drifted in from the softly-lit music room: a sound that carried me back to my childhood days.

In such tranquil surrounding the nightmare of the war faded away and the dreary months spent in the mud and slush of the Wolhynias marshes were forgotten.

According to custom, before we sat down to dinner, presents were distributed in the long drawing-room over the entrance hall to all the children of the workers on Father's estate. On this particular night almost the entire village trooped in: some weeping, others laughing for joy at this first reunion after the war.

"My, how you've grown!" chuckled old Riekel Gragart showing her two fanglike yellow teeth. "So you've come back home to help your dad?"

"Well, we'll see," I told her evasively.

The old crone was right enough in saying that I had grown, for I was literally bursting out of my civilian suit. But as for staying at home, well, I was not prepared to commit myself, even to her.

Over Christmas, in the whirl of eating, drinking and amusement, the vexed question of my future was forgotten. Once, however, things returned to normal and I began accompanying my father on his tours of the stables or drove with him across the snowcovered countryside, he began asking me more and more awkward questions and teasing me in his bluff way.

"Why, you can't even tell a cow from a bull when you see one!" he laughed as we stood looking at his cattle nosing the heaps of fodder.

In his mind my father had somehow managed to link the present revolution with what he disparagingly called the "officer class".

"They'd rather play at soldiers than look after their estates," he growled. "They care nothing and know less about farming and leave everything to their agents. No wonder the workers revolt!"

Father himself was a highly efficient farmer. Winter and summer, not a day passed that he was not out soon after daybreak supervising the farmhands. In fact, farming was his sole interest. So far as I can remember he only went abroad about twice in his life, on trips to Italy with my mother, neither of which I suspect he enjoyed particularly. He scarcely ever read a book or looked at a picture, although he did enjoy my mother's piano playing. But he would not hesitate to interrupt a Chopin nocturne or make her get up from the piano if a dairy foreman needed some disinfectant or a worker in the distillery wanted something from the storeroom. He was almost oblivious of the fact that in the course of years my mother had transformed the ugly, austere castle at Laaske into a show place. He himself was perfectly content sitting on an old horsehair sofa and sleeping on an iron camp bed.

Father hardly ever missed being in the cowshed at milking time, and when we were at home he insisted that we boys went with him. Now that we were back from the war, the old habits were revived. I remember an afternoon when my brother

11

and I stood with Father in the calves' enclosure while he decided whether or not a new bull calf was fit for breeding or should be fattened for market. In the nearby stable the mother started lowing mournfully for her offspring, and all the rest of the cows joined her in chorus. Above the din Father shouted to everyone in general and no-one in particular, expounding upon his pet subject of estates being run by agents. I could see the women in the dairy washing the milk cans and, among them, Anna Busse. When we were children she had been a playmate of ours. Now she had recently married one of the grooms, Heinrich Busse, who like myself was just back from the front, and the pair had moved into a cottage on the estate.

Anna came from the dairy to grumble to my father about a smoking stove in her kitchen.

"Sir, it'll have to be shifted," she complained. "It's quite useless."

"I'll be round to look at it this evening, Anna," my father told her.

When she had gone back to her cans, Father turned to Gebhard and myself. "Boys, I can't cope with all this on my own much longer, it's too much for me. But I refuse to have hired agents," he added meaningly.

I carefully avoided answering him, for it was not merely a question of being uninterested in Anna's stove, but a matter of principle which would affect my entire life. I knew that Father treated his farm-hands exactly as he did us. None of us was allowed to make a move without first consulting him. Now, whether I liked it or not, I was to be included in his scheme of things. Yet it would be unjust to suggest that my father was a sort of ogre, for he was nothing of the kind. Actually, he did not live for himself at all, but for his farming and his family, and one can be certain that in no time at all after that conversation in the cowshed Anna's stove smoked no more. But while I respected him for his conscientiousness, I had not the slightest wish to become part of his system.

Nevertheless, a showdown could not be postponed indefinitely. The climax came one evening when my sister, Armgard, and my little brother, Walter, had been sent to bed, and Gebhard and I were sitting with Father in his study. The old man did not waste words, but told us briefly that he had been in touch with two first-class farmers who had agreed to take us as apprentices.

"Gebhard, you are going to an estate on the Elbwische, where they specialise in breeding cattle," Father said, "and you, Wolfgang, to a farm near Berlin which is famous for its intensive research into seed farming."

In this way, the old man planned that Gebhard and I should be interchangeable on our estates. There was, however, only one snag to his plan and that was that neither of the farms where we were to serve our apprenticeship had a distillery, while there were two on our estates at Laaske and Putlitz. But we could learn all about the distilling of spirits later on.

When Father had finished, a silence fell. One glance at Gebhard was enough to tell me that he was perfectly happy with the plans for his future. So far as he was concerned, he had always had both a liking and a gift for farming. But for my part, I simply could not and would not give in without a fight. Taking my courage in both hands, I said: "Father, you're still a young man and it will be years before I take over Laaske from you. There are heaps of things I want to study before then."

To my relief, he raised no immediate objections and even said that he thought it useful for a farmer to know other things besides farming, although he himself had settled down at Laaske when he was only twenty-three.

"However, there will be time enough for that later on," he added. "First of all, you must learn farming from the bottom up. Then you can go to one or other of the universities. The best would be Goettingen, where they have a good agricultural school as well as the Saxo-Borussia—a decent Corps that will teach you good manners."

My heart was in my boots. The mere thought of the Saxo-

13

Borussia filled me with disgust. I had already had my fill of organised drinking bouts at the official dinners in the officers' mess in Potsdam. I had seen enough of those arrogant, sabre-rattling bores with their slashed faces. I had only to conjure up a picture of my uncle Jochen, who was a typical product of those Goettingen Saxons. Somehow or other I would have to talk Father out of this idea of his.

I started cautiously. "You know, Father, the world's changing fast. This revolution isn't over yet, and, who knows, they may even confiscate our estates. Then what will happen to me if I know nothing except farming? Let me learn about something else so that if we're all kicked out of here I can at least make a living. Let Gebhard learn farming, but let me study something else. After all," I wheedled, "Uncle Wolfgang played soldiers, as you call it, until he was nearly thirty and still became a good farmer."

Father looked at me sharply. "It seems to me," he said, "that you're already infected with these ridiculous modern ideas. All this red rabble should roast in hell! If you think like them, I'll throw you out of the house!"

Struggling to remain calm, I replied: "Father, you've never set eyes on a red in your life. If they are as bad as you say, I wouldn't be here now. I should have been killed by those sailors at the Palace."

But it was useless to argue, for the old man had worked himself into a rage. It was waste of time to tell him that I was just as proud as he was that Putlitz had been our family seat since 1128 and that the Hohenzollerns had come three hundred years later than ourselves to the Brandenburg Mark. I, too, knew that compared with us they were mere newcomers. Now they were gone, but we still owned the old castle of Putlitz on the Stepenitz.

That night in our bedroom I told Gebhard that I was going to run away. "I can't stick it any longer!" I said fiercely. The next morning, without saying good-bye to the family, I packed a

14

suitcase and caught the six o'clock train to Potsdam.

I went there because it seemed the only place to go to. At the barracks I found they were forming a squadron from the remains of my old regiment to send to Upper Silesia to defend the frontier against the Poles. I was accepted immediately, but no sooner had we arrived at our destination than I bitterly regretted my impetuosity. Nothing could have been more depressing than those winter months unless it was the early spring when the snows began to melt and we waded knee-deep in mud. We never saw an enemy, and the only shot I heard fired was loosed off by a soldier, who aimed at a running hare and hit an ox pulling a plough. For a couple of months we hung about menacing the local farmers and their daughters, but still I could not bring myself to eat humble pie and go home. However, in the middle of March, when it was rumoured that we were to be shipped to Munich to fight the Communists, I decided to get out. Never again, I told myself, would I fight my fellow-countrymen. Luckily for me, my major, Baron von Esebeck, was a distant cousin of my mother's, and since he had been bombarded with letters from home begging him to make me see sense, I had no difficulty in getting him to discharge me.

CHAPTER THREE

WESENDAHL WAS THE name of the estate which my father had chosen for me, and its owner was Herr Schmidt. The latter's father was a self-made man who had passed on his property to his son. I was immediately conscious of the vast difference between great estates such as ours, run for hundreds of years under almost feudal conditions, and a property like Wesendahl, organised purely as a business concern. There were no traditional, patriarchal or other human ties between Schmidt and his farm-hands. While he overworked them mercilessly, they retaliated by robbing him whenever they got the chance.

Schmidt was a fierce martinet who was not above slashing his workmen across the face with his riding whip, while they did not hesitate to go for him with a pitchfork. I found the whole atmosphere of the farm little different from the barrack square at Potsdam, with its red-faced, bawling sergeants. At Wesendahl, the foreman shouted at the workers, the supervisors at the foreman, and Wilhelm Schmidt at everyone, including his wife. In such conditions it was small wonder that the labour was constantly changing and consisted mostly of shifting, demoralised, Berlin cockneys and a whole army of Polish men and women, who did not understand a word of German.

My arrival coincided with the beginning of the great famine in the cities, and the nearby villages were overrun by swarms of black marketeers from Berlin. Everything that was not clamped or riveted to the ground was stolen. These conditions were by no means improved by Schmidt, who, like many others, took on

16

groups of volunteers from the Corps Luettwitz—later to become famous through the Kapp *putsch*—who were supposed to mount guard over the potato stores and granaries, and who indiscriminately blazed away with their rifles all night.

To give him his due, Schmidt was an extraordinarily efficient farmer who grew excellent crops and ran his farm on thoroughly economic lines. I could not help but feel that, if my father had taken a leaf out of his book, we should all have been rolling in money. But for Father, making money was a matter of secondary importance. He lived only to improve Laaske; for the pleasure of seeing the pretty cottages standing in the shade of the gnarled and ancient lime trees. If he had any ambition at all, it was that people should say: "If conditions were as good everywhere as they are on the Laaske estate there would be no social democracy in Prussia."

The brutal atmosphere at Wesendahl depressed me almost to the point of suicide, so that my dislike for farming grew daily. But while I knew I would never be happy as a farmer, I had no idea how to escape. After all, I was the heir to Laaske and, with my upbringing, to throw over my inherited duties would have seemed like desertion. What, I asked myself, would old Riekel Gragart, Anna Busse and the rest of them think of me if I suddenly left them to the mercies of some strange agent? Yet it was good to know that I had two brothers whose name was Putlitz. Gebhard I was certain would uphold the family tradition, and there were times when I longed to hand over to him my rights as heir. But, whatever happened, I was determined to leave Wesendahl.

As often as I could I made the short journey to Berlin, where, to begin with, I spent most of my time with old school friends and pals from my regiment. The Cavalry Division of the Guard had at that time found quarters in the Schadowstrasse, near the Unter den Linden, on the first floor of the Union Club. Here they had furnished their club with the best pieces from the various messes. On the walls hung huge battle pictures of the

Bismarck wars and portraits of generals in their splendid uniforms, and the dining tables glistened with silver engraved with the cyphers and royal crown of Prussia, as well as rosebowls and épergnes presented to the Guards by long forgotten Kings and Emperors. The food was good and relatively cheap.

Sooner or later in this club one met everyone one knew. From there I used to wander on to the bar of the Bristol Hotel, in the Unter den Linden, which was particularly popular with the younger set. On Sunday mornings the Bristol bar was packed to its doors, and I shall always remember one such occasion when I found myself sitting in a corner near the fair-haired Rochow, who had with him Lya de Putti, the film actress, with her fantastically long black eyelashes. He grinned acros at me with his staring, puglike eyes. Since I had last seen him he had inherited an estate of some 20,000 acres, and now divided his time between his castles in Stuelpe and Plessow.

"Why, Puttchen, you old idiot," he called to me, "you haven't got on your red tie this morning!" Then he asked me to his table to join him and Lya in a bottle of champagne. Soon the tubby little Kriegsheim came and sat down with us. But that morning he was not at his best, for across the room, between two strange men, sat the beautiful Fern Andra, with whom he was passionately in love.

"Tell me, Tubby, who are those two?" I asked.

"The one on Fern's right is Prince Phillip of Hess, a nephew of the Kaiser," he said. "The fat one on his left is a commoner in some infantry regiment who later became Ruetger's echelon commander. I think his name is Hermann Goering."

I soon became utterly bored by the Berlin set, the Rochows, Buelows, Hohenlohes, Fuerstenbergs and the rest of them, for by then they were little better than museum pieces. So in the end, when I could escape from Wesendahl, I studied at the High School for Agriculture and, to my surprise, Father raised no objection. My real ambition, however, was to go to

18

a university because I was becoming increasingly aware of the narrowness of my horizon. I felt that I would never amount to anything until I had broadened my outlook. So, in the summer of 1919, I matriculated, although as I was still not living in Berlin I could not attend many lectures.

It was about this time that, somewhat against the wishes of the family, I made friends with a cousin of mine who had married a certain Herr von Raumer. The latter was one of the few men, in my opinion, who really understood the situation in Germany in those days. Before the war he had been chairman of a rural district council, but later had joined the great electrical combine of A.E.G. He often boasted that it was largely due to him that the revolution did not entirely destroy social life in Germany. Indeed, it was in his house in 1918 that Walter Rathenau, the head of A.E.G., and Legien, the boss of the Trades Unions, negotiated the so-called *Arbeitsgemeinschaft* between the employers and the workers, which prevented all the worst strikes in those days.

Raumer liked to show his friends the deep, red leather armchair in which Legien had sat drinking red wine and smoking a cigar, while he and Rathenau discussed the nation's future. Indeed, Raumer still insisted that the success of those negotiations was mainly due to the excellence of the wine and cigars he had provided.

By the time that I knew him, Raumer was not only Managing Director of A.E.G. but a Deputy of the Reichstag for the German Liberal Party, and for a while Minister of the Treasury and Economics. He lived in magnificent style in a flat in the Koenigin Augusta Strasse—now the Reichpietsch—in the old West End of Berlin. It was beautifully decorated, mainly with Chinese works of art which he had inherited from his father-in-law, the German Ambassador to Pekin, and most of these treasures had come from the Imperial Palace during the Boxer Rising.

From the moment that I first went to Raumer's flat, I stepped

19

into a new and exciting world. I met there an extraordinary cross-section of society, as well as many famous people whose names I had known only through the newspapers. Walther Rathenau was often there, and I would sit for hours in reverent silence while he held forth. Another fascinating visitor to Raumer's flat was Krassin, who came to negotiate with the German Electrical Industry for the electrification of the Soviet Union. The Peoples' Commissar would arrive for dinner in an immaculate dinner jacket; a shrewd, polished man of the world. Sometimes he was accompanied by a fellow countryman, Lunatscharski, and the latter's wife, always dressed in the latest Paris fashion.

At Raumer's I met, too, the genial French industrialist, Loucheur, the somewhat inaccessible Governor of the Bank of England, the bearded Montague Norman, the boyishly naïve dollar kings from America, and the swaggering German financial magnates. The fortunes of those who frequented Raumer's drawing-room must have amounted to milliards.

From the very beginning I was treated like a son by Raumer, although I never quite succeeded in breaking through his reserve. He was a little hunched man with fine-cut features. His left eye was artificial as the result of a shooting accident, and into his good eye he screwed a monocle as a sort of accompaniment to his witticisms.

"What they call public opinion, my dear Wolfgang, is nothing but the rattling of the boards that people have in their heads for brainboxes!" he once lectured me.

He had a wholesome contempt for mankind that led him to be called the Prussian Voltaire. Nevertheless, he understood my own particular problems, and, at twenty, I felt flattered that such a man should take me seriously.

"It is too much, my dear boy, to expect your august father to understand the world to-day," he told me. "You will have to extricate yourself from Laaske and stand on your own feet. I, too, had to create my own life. Quite obviously I would never

20

have been successful had I looked at life through the eyes of a narrow-minded squire."

While I understood all this only too well, I was forced to point out that if I gave up farming against my father's wishes it was unlikely that he would provide me with a penny.

"There are always ways and means," Raumer assured me, "and I will help you to find a job."

Several months after this conversation, I received a telegram at Wesendahl that read: "Would be pleased to see you here next Wednesday evening. May be very important for your future. Raumer."

I arrived at the flat to find that most of the guests present were men old enough to be my father. Before dinner Raumer took me aside and said: "Make the best of yourself." But in spite of his advice, I sat silent throughout the superbly cooked dinner. Only afterwards in the drawing-room did I do my best to appear polite, hastening to fill empty glasses with claret and to light cigars.

In the historic Legien armchair sat the famous Hugo Stinnes. In his somewhat shabby dinner-jacket and with his untidy black beard, he did not cut much of a figure. Yet I knew him to be the greatest genius in German commerce and industry; the financial wizard into whose lap billions poured. For most of the evening he sat there with his eyes half closed, listening while the others talked. But as I helped him into his coat in the hall, he turned to Raumer and asked: "Is this the young man whom you told me about the other day?" Then he looked me up and down and said with a wry smile: "My boy, I wish I were your age. The whole world is open to you."

Raumer, I remember, made some flattering remarks about my intelligence and family background. When the great man had gone, my host said: "Stinnes likes people with old names and good manners. I think you've taken his fancy."

Again several months went by before I heard any news. Then I received a letter from Stinnes offering me a job with the Hugo

21

Stinnes Steamship and Export Company in Hamburg, which was managed by the old man's second son, Hugo. Even the salary was almost enough to live on.

For the time being even my father had to give in, since his chief threat of cutting off my allowance would no longer work. He did so with good grace. "Go and try your luck. It makes no difference to me. Everyone has to learn by experience, and I see no harm in your trying your hand at business. One day you'll find out that you don't fit in with those pepperjacks, then you'll come running back to me," he chuckled with confidence.

CHAPTER FOUR

IN THOSE DAYS there were quite a number of young men like myself, born of noble families, who were trying to break into the world of commerce. Few of them so far as I can recall ever became successful business men, although one or two of them managed to make their fortunes, while some conveniently married into the rich industrial families. But for the most part they dabbled in the Black Market or became out and out spivs. One way or another, it was easy enough to make a living in Hamburg in the early twenties, for the jumped-up trading companies were only too glad to take on young, enterprising noblemen and ex-officers from crack regiments. In fact, the Stinnes firm on the Jungfernstieg was crowded with them.

The old Hanseatic aristocracy, however, looked upon us with a certain amount of suspicion, and although we were asked to their dances and dinner parties, few of us ever managed to get jobs with them.

I was not particularly thrilled by my new appointment, and soon became bored writing invoices and sticking price tabs on tawdry images of saints destined for the Latin-American market. But I put up with it all because at least life in Hamburg was freer and gayer than anything I had yet experienced. I congratulated myself that I had escaped from the Guards' Cavalry Club and the officers' cliques, and that even if the Hanseatic merchants seemed a little bourgeois in their sumptuous villas along the Alster and the Elbe, the atmosphere was a good deal less stultifying than that of Berlin.

I lodged in a charming house in Fonteney, not more than five minutes' walk from the Lombarde Bridge, and through the trees in the garden I could see the swans and the boats on the river. My "landlady", Frau Waechter, was a woman of seventy and a member of the old Hamburg society. Her husband had left her a fortune, which by the time that I met her had been swallowed up by inflation. She lived for her collection of Pekinese dogs and smoked endless cigarettes through a long ivory holder. Her passion was Bridge, and every day she kept open house to her friends who came to play far into the night. She entertained not only her women friends but also most of the big business men in Hamburg who played for vast stakes. Sometimes I found myself taking a hand, and I had a suspicion that Frau Waechter's guests saw to it that their hostess won.

It was not long before I found myself being invited to the houses of all the leading families in Hamburg. Some of them were absurdly pretentious and vulgar, but a great many of them were veritable museums with fabulous art collections, for at that time the French Impressionists were the rage and the drawing-rooms of the houses I visited were crowded with Manets, Renoirs, Sisleys and Cézannes. "Culture" was in vogue and concert soirées the fashion, and the rich Hamburg merchants vied with one another to engage the finest singers and musicians from all over Europe to entertain their guests. The tables at their parties groaned with food, and the wine literally flowed like water. Yet through this crazy world stalked the spectre of Inflation. The salary which one drew at the beginning of a week became worthless seven days later, and the bulk of the people had not enough money to buy even the bare necessities of life. At the university where I went for lectures the professors talked to us endlessly of trusts and combines, and their usefulness in the national economy. Yet I had only to look at the Stinnes combine where I worked to realise that theory and practice simply did not match.

It was not long before I realised that I was no more happy working for Stinnes than I had been on Herr Schmidt's farm at Wesendahl. I think I became aware of this one morning when I took the mail up to Hugo Stinnes's office. Known to us all as "Junior", he was sitting at his desk with the telephone receiver clamped to his ear. As I came into the room he waved to me to wait. He was on the line to London, and while he talked I gazed out of the window on to the Jungfernstieg. By contrast with life outside, the vast office of my boss seemed cold and soulless with its huge safe, wooden shelves laden with files, its maps and ships' models. The only human touch was the photograph of Hugo's wife which stood on his desk.

"Junior" was excited as he shouted into the telephone. "What, as soon as that? Are you sure? You mean, the French won't listen to reason?"

So far as I could gather, the reply from London did nothing to reassure him.

"But don't you people in London realise that you're cutting your own throats? It can't possibly be in their interest for the French to seize all the coal as well as the steel industry in the Ruhr! I can't believe it. Damn it, it sounds like blackmail to me! But if you're quite sure........."

Whoever Hugo was speaking to in London was evidently quite sure.

"Thanks, anyhow, for your information. But keep it under your hat so as not to upset the market," Stinnes advised.

The conversation was over, but Hugo was still not ready to open his mail, and a second later he picked up the receiver again and asked for Tillmann, the Hamburg banker.

"Hullo, my dear Tillmann, how are you?" he purred. "Look, this is important—I know the market hasn't opened yet, so will you please cancel my last night's order? Instead spread the fifty thousand about. Some in London and the remainder between here and Frankfurt so as to avoid any panic."

Tillmann apparently was a little shaken, but Stinnes quickly reassured him and, having done so, rang off.

As he looked through his letters, I longed to tell him what I

25

thought of such shady speculations against the mark which brought him huge profits at his country's expense. Yet on reflection I wondered if I would not have done exactly the same thing had I been in his shoes. In my small way I was already operating on the Black Market, for, like everyone else, thanks to Inflation, my weekly salary was spent as soon as it was paid to me. Placed as I was, I was able to provide useful inside information about the stock market to my old army friends and, among them, Count Schimmelmann von Ahrensburg, who was rolling in money. Quite a lot of these friends needed waggon-loads of potassium and other fertilizers for their farms, and through the chemical department of Stinnes I was able to oblige them. With the commissions I made on these deals I gambled on the stock market and, through a friend in the Tillmann Bank, I bought foreign currency, exchanging it for Reichsmarks only when I needed them. In those days it was quite simple for someone like myself, sitting in Stinnes's office, to make money on the side. Indeed, in the winter of 1923, when the dollar was worth billions of paper marks, I made six hundred per cent profit in one deal over Gold Loan certificates. But, in spite of this, I was unhappy with the Stinnes Combine. I felt like a parasite and longed to escape to a job in which I would be doing some good. By now, my ambition was to become a diplomat, but in order to do so I realised that I must finish my university education and take the necessary degrees. To this end, I threw up my job with Stinnes and, in the early spring of 1924, took my degree in Economics at Hamburg University, and then handed in my application to the Foreign Office in Berlin.

CHAPTER FIVE

IN ORDER TO get into the Foreign Office it was necessary for me to know two languages besides my own. Thanks to a Swiss governess I spoke French fluently, but as I knew hardly a word of English I made up my mind to go to England. Luckily, I had no need to ask my father for any money, for, as a result of my flutters on the Black Market, I had several hundred pounds to my credit. With these safely hidden in a cigar box in my suitcase, I set off for London. I was also armed with a number of letters of introduction, one of the most useful being from Raumer to the London correspondent of a German newspaper, whom I will call Paul X. Although he had served in the German army during the war, he had been partly educated in England, and his wife, Gabrielle, was the daughter of a well-known French painter and herself a talented artist. So neither of these two charming people was looked upon as being entirely German by their English friends at a time when even the German Ambassador in London was to some extent under a cloud.

I was not a little shocked to find how unpopular we Germans still were in England. When I called with my letters of introduction I was sometimes coldly received, and on occasions the front door was firmly shut in my face. In retrospect, it seems almost fantastic that amongst those who refused to receive me in 1924 was Lady Redesdale, one of whose daughters later married Oswald Mosley, and another, Unity Mitford, became completely infatuated by Hitler. Yet it is true to say that in those days it was pretty well impossible for a German to be accepted into English society.

In London, the German Ambassador, Sthamer, and his wife, who were old friends of Frau Waechter, took me under their wing. They both came from Hamburg where they had a lovely house near the Lombarde Bridge. The Counsellor of the Embassy was Count Albrecht Bernstorff, who came from Schleswig-Holstein, and whose brother and I had served together in the same regiment. It was Bernstorff who advised me not to become involved in the hectic life of post-war London but to go to Oxford, where I could meet plenty of young Englishmen of my own age. At that time there were only two German students—youngsters from Cologne—up at Oxford, and I had the impression that Bernstorff planned to use me as a sort of exhibit at the University.

On a beautiful spring morning he drove me to Oxford in his car and, among others, introduced me to a young Frenchman called Michel Leroy-Beaulieu, who was then up at Balliol. Now, I believe, he is an ambassador somewhere in South America. Then, he was fascinated to meet his first German and, in turn, introduced me to his friends, most of whom were English. I found it desperately hard to get to know them, not only because we had no common language, but because the majority of them were still deeply prejudiced against "the Huns". They looked upon me as a a sort of wild beast who ate his young! But gradually I overcame their prejudices and managed to break through their reserve, and because there was no-one with whom I could talk German, my English improved rapidly. Some of these undergraduates I remember are now famous men, such as the novelist Graham Greene.

I do not think that at any time in my life, before or since, have I been so happy as I was at Oxford in the early twenties. In those days, it had yet to become commercialised and was still a lovely, tranquil, university city; a paradise of tall spires and lush meadows through which the Isis meandered lazily. In those days, too, the undergraduates still lived spaciously and in almost patriarchal style, waited on by their "scouts" in their comfortably furnished rooms. Most of them owned fast motor-cars in which they raced about the countryside and up to London, and although my own parents were well-to-do and I was accustomed to good living, the luxury in which these young Englishmen lived left me aghast. Only the food they ate appalled me. While their dining tables were laid with beautiful silver, handsome candlesticks and Waterford glass, the food served seemed to consist of dried-up fish, watery meat and pap-like puddings of indescribable nastiness.

At Oxford there seemed to be no subject under the sun that one could not study; Egyptian mythology, Assyrian architecture, Tibetan flora, Mexican fauna, Chinese philosophy and French post-Impressionist painting. But I think what impressed me most was the astonishing classical knowledge of these young Englishmen. I had been to the Brandenburg Ritter Akademie, where I had taken my finals, but I was still unable to read either Latin or Greek without a dictionary. Yet, here in Oxford, young men sat in the shade of a Himalayan cypress or weeping willow by the river bank reading their Homer, Sophocles or Ovid as easily as they would read Galsworthy, Bennett or Michael Arlen. By comparison with them, my Kriegsheims, Schimmelmanns, and Rochows were little better than barbarians. Beside them, even the more cultured specimens of Berlin and Hamburg Universities were uncouth louts. The English boys were far more erudite than their German contemporaries, and their outlook infinitely more catholic. As for their manners, well, I hesitated to draw any comparisons. Yet they lacked the thorough and expert knowledge, as well as the tremendous power of concentration of the Germans, and most of them were hopelessly and helplessly impractical. I doubt whether many of them could have fried an egg or told the difference between wheat and barley.

With Michel I often used to laugh about these gilded young Englishmen and argue whether they really were as effete and degenerate as they appeared. I shall always remember one night

29

at Oxford when Michel and I sat around the fire in Anthony Russell's rooms. Anthony was the nephew of the then Duke of Bedford and a grandson of Sir Odo Russell, the famous British Ambassador in Berlin in the days of Bismarck. He loved Burgundy and always kept a splendid cellar. While we sat drinking one of his favourite vintages, Michel started to air his views.

"You Englishmen," he harangued Anthony, "have two distinct sides to your characters. One is barbarian, which you inherited from Wolfgang and his lot: the other—the cultured one—you got from us. Yet, oddly enough, that doesn't apply in your case, or, for that matter, in any of our cases, because we are cultured. Both of you are far closer to me than any scavenger on the Paris streets with whom I have nothing in common except our language."

Full of Burgundy, Michel grew more and more talkative and excited. Suddenly he jumped up and took down Anthony's shotgun which was hanging on the wall. "Any war between us is unthinkable! Let the common people shoot each other, but not us!" he shouted. Then he jabbed the gun in my ribs. "Wolfgang, you old boche, swear that to me on your word of honour."

"Whatever happens, I promise you that," I swore, edging away from the gun.

Yet, secretly, I did not quite agree with Michel. Certainly I was much more in sympathy with him and Anthony than with any of my friends in the Guards' Club. But there were other things that I had in common with old Riekel Gragert from Laaske and my sailor from the Imperial Palace; things that Michel did not understand. When I tried to explain this to him, he roared with laughter.

"You always have been and always will be an incorrigible old boche—boorish and provincial! I must take you to France to broaden your mind!"

Michel was a good as his word, and at the end of that term

he insisted that I should go with him to France. My first visit to Paris was a wonderful experience that I shall never forget. But that spirit of international understanding about which Michel had spoken was not quite as marked as he would have had me believe. Soon after we arrived in Paris, he shamefacedly had to admit that his family were none too anxious to meet me. As it was high summer, the family flat in the Avenue Kléber was closed and Michel's parents were living in their country place near Montpellier. For a time we camped out in the flat, while Michel tackled the problem of my meeting his family. Finally, I was invited to Montpellier, but no sooner had I arrived than it was made perfectly clear to me that I could not stay long, since, as Michel explained, the presence of a German was causing gossip amongst the servants and villagers. So, after a day or so, I set off with Michel and his two brothers for a fortnight's tour of France. Before we started, it was decided that I should be introduced everywhere as Michel's "Norwegian friend from Oxford", and I gave him my solemn undertaking not to admit that I was a "boche".

"Unless you want to sleep out of doors," he told me, "you must promise to do that."

At the end of our trip, when I bade good-bye to Michel in Paris, I said to him: "One day, Michel, you will be Ambassador in Berlin and I in Paris. Then we can see to it that there will be no more wars!"

I could not drag myself away from Paris. I was bewitched by it, and only left when I had practically run out of money. I journeyed home by way of Amsterdam, and then went to stay with an old army friend who lived in Haarlem. In the end, I was forced to pawn my gold wrist watch which I had bought with the money I had made out of my deals with Schimmel-mann, so that I arrived back in Berlin in October 1924 without a penny.

*　　*　　*

31

Since I had still heard nothing from the Foreign Office and did not want to go home, I called on Raumer, who promptly gave me a job as his private secretary with a salary of four hundred marks a month. Working in the central offices of the A.E.G. in the Cornelius Strasse, I had ample opportunity of watching the intrigues and struggles for power that were going on in Germany. Raumer, as representative of the electrical industry, was up to his eyes in it all. He was a recognised master of intrigue, so much so that, one day, when I was looking for him in the Reichstag Building, I was told: "Deputy Raumer is plotting in room 203." That he plotted with benefit to his companies and profit to himself was proved by the fact that the following summer he left his flat in the Koenigin Augusta Strasse and acquired a magnificent villa in the Grunewald.

While I was with Raumer, I had the chance, too, to learn a little about "big business' and watch the jungle war that was being waged between private enterprise and the great industrial combines. It was my job to write the reports of the battle for Raumer, and one did not need to be particularly brilliant to understand what was happening. I soon realised that all the high falutin talk about working for the nation's interests was so much nonsense and that every man was for himself. The strongest, richest and most ruthless were inevitably the winners.

Once again, what I saw filled me with revulsion and I was determined to escape from it all. But still no word came from the Foreign Office. When I went home to Laaske, Father refused to believe that I had set my heart on becoming a diplomat.

"The best thing you can do is to stay here," he told me. Yet I had the feeling that he knew I had outgrown his old feudal world. I think he was reconciled to the fact and his disappointment in me was somewhat mollified now that Gebhard had finished his training and had taken over the management of his Gut Burghof property in Putlitz. He was delighted, too, that Walter, my youngest brother, had also decided to become a

32

farmer. Nevertheless, he was far from enthusiastic at the prospect of a Putlitz of monarchist Brandenburg descent becoming a servant of what he called the "Red Republic". However, he was forced to admit that that was better than being a "shopkeeper", for, in his eyes, there was still a certain *cachet* in being a diplomat.

Now that the mad days of Inflation were over, life in Berlin became more normal and I threw myself into it with gusto. Once more I went the round of parties and, instinctively perhaps, picked those at which I could meet foreign diplomats and the heads of the Foreign Office. The Secretary of State, von Schubert, then lived in the Margaretenstrasse, almost opposite Frau von Dircksen, the mother of the man who was later to become Hitler's Ambassador to Moscow and London. Frau von Schubert was a cousin of Frau von Raumer, and so her house was always open to me. But I was chiefly interested in the Foreign Minister's wife, Frau Kaete Stresemann, who had a penchant for young people and who took me under her wing.

But of all the foreign diplomats, the one who attracted me most was Monsieur de Margérie, who lived in the beautiful embassy on the Pariser Platz. His daughter-in-law, Jennie, was heiress to one of the greatest fortunes in France, her family being the biggest shareholders in the Crédit Lyonnais. At that time she was not only one of the most charming and elegant girls in Berlin society but also the most intelligent and cultured. These visits to the Margérie family soon began to cause gossip in the Horse Guards' Club, and, because of them, I was in the Guards' Club, and, because of them, I was officially hauled over the coals by Rittmeister von Heyden, the Chairman.

One evening at supper, in the presence of many of the members, he confronted me with my behaviour.

"Herr von Putlitz," he said pompously," we wish to draw your attention to the fact that according to our rules none of our members is allowed to associate with subjects of enemy States except on official business. It has come to our notice that you are not only a frequent visitor to the Italian Embassy but also to the French."

I replied that for anyone like myself who was joining the Foreign Office it was only normal that I should behave as I did.

"But you are not yet in the Foreign Office," von Heyden pointed out," and we insist that you stop behaving in this way at once. You must realise that in this Club we preserve all the discipline of our Officers' Corps."

The whole thing was so ridiculous that I am afraid I was rather rude to the Chairman, who threatened to call me before the Committee.

"Do as you please," I told him. "But here's my resignation."

With that I bowed and left the Club without saying good-bye to anyone, and have never set foot in it since.

In May, 1925, I passed my languages examination for the Foreign Office and, in the following July, on a lovely sunny morning, I walked through the doors of 73—75, Wilhelm-strasse to report for duty.

CHAPTER SIX

THE GREAT IRON-HINGED door of the main entrance of the Foreign Office was only opened on special ceremonial occasions. The ordinary visitor had to ring, and after a brief pause a small wicket would be opened. Immediately inside one was confronted by two life-sized statues of the Sphinx, sculpted in granite, which lent an air of mystery to the interior of the vast hall. Behind the Sphinxes was a white entrance hall lit by a bronze chandelier, and to the right a wide marble straircase swept up to the first floor where were the reception rooms, offices of the Minister and Secretaries of State as well as of the Personnel Section. The corridors were laid with deep-piled red carpet and the rest of the furniture was equally luxurious. For this reason this floor was called the "Vintage Wine Section", while the other offices, which were old-fashioned and furnished with spartan simplicity, were known as the "Saloon Bar Section".

It was in the former section that I found myself on that morning in July, 1925, together with fifteen other newly appointed attachés. As we talked together, we congratulated one another, for over three hundred had applied to join the Foreign Office and of that number we were the only ones to be selected. Many of us knew one another already, for we had met once or twice during the examinations.

Looking over the little group of men I realised with what care the Foreign Office had chosen us so as to give no one party or particular vested interest an excuse to say that it had been neglected. Naturally, none of us could be described as coming from the working class, but within these limits the Foreign Office had made a very careful choice. We came from all over Germany, and no two of us belonged to the same category. We were the sons of, amongst others, a Rhineland industrialist, a Hamburg shipowner, an executive of I. G. Farben, a newspaper publisher in Saxony, a Bremen businessman, a Bavarian banker, and even a Mecklenburg parson who belonged to the Social Democratic Party. Altogether there were four noblemen among us. Only two of us could be properly described as Junkers— Count Strachwitz and myself. But even we had rather different backgrounds, for Rudi Strachwitz came from a strong Catholic family in Silesia, whereas the Putlitzes are Protestant to the backbone.

For the first year we were put through a course of instruction that was like a school curriculum. Every day we went to class and sat down with nicely sharpened pencils to listen to lectures or hold seminars and write essays. Sometimes we made interesting educational trips into the country, going, for instance, for several days to the Ruhr to see how the steel combines were run. By the end of the course we were most of us on very friendly terms. Later, I was to discover that this sense of *esprit de corps* was illusory, and that anyone who lost favour in high places was quickly dropped by the rest. To a certain extent we looked upon ourselves as the élite of the German Nation: we were the pillars of the State. Political parties and ministers might come and go, but we remained. We belonged to the indispensable apparatus of government on which everything depended. Also, we were pampered, which encouraged us in our delusions of grandeur. In fact, no other section of the administration under the Weimar Republic was so divorced from social reality or so opportunist as the high level officials of the Foreign Office.

Having completed my training, I was appointed to our Embassy in Washington. The trip from Hamburg to New York lasted ten days, during which time, apart from putting in briefly at Southampton and Cherbourg, one saw little but the endless expanse of the ocean. The first sight of New York, as the tops of the skyscrapers emerge over the horizon, is unforgettable. It seemed to me incredible that these buildings were the work of man, for they rose out of the sea like the towers of Atlantis.

Despite the hurry and bustle, the same air of unreality pervades one's first hours in New York. Only gradually did I become accustomed to the great canyons of streets, the seething crowds and the deafening noise. American civilisation struck me as at once wonderful and hideous. Behind the glittering sky signs, I was aware of a cold and impersonal atmosphere that was slightly terrifying. Tradition, sentiment and the finer feelings seemed to have little place in this city of steel and concrete. I felt that the dollar ruled in New York and the individual counted for less than his bank balance.

In the year 1927, the United States was at the peak of the great American boom. Money was as easy to come by as ice cream. There was a market for everything, from gleaming automobiles to frigidaires that were rolling off the conveyor-belts in an endless stream. The so-called "American miracle" was providing a standard of living that rocketed up and up every day. Soon, they said, even the most humble lavatory attendant would have his Ford in the garage and his refrigerator in the kitchen.

Yet, for me, New York, despite its confusing immensity, made sense. It had grown to be what it was. Washington, on the other hand, beautifully and extravagantly laid out, struck me as being a curiously artificial city. Its main *raison d'être* is that it is the centre of government. There is neither industry nor market, not even a resident population. I came to think of it as an enormous modern hotel in which the faces changed all the time. There were new ones at the opening of every session of Congress.

Social life in Washington is strictly pragmatic. If one is invited out, it is for a reason, whether it be a millionairess from the Middle West trying to find a titled husband for her daughter, a journalist looking for a scandal, a senator pursuing an intrigue or a big-business man after a million-dollar contract.

In these circumstances, the foreign embassies in Washington are greater centres of attraction than they are in the capitals of other countries—and in 1927 this was so for a special and irresistible reason. For then the Americans were still suffering under Prohibition, and, while gangsters and racketeers made fortunes selling hooch on the Black Market, we, as diplomats, could import any and every kind of alcoholic drink.

What we had to offer was genuine and plentiful, so it was small wonder that invitations to foreign embassies were much sought after.

Many of the young American attachés whom I met at this time later rose to occupy high posts in the U.S. Foreign Service after the war. I still look back with pleasure on the many happy evenings we spent in my flat on Massachusetts Avenue, little thinking that less that twenty years later many of these young men would emerge as rulers of my own country on the U.S. Commission in Germany. I still count them as my friends, but only after long and bitter experience have I grasped the fact that friendships such as these have not the smallest influence upon the history of nations.

One of my most stimulating memories of America in those days belongs to a misty evening in late autumn on Lakehurst Airfield in New Jersey, whither we had travelled to see the arrival of the first Zeppelin to cross the Atlantic. There were tens of thousands of spectators at Lakehurst. The airship was four hours late. The sky gradually darkened and the weather became more unsettled, until finally it began to rain. The hot-dog stands sold out, but still the crowd waited. Then, at last, we heard the distant drone of the airship's motors. A searchlight pierced the mist, and in a few minutes the great silver hull of the Zeppelin hovered majestically over the landing field, now so brilliantly illuminated that it was like day. I saw the black, red and gold insignia of the German Republic, and the letters *ZR3 Friedrichshafen*. An American band struck up the German National Anthem, but the music was quickly drowned by the great roar that went up from the crowd.

As representative of the Embassy, we were the first to go forward to greet the Captain, Doctor Hugo Eckener, who was looking down from the open window of the airship like a ruffled old bear. Frau Kiep, wife of the Consul, a great, blonde giant of a woman, offered him a bouquet of roses.

"For goodness' sake, let's leave all that till I get the ship anchored to her mast!" Eckener shouted. So far as I know, Frau Kiep never managed to hand over her roses.

There were other scenes in the U.S.A. during those years which gratified one's patriotism as a German. I shall never forget the great chorus of sirens from every ship in New York Harbour when the *Bremen* arrived to win the Blue Riband of the Atlantic crossing; the snowstorm of confetti and ticker-tape which showered down when the German trans-Atlantic fliers, Koehl and Huenefeld, drove along Broadway; the night when Max Schmeling won the world's heavyweight title at Madison Square Garden; the première of Marlene Dietrich in "The Blue Angel"; Einstein's reception at the White House; the visit of the German Theatre under Max Reinhardt; Lotte Lehmann in "Rosenkavalier", and Elizabeth Schumann in the "Marriage of Figaro" at the Metropolitan Opera House; the Berlin Philharmonic Orchestra under Furtwaengler at the Carnegie Hall. One of the best-selling books in America then was Erich Maria Remarque's "All Quiet on the Western Front", while the Americans were dancing to German tunes like "I Lost my Heart in Heidelberg" and "I Kiss your Little Hand, Madame". In fact, Germany's achievements were a constant topic of admiring comment in the United States. We had no need to make propaganda; the enmity of the first World War was forgotten. It seemed to us then that the era of the jackboot and the Potsdam monocle had gone for ever, and that we Germans had become peace-loving and responsible members of the civilised community of nations at last.

Our Ambassador to Washington was von Prittwitz, not a genius, but a man of considerable ability and personality. Like myself, he came from a Guard Cavalry Regiment, but he had prised himself loose from his reactionary background. He was a Democrat by conviction, and since he was only forty-two, Stresemann had to overcome a great deal of opposition in promoting this renegade from the aristocracy to the important diplomatic post of Ambassador to Washington. I liked von Prittwitz and felt I could learn much from his experience.

I remember that one evening around Christmas-time, when we were sitting with his wife in the huge salon of the Embassy, I took the opportunity of asking him a question which preoccupied me.

"Ambassador," I said. "you were an officer in one of the most monarchist regiments in Germany. How is it that you have become such a convinced upholder of the Republic?"

He replied: "Believe me, I saw enough to convince me of the irresponsibility of the Kaiser's régime. By 1916 there was not a man in the Chancellery who did not know that Germany had lost the war. To go on with the useless slaughter of thousands of German soldiers was futile. But nobody had the courage to oppose the plans of the High Command and in particular those of that megalomaniac Ludendorff. We muddled on until even the brasshats had to admit defeat. But in the meantime, millions of soldiers had to die because the men at the top were without conscience or would not risk their jobs. Doesn't that rank as one of the greatest crimes in history? Now you will understand why I never want to set eyes on the Kaiser's flag again."

It was Prittwitz who signed the Kellogg Pact, outlawing war, for Germany, and I am convinced that nobody could have done it with a better conscience that he. When Hitler came to power, he was the only German Ambassador who immediately handed in his resignation and retired into private life.

In 1929 my youngest brother, Walter, came to the States to study modern American farming methods in Missouri. Before he went home, we spent a few days together in New York. One night, after seeing the famous coloured revue "Blackbirds", then running on Broadway, we walked slowly back to our hotel through the cubist landscape of New York and the electric signs. When we reached Fifth Avenue we heard the newspaper sellers calling; "Late Extra! Stresemann dead! Sensation in Germany!"

"God, how terrible!" Walter said.

"Yes," I answered, for there seemed nothing else to say.

The gay, haunting music of "Blackbirds" suddenly seemed to have lost its lilt. We walked silently back to the hotel where the reception clerk, a German-born American, had not heard the news. When we told him, he said gloomily: "What is going to happen to Germany now?"

A few weeks later came the next shock. Black Friday. With a terrible suddenness the New York Stock Market collapsed. Up till that moment it would have been little short of blasphemy to suggest that the "American miracle" might one day be over. The panic was indescribable. One of my colleagues had made a considerable amount of money playing the Stock Market. He used to do business in the Mayflower Hotel in Washington, where one of the biggest broking firms had its luxurious offices. I often went there with him to watch the ticker-tapes flashing the latest New York prices while the speculators sat about in club chairs. I used to study their faces. They sat there like a funeral party and stared at the figures flickering across the screen that told them whether they had made or lost a few hundred thousand dollars in the last five minutes.

Although I had read Economics at the university and taken a Doctor's degree, I still could not grasp what had happened. The real basis of American economy—the enormous factories, the raw materials, the great stocks of goods and the labour force, were all still there. How then was it possible that mere figures

41

on the ticker-tapes had the power to throw the entire economic machinery out of gear, so that the factories had to close their gates and throw the workers out on to the streets, and everyone suddenly became broke?

One fact, however, was abundantly clear to us all; the American crisis was going to have a terrible reaction in Germany. There were many clever men there who had believed that the economic boom which had followed the end of Inflation was illusory. The fact was, it would never have been possible without enormous foreign loans, especially from America, which were pumped into the country. As a result, our economy underwent a great expansion, but it no longer belonged to us entirely—it was a dangerously dependent subvention for which interest, at uneconomic rates, was paid to Wall Street. Twelve per cent or more was not unusual. This was managed by raising further loans to pay the interest on the earlier loans. The financiers made huge fortunes, but the economy sank ever deeper into debt. Eventually, it had to lead to bankcruptcy. The really clever German financiers—amongst them Doctor Hjalmar Schacht, who visited us several times in Washington—actually calculated upon this happening in order to trick the Americans out of their money. Cynically, they said: "A really good slump will put us on our feet again."

For the time being it did not seem to work out that way. America stopped lending money, but saw no reason why she should not demand the interest that was due to her on private or state loans.

The peak of the world economic crisis came in the summer of 1931, after the great failure of the Berlin banks. In the damp heat of those July and August weeks in Washington we sat sweating into the small hours of the night with our code books as we deciphered the endless S.O.S. messages that were pouring in from Berlin. I can still see my colleague, Alex Wuthenau, sitting opposite me with his damp hair falling over his eyes and the sweat running down his chest under his open shirt.

"How far have you got?"

"I've just got: 'Complete standstill of whole economy."

"And the next group reads: 'Anticipate catastrophic effects."

"And then?"

"The next word looks like Chinese. I make it: cho—I can't read it. It's a balls-up."

"It must be chaos—or chaotic."

"Chaotic—of course! You're right. After that, I've got 'situation'. That's it—chaotic situation."

Almost every European Embassy in Washington was being bombarded with similar telegrams. The Chargé d'Affaires was continually employed carrying one urgent memorandum after another to the State Department. Even our pay stopped, and for weeks we had to live on tick.

Then eventually President Herbert Hoover was forced to declare his famous Moratorium. For a moment at any rate we could breathe again. I remember a small party given at this time by the French Ambassador, the famous Catholic poet, Paul Claudel. He raised his champagne glass for the first toast: "Here's to the brief interval which remains to us between the crisis and the catastrophe." ("Au petit moment qui nous reste entre la crise et la catastrophe.")

In Washington we caught the echoes of the degenerating political situation in Germany. After Stresemann's death the old Prussian militaristic spirit began to reassert itself, and the political centre of gravity moved perceptibly from the Foreign Office in the Wilhelmstrasse to the Ministry of Defence in the Bendlerstrasse. Otherwise, how was it possible to explain that, in spite of this crisis, Germany began to build the most expensive "pocket" battleships in the world? And why did Brüning, the new Chancellor of Germany, choose this moment to bring up "German equality in Rearmament?" Why, again, did the Minister of the Interior, Treviranus, stretch German—Polish relations to breaking point by openly demanding the return of Danzig and the Polish Corridor?

The first swallows of spring for the rearmament faction had already flown in 1930. Two men from the Bendlerstrasse were sent to us in Washington to work on the defence question. They were Warlimont and Speidel. Their names became famous in the Third Reich, for they helped to build up Germany's new fascist army.

* * *

After five years abroad—latterly as Chargé d'Affaires in the beautiful island of Haïti—I was due for four months' home leave. In May 1932, at Port-au-Prince, I boarded a freighter of the American United Fruit Company which was to take me to New York, where I would re-embark for the Atlantic crossing in the *Bremen*.

Conditions in the United States had greatly deteriorated during the brief year I had been away in Haïti. The unemployed stood in their dozens on street corners selling apples, shoelaces or matches. Organ grinders and street musicians were churning out the hit tunes from Hollywood and Broadway, the most popular of which was, "Brother Can You Spare a Dime?"

I stopped off in England and spent three days in London looking up old friends. Our Ambassador to St. James's at this time was the Freiherr Konstantin von Neurath, who as a young man in Stuttgart had been a dancing partner of my mother. He invited me to luncheon with his family, and the conversation at table inevitably turned to the critical situation in Germany. Hindenburg had just dismissed Brüning, and Germany was for the time being without a Government. Von Neurath seemed not in the least worried by the situation. He was far more concerned as to how the hunting season would turn out in his native Swabia.

The following day in Paris I read in the evening papers that Neurath had been appointed German Foreign Minister, and that the new Chancellor was Franz von Papen. The latter name was not unknown to me. In Washington I had met young Franz von Papen, his son, who was studying law at the Catholic University of Georgetown. By chance, young Franz was one of the first people I ran into when I returned to the Foreign Office building. The new Chancellor was living next door at No. 74, Wilhelmstrasse, and I was invited to luncheon.

Germany was collapsing in ruins, yet the atmosphere in the Papen household seemed serene, almost sunny. We chatted inconsequently at luncheon and then went out to the verandah for coffee and cigars. At about three o'clock Papen suddenly said: "Good Lord, I have to be at a cocktail party with the Americans in two hours. After that, there's another reception, and at eight I have to dine at the French Embassy. I shall hardly have time to change between the two. But shall we get some fresh air while we can? What do you say to a game of tennis?"

And off we trooped to the tennis court.

I often asked myself if Papen ever went to his office at all. He was an elegant man of the world, smooth as butter. He worked obliquely through intrigue and gossip, but he kept constantly in touch with the "old gentleman"—Hindenburg—who lived at the other end of the garden. It was well known that the old boy, an unimaginative "blimp", was quite captivated by the worldly-wise and accomplished Papen.

Now there was no doubt about the change in the political climate in Germany. The spirit of Potsdam, which I had thought dead for ever, was in the ascendant again, and Papen's "Cabinet of Barons" was exclusively composed of Prussian Junkers.

The only element missing to complete the picture was His Imperial Majesty the Kaiser. The place of the Kaiser was symbolically filled by the "heroic figure of the old Field Marshal". I remember my mother telling me a few years before how she had sat beside Hindenburg at dinner in Brandenburg. He was so far advanced in senility, she said, that she could not get a sensible word out of him. The truth was, of course, that

Hindenburg wished for nothing more than to lay his office at the feet of a German Kaiser. If the monarchy could not be restored for the time being, at any rate efforts could be made to introduce its outward forms. It was extraordinary how many Royal Highnesses, Serene Highnesses and Excellencies suddenly reappeared after a temporary eclipse under the Weimar Republic. The big hotels of the Brandenburger Tor were swarming with them. They were all there—the Crown Prince and his brothers; the Duchess of Brunswick, the Kaiser's daughter; the Duke of Saxe Coburg-Gotha; the Landgraf von Hessen; the Prince of Sachsen-Weimar, and the rest of them.

There was only one topic of conversation during that ominous summer—who will it be? Every day there were new political combinations, depending upon which prince had dined with which minister the previous evening. One thing was clear; the decision would be made by the "Old Gentleman" and the generals of the Bendlerstrasse.

I learned what "restoration" meant in the Papen era. Germany was in chaos, but there seemed to be no bridge between the burning problems of the nation and the antiquated Royalist preoccupations of the ruling classes.

CHAPTER SEVEN

LAASKE WAS ON the verge of bankruptcy. The farmers in the surrounding villages were so deep in debt that there was hardly a bundle of straw in the yard that they could call their own. The unemployed roamed the countryside begging, and from the kitchen we dished out free soup to as many as fifty in a single day.

In Berlin conditions were, if possible, even worse. I felt ashamed as I walked down the Potsdamerstrasse and saw how enviously the pitiful, ragged men at the street corners stared at my English clothes. This state of affairs simply could not continue. The blue skies of Stresemann's democracy had clouded over for good. After Papen and his barons there could only be catastrophe. Germany stood on the brink of a great historical change. Something revolutionary had to happen. But what? There were only two great forces among the people which could revolutionise Germany: the Nazis and the Communists.

Of the Communists I knew nothing, but I had contacts with the Nazi Party through a former colleague of mine in the Foreign Office now working with Goebbels in the Berlin branch of the Party. His name was Johan von Leers. We had one thing in common from our childhood: the same nurse.

I used to meet him from time to time and he would say: "Putlitz, you know a man like you really belongs to us."

I was sceptical, but, nevertheless, I went to look him up one day in his office. More often we met in the local Nazi pub. He introduced me to his friends and sometimes we talked well into the night.

That day, in his office, I agreed that something had to be done to clear up the mess in Germany once and for all. I also admitted that I agreed with some of the Nazi ideas.

"Put the community first, and I'm with you," I told him. "But some of your other ideas I find childish and barbaric. Do you really believe in this race propaganda? Do you honestly think that everything will be fine if only we can get rid of the Jews?"

"My dear Putlitz, you are taking things too literally. We know there are good Jews and bad Jews. We are Socialists and our real fight is against the parasites and racketeers," he explained. "We will fight them to the death, especially the ones who are always trying to call the political tune. You know as well as I do that these Jewish spivs occupy all the key positions in the newspaper offices and banks in this country to-day. Types like Sklarek, Barmat and Kutisker—we've got to get rid of them."

"You mean," I asked, "that you would not touch the professional Jews? I'm thinking of my doctor, Doctor G. None of your Aryan doctors could do for me what he did. Would you throw him out?"

Leers laughed. "So long as he sticks to his job and behaves himself, certainly not."

I told him that I was glad to hear that he and his Party were open to reason on this question of the Jews. "But what," I asked, "about your attitude towards the Communists? They're Germans and, as far as I can see, many of their ideals are much the same as yours. So why these brawls and fights every night?"

Leers shook his head sadly. "That's a tragic business," he said. "The average Communist is really one of us. The trouble is that international Jewry wields tremendous power in the Communist Party leadership and is inciting its supporters against us."

It was my turn to laugh. "I absolutely refuse to believe that the Communist Party leaders are all international Jews! In my opinion, the real reason why the genuine Communists refuse to join you is because your Herr Hitler not only signs friendly

48

agreements but actually forms an alliance with Hindenburg and Seldte's Stahlhelm. Not content with that, he's making friends with the most reactionary financial interests by forming the so-called 'Harzburg Front'."

As I warmed to my subject, I told Leers that his Party cursed the reactionaries in its propaganda, called von Papen the devil himself, and yet even the simplest fool knew that neither would harm the other.

"If your S.A. men would go into action seriously," I said, "I'm convinced you would get enough people behind you to throw Papen and company out of office in twenty-four hours. Why don't you do that?" I challenged.

"My dear Putlitz," Leers said archly, "this is a question of high politics which neither of us understand. You don't know our Führer, but you can take it from me that he will choose the right moment when it comes. Until then, we must make our plans. You wait a bit—one day Adolf Hitler will give Papen and Co. a kick in the pants that will take their breath away! Then we shall be in power, and the outlook for Germany will be very different."

Nothing, I told myself as I left Leer's office, that these Nazis said made sense. At the same time, I could not help feeling that if they came into power they would at least get a move on by sweeping away the reactionaries. I would be dishonest if I said that in those days I had seen through the calculated deception of the Nazi slogans. The contrary was nearer the truth; I thought then that a spirit of real sacrifice for certain ideals which seemed to me well worth fighting for underlay the bullying Nazi manner. In that summer of 1932, if they had only attempted a coup against von Papen's "Cabinet of Barons", I would have been one of their most ardent supporters.

I think that I first began to have doubts about the Nazis in the autum of that year when my leave came to an end and I was appointed to the Press Department of the Government in the Wilhelmplatz. There I was able to watch from close range what was going on behind the scenes. I was in charge of the Government's relations with the British and American Press, so, in order to put me in the picture, I was sent to our Embassy in London for a few weeks. Since von Neurath's departure, my old friend Count Bernstorff was acting as Chargé d'Affaires, and he and Paul X introduced me to the world of Fleet Street. Now in London, in contrast to ten years before, Germans were hospitably received everywhere.

Soon after my return to Berlin von Papen's Government fell, and immediately the haggling inseparable from the formation of a new Cabinet began. The military party, which had previously spun its web only indirectly around the "revered Field Marshal", now found itself obliged to take up the reins in earnest. For the first time, the mysterious General von Schleicher, the genius behind the Bendlerstrasse, was forced to step into the limelight. At this stage, it was no longer possible to depend only on the support of the Reichswehr; it was imperative to capture the imagination of the masses. Gone, anyhow for the moment, were dreams of a restoration of the monarchy.

Now the hour of the "Peoples' Tribune"—Adolf Hitler— seemed at hand, for he alone was in the position to rally the population behind the Generals.

The Party leaders of the Brown Shirts in Munich were invited to Berlin to take part in the negotiations to form a government. They made their appearance in a long column of limousines, and put up at the ultra-snobbish Hotel Kaiserhof in the Wilhelm-platz from which all the other guests were told to take their leave, at least for the time being. As my office in the Press Department was directly opposite, I was able to watch the flamboyant arrival of this uniformed herd. From what I saw one might have been forgiven for believing that carnival time had arrived several months too soon—at least that was the impression made on me by the men to whom the German people now looked for rescue from their poverty. I pointed out the incongruous nature of these proceedings to Leers. Even he found their humbug repulsive. Nevertheless, he said loyally: "It all depends on the Führer. He is a man of the people himself and his feet are firmly planted on the ground. At the right moment, he'll stop all this junketing."

Every evening we issued a communiqué on the course of the negotiations. Our material consisted chiefly of a polite and formal exchange of letters in which Herr Hitler and Herr Meissner, Chief of President Hindenburg's Chancellery, assured one another of their mutual regard. Beyond this, however, there was not the slightest sign of agreement. Hitler wanted to be Chancellor and demanded full powers. The military clique wished to propitiate him with the offer of a few ministerial posts, while the "old gentleman" did not want any part of this Adolf Hitler. When, however, he finally found himself obliged to receive him, he let him remain standing, and muttered under his breath to Meissner: "I absolutely refuse to sit down with this Bohemian corporal! So this is the man you want me to make Chancellor? I would not entrust a squad of recruits to such a Slavonic-looking fellow!"

So the powerful limousines, with their swastika pennants and uniformed passengers, drove back to Munich having achieved nothing. It was left to General von Schleicher to form a government as best he could. In contrast with von Papen and his barons, the General possessed a certain liberal outlook. He was quite pleased to be known as "the thinker in military uniform" or "the General with the social conscience". One of his favourite "ideologists" was my immediate predecessor, Major Marcks, now Chief of the Government Press Department, a son of a well-known historian at Göttingen and himself a bespectacled intellectual product of the General Staff in the Bendlerstrasse.

Day after day Marcks held conferences with one or another of the optimistic would-be reformers of State and Society. The more I saw of it the more astonished I was at the political

51

cloud-cuckooland in which these otherwise reasonable and shrewd members of the General Staff, such as Schleicher, actually lived.

Meanwhile, the situation throughout the country drifted steadily towards chaos. I remember attending the first sitting of the Reichstag summoned by Schleicher in December, 1932. No debate, however, took place. Instead, there was a great deal of shouting, inkpots and paperweights were flung about and the chandeliers shattered, until finally we on the Government benches were forced to take cover under our seats, while the opposing members fought it out.

The reactionary Government of the Barons had failed. The Generals from the Bendlerstrasse had proved unable to cope with the situation, and no-one, least of all myself, could say how it was all going to end.

About the middle of January, 1933, my old friend Count Gottfried Bismarck, grandson of the Iron Chancellor, who had spent many years on his Pomeranian estate, invited me to luncheon at the Union Club in the Schadowstrasse.

"I think," he told me over our coffee," I've done something rather silly. I joined the Nazi Party some time ago. To say the least of it I feel that I acted a little hastily. It looks to me as if the Nazi following is on the decline. You're at the centre of things, what do you advise me to do?"

"Well, Gottfried," I answered, "I can't tell you anything for certain. Something is going to happen, but what it will be, God alone knows!"

We were discussing this and that, when suddenly everyone in the room turned towards the door. Von Papen walked in accompanied by a friend. Bowing affably, he walked through the room and disappeared with his companion into the small adjoining dining-room.

"I seem to know that chap with Papen," I said to Gottfried.

"Of course you do," he laughed, "Don't you remember those two fellows in tails who used to stand about the corners at the

52

dances here a few years ago—Ribbentrop and Tettelmann?"
Gottfried added that Papen's friend was the bounderish Ribbentrop, with his assumed "von". I remember well his turning up
with his friend at all the fashionable parties in Berlin in the
twenties, whether they were asked or not. We always used to
whisper to each other, with Shakespeare's Rosenkrantz and
Guilderstern in mind: "Ribbentrop and Tettelmann!"

"But I thought he was in the champagne or whisky trade," I
said. "How comes it that he's friendly enough with Papen to be
asked to luncheon at the Union Club?"

"I believe there's something behind this," Gottfried answered
thoughtfully. "I've heard that Ribbentrop has been making up
to Hitler. So possibly Papen is about to do a deal with him.
I've an idea that the Cologne banker, Schröder, and other big
financiers have also got a finger in the pie. During the past
few days, rumours have been flying around in Hugenberg
circles to that effect."

"You know much more than I do, Gottfried," I told him, "so
it's quite possible you're right."

As I said good-bye to him, Gottfried remarked: "I think I'd
better hang on for a time or I may miss the chance of one
day ranking as an old fighter for the Nazi cause!"

Schleicher's régime lasted a mere two months; then the negotiations for another government started all over again. Once
more the big limousines from Munich streamed into the Wilhelmplatz. But this time there was no formal exchange of letters
between Hitler and Meissner. This time, the Bohemian corporal
was ushered immediately into Hindenburg's presence and
permitted to sit down.

So that Hitler might be kept within certain limits by men of
experience, Hindenburg summoned Hugenberg, the so-called
"silver fox", to attend the meeting. This former director of
Krupps had the reputation of managing to induce industrial
magnates and great landowners to sink their differences.

On January 29th, 1933, the day when this decisive discussion took place, I happened to be alone in the Press Department, for it was Sunday and my turn of duty. I had arranged to have luncheon with Steltzer, a colleague who had just arrived in Berlin on leave from Moscow. The Press was constantly ringing me up, but so far I had nothing to tell anyone. Steltzer arrived at about one o'clock, but as it was impossible for me to get away from the telephone, we decided to wait until things quietened down. Finally, I suggested that we slipped across to the Kaiserhof for a snack.

By now it was between three and four in the afternoon, and the hotel dining-room was empty except for a large table by the window which was still occupied. Around it sat the élite of the Nazi Party—the Brown Shirt big-shots, most of whom were in uniform. Who they all were did not interest either of us very much at the time. But this was the first occasion on which we actually saw the Charlie Chaplin face, so familiar from photographs, of the so-called Führer. He wore an ill-fitting blue suit, and had a bottle of lemonade before him, while his companions were swigging beer.

We sat at a small table near the door so that we could watch them. Just before we had finished luncheon, a hotel page came in and handed Hitler a note on a silver salver. He read it, and, making some remark to his friends, strode out of the room. Close to the door stood a trolley laden with hors d'oeuvres, paté de foie gras, and the rest. As Hitler passed it, on the spur of the moment, I said to Steltzer: "Mark my words, that looks to me like the sort of barricade over which a modern revolutionary climbs to power!"

We paid our bill, and in the entrance came face to face with the uniformed bodyguard who had escorted Hitler to the car in which he had just raced across the hundred yards separating the Kaiserhof from the Chancellery. The deal was well under way.

That same evening I telephoned Leers and told him that by the next day his Leader would be Chancellor in a cabinet which included the gentleman rider, von Papen, the reactionary "silver fox", and Seldte, head of the Stahlhelm.

"If that's true," shouted Leers, "he has sold us down the drain and betrayed our movement!"

"It's true and he's sold you all!" I insisted.

After a pause I heard Leers's voice saying: "If it is true, he must have had a good reason for it which we know nothing about. The time will come when he will break off this unholy alliance. We shall see who is the stronger."

A few days later, under a vow of secrecy, he quoted me a new version of the Horst Wessel song which was in circulation in certain quarters. I never saw Leers again. After the failure of the attemped second revolution upon which he had placed his hopes and which was crushed by the "Röhm Putsch" on June 30th, 1934, he accepted the existing order of things and became a well-known writer of anti-Semitic, race-antagonising pamphlets. That notorious rubbish, "The Jews are watching you", was from his pen.

Shortly after, I ran into von Papen's son, Franz, in the Wilhelmstrasse. "Tell me," I asked him, "has your father been left in the lurch by all his shrewd advisers?"

Young Franz eyed me thoughtfully. "I'll tell you something in confidence," he said. "When the newly-formed cabinet was preparing to leave after a decisive conference with Hindenburg, my father was putting his coat on when that upstart Hitler came up to him like a lackey and helped him. If you consider what that gesture indicates, I don't think that you will judge my father too harshly."

As I turned the corner into the Unter den Linden, I noticed an enormous red banner hanging from a rooftop, bearing in large letters the words "Berlin is remaining Red!". It was still there the following evening, on January 30th, when a great Nazi torchlight procession paraded along the street. But the next day, after the night on which "Germany awoke", it had disappeared. At the street corners where formerly one policeman

55

stood, there were now three upholders of the law—one of the old green police, a member of the Stahlhelm in field grey, and a brown-shirted S.A. man.

At first things were not so bad as many pessimists had feared. Nevertheless, the public experienced a brief shiver of apprehension when they read in their newspapers the first decree issued by the new Prussian Minister of the Interior, Hermann Goering. This was the so-called "Order to shoot for the maintenance of law and order". In it the police were instructed to make ruthless use of their weapons in certain circumstances, and were assured that the Minister himself would take full responsibility should innocent people be injured as a result of such action.

From now on, the average citizen had to tread more warily so far as politics were concerned. This he accepted, and, after all, it was not really so intolerable. Indeed, jubilation now reigned in the ranks of the old Military Association and Soldiers' Union, and among all those who had secretly longed for the return of the good old days when youth would once again know the meaning of discipline and acquire a soldierly bearing. It was high time there was an end to loose and slovenly behaviour.

Even my own Regimental Association gave a dinner to celebrate the "National Revival" and "the coming together of the officers and soldiers of the old army with young Germany". It was at this function, after a lapse of many years, that I saw the now white haired General von Tschirschky. As on that famous day when he had reviewed his regiment for the last time, a few tears trickled on to his bristling Kaiser Wilhelm moustache. But now they were tears of joy, and in the course of the evening he made no attempt to control his feelings, but, tapping his glass, proposed a toast of eternal loyalty to the memory of our former Supreme War Lord in his solitude at Doorn.

I had gone to the dinner expecting a somewhat different evening. I was particularly horrified when my uncle, whom I had always considered a more or less balanced man, in an outburst of enthusiasm referred to Hindenburg and Hitler as "the saviours of Germany".

I walked home that night in a depressed mood, remembering the old saying that "only the stupidest calves choose their own butchers". Even Major Marcks, when I asked him how he felt about the present state of affairs, answered: "Perhaps what has happened is all for the best. An iron hand is sometimes needed to restore order."

However, the fusion of the old and the new Germany did not proceed so smoothly—The two "saviours of the Nation" had made conspicuous appearances on two separate balconies at the torchlight parade on January 30th. The new Chancellor of the Reich had declared to his Brown Shirts: "Give me four years and you will not recognise Germany!" The "Old Gentleman", a few hundred yards farther on, watched the parade in silence and seemed more pleased at the sight of the helmets of the Stahlhelm than the foreign-looking brown képis of the Nazis as they marched past. He was, indeed, well aware that he had scarcely more than four years to live, and Adolf Hitler knew it too.

Even the cunning "silver fox" had his troubles. He had always been so successful at combining politics and business. In addition to endless directorships, he was the principal shareholder in UFA, Germany's biggest film company. The latter had just completed a patriotic film called "Morgenrot", which glorified the gallantry of "our sailors" in a German U-boat in the first world war. Hugenberg had decided that the première of this picture should be the initial act of the new régime, at which the Cabinet of national solidarity would appear for the first time seated all together in a box.

We of the Press Department were also invited. For several days there had been rumours that the Führer had no intention of letting himself be made use of by the "silver fox". In a mild state of tension, we sat among the select gathering in the stalls of the Capitol Cinema and watched the Cabinet box, where the dress-coated Hugenberg did the honours of the evening. One after the other they appeared; von Papen, Seldte, Count Schwerin-Krosigk, Baron von Neurath, and nearly all the other ministers. After General von Blomberg, in full uniform, had taken his seat, nothing happened for some time. Finally, the lights went out and the curtains parted. Adolf Hitler had not put in an appearance.

The following day Walter Funk, who had succeeded Major Marcks as Chief of the Press Department, passed an article to us for publication. It was an account of the première of "Morgenrot", and stated that the film was merely a glorification of the officer caste and paid no tribute to the heroism of the crew. It was a typical example of Nazi tactics, which attempted to hoodwink the masses into believing that the bigwigs of the Third Reich were genuine fighters against the reactionaries and had the welfare of the people at heart.

CHAPTER EIGHT

OUR CHIEF UNDER the new régime, Walter Funk, was a truly extraordinary creature to be working in a government department. A hard-drinking journalist, he had at one time been on the staff of the *Börsenzeitung*, but had been sacked for laziness. Later, he had found favour with the Nazis through his connections on the Stock Exchange. He was a fat, bloated man with bleary eyes, who spoke with a strong East Prussian accent, and to work with him was practically impossible, for one never knew when he would put in an appearance at his office. He was seldom there for more than a couple of hours. Whenever I had to introduce British and American correspondents to him, I took the precaution of having our usher, Mehlis, in attendance, because he had acquired the knack of mixing potent cocktails. When, however, Funk was receiving the German Press he shouted for good, old-fashioned rye brandy.

Immediately the Nazis came into power things started moving in the Press Department. There was a sudden and vast increase in the number of documents with which we had to deal. Every morning we found stacks of shorthand reports on our desks of the tapped telephone conversations of foreign correspondents during the past twenty-four hours. I found it extremely unpleasant to have to read the personal secrets of my friends in this way and so hastened to warn them of what was going on.

One of our most frequent visitors at this time was a tall, lank, Bohemian-looking man known universally as "Putzi". He was a member of the well-known family of Munich art publishers,

Hanfstaengl, who produced the majority of those religious coloured prints which adorned all the spare rooms at Laaske when I was a child. After the unsuccessful "Bierkeller Putsch" in 1923, Putzi had hidden Adolf Hitler, then wanted by the police, for some months in his house in Munich, thus winning the great man's friendship. Putzi was a thoroughly bad painter but a brilliant pianist. He told me that he spent whole nights in the Chancellery playing selections form Wagner and Franz Lehar to soothe the insomnia-stricken Führer. I remember him telling me that one of Hitler's favourite numbers was a popular song entitled "How could I have lived without you?". I have often thought since that, as he listened to it, Hitler must have had the German people in mind.

As Putzi had spent many years in America and spoke English fluently, Hitler appointed him as his personal adviser in his relations with the Anglo-American Press. But since he was, in fact, a somewhat naive creature, he nearly always came to us for advice.

The British and American newspapermen were often summoned to interviews with Hitler. Sometimes I attended these on my own, but more often in company with either Hanfstaengl or Funk. If the audience was a large one, we remained standing; otherwise we all sat in comfortable chairs around a large table in the Chancellor's study.

So it was in those early days that I had ample opportunity of studying the Führer at close quarters, and my colleagues in the Foreign Office, who had only seen him at a distance, often asked me eagerly: "What's he like? What sort of impression does he make on you?"

"It's really impossible to say," I told them. "But his effect on me is that when he looks at me I want to wet my pants like a little boy!"

That comic lock of hair on his forehead, the ridiculous little moustache and the twisted features made him look like a caricature. With his long body and short legs one could not help thinking of him as a somewhat crazy comedian from a third-rate provincial music-hall. Sitting silently in my corner, I did my best to find something impressive in Hitler. I failed hopelessly. Yet the moment I felt the piercing gaze of his fanatical steel-grey eyes focussed upon me, everything changed. Only once in my life had I seen such ice-cold eyes. That was many years earlier when I was travelling on a mountain railway on the Wendelstein. Opposite us sat a man with eyes just like Hitler's—dangerously mad-looking eyes. He made us all feel thoroughly uncomfortable, so that none of us spoke for the rest of the journey. But when we got out, one of the party turned to me and said: "Do you know who that was?" When I shook my head, he told me: "General Ludendorff."

Hitler was practically unbearable when carried away by one of his fits of hysteria. Sometimes I brought to the interviews papers relevant to the business under discussion, and I was astonished how quickly the little man, whose only education had been at an elementary school, glanced through them and memorised their contents word for word. He often began one of these interviews by speaking quietly and rationally. Then, suddenly and without warning, he would fly off the handle, ranting and raving and waving his arms like a lunatic. He would shout until the walls shook, and saliva would spurt from his lips. Those who, unlike my phlegmatic English friends, were not amused by these delirious outbursts, positively quaked in their shoes. It was small wonder that rumours were rife that the Führer bit the carpet and the curtains in rage. But it was equally strange how, after these outbursts, he would suddenly calm down again and continue the conversation in a perfectly normal and reasonable manner.

Although I hardly ever opened my mouth at these interviews, I noticed that Hitler often eyed me closely. His eyes would peer fixedly into mine until I felt like a hypnotised rabbit. When I told Raumer this, he advised me to concentrate my gaze on the bridge of Hitler's nose.

61

"That," he assured me," is a certain way of making such an hysterical type feel uncomfortable."

But I was never able to remember this advice in the Führer's presence, and just sat there with my mind a blank.

Hitler did his best at this time to ingratiate himself with the British journalists, in one or two of whom he then felt a certain confidence. I attended a few of the interviews at which all the accredited British and American Berlin correspondents were present. On each occasion, as we were leaving, Hitler said: "Herr Delmer and Herr von Weigand, please stay behind for a moment," and these two would stay on to talk with him privately. Sefton Delmer was then a brilliant young writer on *The Daily Express*, and Karl von Wiegand, who had got to know the Kaiser in the First World War, was employed by the Hearst Press.

So, in spite of the atmosphere of tension, the first month of the Third Reich passed without any startling change so far as I was concerned. Rumours had begun to circulate about the terrible brutalities inflicted upon the detainees in the S.A. barracks, and these were reported in some of the foreign newspapers. I remember that the Hedemannstrasse and the Papestrasse had particularly sinister reputations, but it was generally thought that these excesses were grossly exaggerated.

Nevertheless, we in the Press Department saw pretty clearly that this new régime was indulging in propaganda that consisted chiefly of shameless lies. One afternoon, for instance, we received a number of pamphlets reputed to be of Communist origin that were said to have been dropped on Berlin during the night by planes of an unknown nationality. We were instructed to give this story to the press, but since the print on the pamphlets was not even dry and the night in question was still several hours away, there could manifestly have been little truth in it!

No-one wanted to take the Nazis seriously. When we were alone we told jokes against them and laughed at them, for we were certain that they were but a flash in the pan. A few spies were appointed to keep an eye on us, but even they were not taken seriously.

Such, then, was the situation when, at the end of February, just before the General Election, events took a sensational turn. In those days I knew a woman who kept a bar in Charlottenburg where I sometimes went to buy a snack when I was on night-duty. If I had time, I would spend half an hour or so chatting with her. One evening, when I was in the bar, a tart came in and said: "There's a fire somewhere over there. They say it's the Reichstag."

Before setting out for home, I looked along the Charlottenburger Chaussee towards the Brandenburger Tor and saw the glow of a fire in the night sky. The following morning as I walked down the Regentenstrasse I ran into Sefton Delmer and Putzi emerging from a car. They told me that they had just had breakfast after spending the night in the burning Reichstag in company with Goering, who had informed them of the alleged "frustrated conspiracy of Communist incendiaries". Delmer was duly cynical on the subject.

That same morning, at the usual eleven o'clock press conference, I noticed an unfamiliar face. It belonged to Rudolf Diels, the newly appointed Chief of Goering's Secret Police. From that day onwards, he was to appear almost daily and produce from his briefcase the most amazing documentary evedence about the alleged Communist conspiracy. He was an ex-Corps student, barely thirty, with the typical sabre cuts on his face. A few years previously he had been appointed to the Prussian Ministry of Home Affairs under Severing, where he was the official responsible for all matters connected with the Communist Party. Now it was apparent that from the very beginning he had been a Nazi agent.

Who actually set the Reichstag on fire remained a mystery for a long time. From the very beginning, certain foreign journalists suspected that Goering himself had been responsible. But hardly anyone seriously believed that the Communists were to blame. Diels's documents were too obviously forgeries and his arguments too far fetched to convince anyone. Besides, the whole object of the propaganda was obvious; to intimidate the public with the threat of "Communist Terror" and so get it to vote for the Brown Shirts who had "saved it from Red chaos".

I was present at the notorious meeting of the Reichstag that resulted in the Nazis' final triumph. Adolf Hitler was determined to assume power by legal and democratic means and demanded an overwhelming majority to vote him Dictator of Germany with absolute power.

As the Reichstag building had been burnt out, the session took place in the Kroll Opera House. From our reserved box I looked down on the stalls below. S. A. men in their brown shirts, with rubber truncheons in their hands, lounged against the walls. The deputies, who were slowly filling the auditorium, were closely scrutinized. Never before in history had a German Chancellor had the impudence to put such pressure on members of the Reichstag. The atmosphere was electric. The Communist Party had already been banned, and many of its deputies, in spite of their immunity from arrest, were already under lock and key. Had they been present, they would have made a two-thirds majority in favour of the Nazis impossible.

So now the vital question was, what would the Social Democrats do? Would they even put in an appearance? But they did turn up and, with a somewhat subdued air, took their seats.

The session began. Hitler spoke first. After him, Otto Wels, chairman of the S.P.D., asked to speak. Everyone felt that he was terribly excited and alarmed, but he put forward no clear programme. He agreed with the foreign policy of Hitler and the demands for German equality all over the world. Then indeed he turned against the Government and demanded the cessation of any persecution of the Social Democrats, and that the Government should rule according to the Constitution. Catcalls interrupted him and in many parts of his speech laughter was heard from the rows of the Nazi deputies. Finally, Wels declared that no authority should be given to the Government to enable them to rule with force and terror, and for this reason the S.P.D. would vote against this new law.

When Wels had finished speaking, Hitler got up and strode theatrically amid loud applause to the Speaker's desk. He crossed his arms and let his eyes sweep along the rows of deputies. He then began in his sharp staccato voice, in an accent which belonged to no particular part of Germany, to abuse the Social Democrats, and especially Herr Wels as if he was a naughty schoolboy. With intense scorn, he accused his opposers of arriving too late, if indeed they had arrived at all. But whether they had arrived or not, they could alter nothing, and anyhow they were no longer needed. At this Goering could not suppress a triumphant shout.

It came to the voting.

The Social Democrat deputies who were present all voted against the new law, but their cries of "No" no longer disturbed Hitler.

He received the requisite majority without difficulty, in some cases with great acclamation. Hitler had received democratically, legally and within the framework of the Constitution the right to be a dictator. The Nazi party members rose and sang the opening lines of the Horst-Wessel song.

Amongst the ranks of the so-called Democratic "Staatspartei" was one whose face was familiar to me, as he had been one of the lecturers at the Berlin High School for Politics when I attended a course there. I refer to Herr Theodor Heuss, later head of the Bonn Government. At that time, politicians of his sort were dubbed "Santa Clauses" by the Nazis.

CHAPTER NINE

ONCE HITLER WAS firmly in the saddle, the Reichstag fire was exploited as a convenient excuse for giving his gang of cut-throats a free hand to persecute Jews and Communists. From now on columns of the Anglo-American newspapers were filled each day with accounts of these Nazi atrocities. We, in our turn, were obliged to publish denials, which were received with increasing scepticism. It is possible that sometimes these reports in the London and New York papers were exagger-ations. At the same time, I had myself daily incontestable evidence that not only were revolting bestialities being per-petrated but that they were carried out on instructions received from the highest level.

The first man to convince me completely was an SS man who belonged to Goebbels's bodyguard. The club-footed Doctor had by then been appointed Minister of Public Enlightenment and Propaganda and was installed in offices in the same building as myself, for it had been decided to incorporate our Press Department into this new Ministry. As a result, whenever Goebbels was upstairs in his office, his personal bodyguard lolled about in the entrance hall. This fellow happened to be an expert mechanic, and often came to my aid when something went wrong with my old Opel car.

One morning when I arrived I noticed that he was as white as a sheet, and asked him if he felt ill.

"No," he said, "not what you might call ill, but I think I'm going mad."

"What makes you think that?" I asked, somewhat astonished.

"Don't breathe a word to a soul," he whispered, "but I can't stick these nights much longer. Last night nearly finished me. Just imagine, we had to search a flat on the fourth floor where a young married couple lived with their old grandfather. We forced our way in by breaking down the door, and then the wife seized her baby from its cot and jumped out of the window with it in her arms. Her husband jumped after her. We managed to get hold of the old man. Whether they were killed outright on the pavement, I don't know. Perhaps I'm too gutless, but that sort of thing knocks me out."

The club-footed Doctor lied as naturally as others breathe. The sly enjoyment he got out of fooling some unsuspecting person was amazing. "Now, how did I manage that?" his eyes seemed to say with a smirk. "Didn't I fool that idiot brilliantly?" The impudence and the agility he displayed in proving that black was white were quite astonishing. Unfortunately, I knew him slightly. His wife's first husband had been the millionaire industrialist Günther Quandt, who came from my home town of Pritzwalk, where he owned a large cloth factory. In 1929 the couple toured the U.S.A., and I spent Christmas Day in their luxurious suite at the Wardman Park Hotel in Washington. Since we came from the same town, we spent a lot of time together in Washington, but when I met the handsome Magda again on the main staircase of our offices in Berlin, I scarcely recognised her. The chestnut haired, fashionable woman of the world whom I had known was now transformed into a typical blonde German "Gretchen". She was obviously none too pleased at meeting me, and we never resumed our former friendship. So far as Goebbels himself was concerned, I immediately decided that the best thing for me to do was to adopt the role of a harmless, cretinous semi-idiot!

The new Minister issued instructions that we were all to give special attention to the so-called "atrocity reports" printed in the foreign press, and whenever possible procure official evidence in order to deny them. In most cases, however, the required evidence was unobtainable, since the facts were irrefutable. I well remember the murder of Jonas, the Jewish owner of the Berlin stores of that name, whose mutilated body was found in the Landwehr Canal and duly inspected by certain foreign journalists. The incident caused something of a sensation at the time and was brought to Goebbels's personal notice. Without a moment's hesitation, he said: "There is not a Jonas store in Berlin, and that's that!" It is just possible that this official statement was believed abroad, but every child in Berlin knew the "Warenhaus Jonas".

Reports of the ill-treatment of arrested Communists also grew more and more numerous in newspapers abroad until one day we received the following directive: "An important interview will be granted to foreign journalists by Hermann Goering at 11 o'clock to-morrow morning".

Fat Hermann was then living in the residence of the President of the Reichstag in the Sommerstrasse, from which ran the now notorious underground passage to the Reichstag Building immediately across the way. We assembled in the large reception room, and then, followed by a large retinue, the great Minister appeared in full war-paint, booted and spurred, with cap, revolver and gloves. He also carried a riding whip in his hand. It was quite some minutes before the fat man had unbuckled all this equipment, laying it aside on a table. Then he delivered a brief address consisting of the usual bombastic clap-trap, in a sharp, truly Prussian manner. He said that Regierungsrat Diels was at the disposal of the correspondents to take them on a tour of inspection of the Police Headquarters in the Alexander Platz where they could see for themselves that the reports of ill-treatment of prisoners were unfounded.

We drove off in a fleet of cars. I was curious, for I had never yet seen the inside of a prison. As we climbed the staircase, we could look down through the barred windows on to the dreary courtyard below where a crowd of prisoners shuffled round at exercise. There were men and women, old and young, looking utterly miserable in their drab clothes. It was a rainy day, and the several hundred who ambled round, penned in by the high red-brick walls, were wet to the skin. Diels conducted us along the corridor and a police inspector unlocked several cells one after another. We noticed, however, that some cells remained closed. At each open door a man or a woman appeared, who, we were told, were either Communist or Social Democrat officials. I had never heard the name of one of them. They all reacted to their visitors differently; some seemed annoyed, others surprised and a few even pleased. I suppose they thought that our presence might offer some hope of release. But the journalists were unable to get anything out of these poor wretches.

At last, one correspondent asked: "Isn't Thaelmann here?" Diels was somewhat taken aback and did not answer. But since one of the warders remarked that we were standing outside Thaelmann's cell, Diels was forced to give way. The iron door was thrown open, and in the bare, white-washed room we saw the rugged features of the well-known working-class leader, of whom even Leers and his cronies at the "Ameise" had spoken with a certain affection as "Teddy".

Immediately he saw us, Thaelmann deliberately walked to the far corner of the cell and, turning his back on us, stood motionless with his hands clasped behind him.

"Thaelmann," Diels told him, "I have brought some foreign journalists who would like to have a word with you."

The man in the corner merely shrugged his shoulders.

"Herr Thaelmann," Diels said again, "I think these gentlemen might be of some service to you."

Still Thaelmann said nothing.

"Isn't there anything you would care to say to the outside world, Herr Thaelmann?"

In spite of Diel's repeated efforts, Thaelmann remained silent, and in the end the cell door was locked again.

Diels flushed and the sabre cuts stood out on his face. "You see, gentlemen, "he said, turning to us, "the man behaves like a pig. It's useless to treat creatures like that as normal human beings. One can only keep them locked up where they can do no harm to anyone."

I drove back with that particularly shrewd, red-headed Chicago newspaperman, Knickerbocker, who turned to me and said: "Thaelmann is made of tougher stuff than most of the others. He impressed me tremendously. I don't believe they could break his spirit if they flogged him every day for a thousand years."

With terrifying speed conditions of unrestricted despotism spread through every government department. Indeed, in ever increasing numbers regular criminals were appointed to posts in which they could quite openly indulge their vileness. Even with us in the Foreign Office there occured incidents that were totally inexcusable. Several armed Brown Shirts arrived one day and arrested one or two high officials, who were known to be dyed-in-the-wool reactionaries. Amongst them was the former Stahlhelm leader and subsequent Ambassador to Brussels, von Bülow-Schwante. It is true that they were released after a few days, but, nevertheless, they were haunted by their experience for weeks afterwards.

Although German militarism has always been one of the most brutal and ruthless institutions of its kind, it has insisted that discipline and obedience to orders prevailed in its ranks. But these savage hordes of SA and SS bullies seemed to be allowed to behave as they liked.

Meanwhile, a relentless struggle for power went on between the Army and the Brown Shirts—in other words, between General von Fritsch and Captain Roehm. For both these men it was vitally important to gain ascendancy with Adolf Hitler. So far as the Army was concerned, it certainly did not regard Hitler, "the Corporal of the First World War", with any particular antipathy. However, he was a difficult customer to deal with. He was not yet the "greatest general of all time", but already in those days he showed little respect for high-ranking officers. His vast multitude of Brown Shirts far outnumbered the Reichswehr, restricted after the war to one hundred thousand men. So there was a very real danger that these strutting Group Leaders might thwart the designs of the professional soldiers and become even more powerful. To the generals it became clear that in order to entice Hitler into their camp, the whole mumbo-jumbo of the Prussian-German Military Tradition must be resorted to and burnished up in its full glory in his honour. To this end, the "Historic Day of Potsdam" was staged. Pictures were distributed by the thousands throughout the country with the caption: "The Führer of the Reich, which has risen again after fourteen years of shame and ignominy, stands in silent communion before the coffin of the Great King of Prussia." Hoffmann, the photographer, was permitted to perpetuate this moving moment when the "Unknown Corporal of the First World War", arrayed in silk hat and morning dress, sealed for ever the unbreakable union of the Old and the New Germany with a touching handshake with the aged Field Marshal, amidst cries of: "To Immortal Germany and her great soldiers, Frederick, Hindenburg and Adolf Hitler!"

No doubt the "Day of Potsdam" had a strong psychological effect both on Hitler and the Reichswehr. There was, however, one discordant note. Old Hindenburg, according to tradition, had insisted on "helmets off for prayer", that is to say on also paying tribute to the "God of Battles". So there was a church service before the patriotic ceremony. But it was distressingly noticeable that Hitler did not attend it. He preferred to spend the time taking a stroll in the gardens of Sans Souci.

I happened to be in the department of the Foreign Office directly opposite the President's residence in the Wilhelmstrasse when Hindenburg returned from Potsdam. A small crowd had collected by the railings as the old man descended stiffly from his carriage, and, with the help of two footmen, moved slowly up the steps to the front door. There he turned

71

to the crowd. His enormous frame, like an ancient German Colossus, almost filled the doorway. His face showed no trace of emotion or pleasure. Slowly, like an automaton, he raised his hand to his helmet, saluted, and disappeared.

What General von Fritsch sought to gain for the Military Party, Herr von Papen attempted to achieve in civil affairs. He strove to bring about a closer understanding between the Führer and the ruling class of the old Germany. As Vice-Chancellor, with this object in view, he gave a large reception in the splendid rooms in the upper part of our official mansion in the Wilhelmplatz. For this the Hotel Adlon had provided of the best, and the wines and food were superb. In spite of the fact that there were rumours that the much heralded "boycott of the Jews" was about to begin, several members of Berlin's Jewish society were among the guests.

I had received an invitation from von Papen's son. I can still see Frau André, sister of the assassinated Walter Rathenau, standing beside Lady Rumbold, wife of the British Ambassador, in animated conversation with Goebbels, and the chic Ullstein correspondent, Bella Fromm, enjoying a glass of champagne with some young men in SS uniform. Herr von Papen had indeed collected an extraordinary mixture of people!

The Führer, who was wearing evening dress, probably for the first time in his life, presented a bizarre figure. His white tie was awry, his coat tails, far too long for his short legs, flapped over his effeminately fat posterior, and his hair looked as if it had not been brushed for days.

His arrival created a sensation. It was revolting to see how this so-called society fawned over the little man. The young women in particular swarmed around him, their eyes glowing with curiosity and even reverence as he kissed their hands. That evening he made a great effort to display his manners.

The young SS men standing guard at the doors were far less enthusiastic, and I heard one of them say: "Why the tails? Isn't a Brown Shirt good enough for him any more?"

For one brief moment there looked as if there would be trouble. But Goebbels, sensing the atmosphere at once, spoke to several of them. What he said to these hot-headed youngsters I shall never know. But his most effective move was to detail our usher, Mehlis, to fix up a special bar for the SS men, at whose disposal he, Goebbels, placed an unlimited supply of champagne.

Meanwhile I had sat down on a sofa with some members of the Bismarck family so that we could watch exactly who laid siege to the tail-coated Adolf. He was standing only a few steps away from us in the centre of the room, but owing to the general buzz of conversation, we could only catch an occasional word of what he said. We noticed, however, that Hugenberg and Seldte tried to persuade him to call off the planned Jewish boycott, telling him that it would have a most damaging effect on our export trade. Immediately Hitler burst into one of his, to me, familiar rages. "I'm not going to be influenced," he yelled. "I'm going straight ahead in my own way!"

His shouting filled the room, and in the silence that fell the only sound was the raving of the incredible Reichs Chancellor. When just as suddenly he calmed down, Hugenberg and Seldte very wisely changed the subject.

I turned to Prince Otto Bismarck: "Do you think this man will ever rank as high in German history as your grandfather, or old Fritz?"

To my utter astonishment Otto looked at me very earnestly and said with great conviction: "Most certainly."

Countess Hanna Bredow, his sister, whispered to me: "If the male members of the family go crazy, we women, at least, should retain our sanity!"

CHAPTER TEN

IN SUCH CONDITIONS it was only natural that all of us in the Foreign Office wondered how long we could continue to serve under the Nazis. We discussed this question endlessly among ourselves. If Hitler remained the ruler of Germany for long the situation could only end in catastrophe.

There were, of course, some who, throwing every scruple to the winds, went over to the new régime and became members of the Party, but they were then in the minority. The rest of us did not know what to do for the best. The majority favoured playing the waiting game, and never before was the famous English saying, "my country, right or wrong", so often quoted in the corridors of the Berlin Foreign Office.

So far as the organisation of our Ministry was concerned, it had met with little interference, as had the Press Department which was now under the control of Goebbels's Ministry of Propaganda. We were still left very much to ourselves, and we knew that Baron von Neurath would remain faithful to the old traditions. At least we hoped that we would be able to retain our independence and so remain a solitary island of reason and common sense in the raging sea of Brown Shirt madness. One thing reassured us, and that was that the Nazis had no-one qualified to handle the delicate and complicated business of international diplomacy.

There were some in the Foreign Office, like von Weizsäcker, later Secretary of State, who held that it was our patriotic duty to defend our independence at all costs; while there were others, the cynical Köpke amongst them, who considered the

Nazis so utterly childish that they would soon destroy themselves through their own incompetence. Even the Jews among us, men like Richard Meyer and the Counsellor of Embassy Sobernheim, treated the situation with light-hearted contempt. Prittwitz was the only one of us who really came to the correct conclusion by resigning. If the rest of us had followed his example, instead of seeking refuge in excuses, a serious blow would have been struck against the Nazi régime. As we failed to do anything of the sort, we were from the very outset morally disarmed and became the easy prey of opportunism that was in the end our most insidious enemy.

There were moments when I wondered, somewhat hysterically, whether I ought not to shoot the Führer. I had many opportunities of doing so, particularly as in those days we were not searched before audiences with him. Short of such action, what could I do? I could not face resigning from the Foreign Office and returning home to Laaske, and the thought of trying to earn a living in business was altogether repulsive to me. I could not contemplate leaving Germany and exiling myself in some foreign country, so there was nothing for it but to remain where I was. At the same time my position was far from happy, for so long as I remained in the service of the Nazis, consciously or unconsciously I felt that I was an accomplice in whatever they did.

Now, perhaps for the first time in my life, I longed to escape from Berlin to one of our embassies abroad where at least I would not be immediately involved in the Nazis' beastliness. They were perfectly aware that we in the Foreign Office did not whole-heartedly co-operate with them, and as a result we were far from popular with the Party. By threats and flattery they did their level best to entice us to join them. More than once Funk and Hanfstaengl hinted at the brilliant future that lay ahead of me if only I would join the Party, but I refused to be moved by their efforts. In the long run, however, such efforts met with quite considerable success among us. But they never managed to bring the entire Foreign Office into line, although they staged a special demonstration for our benefit in the gardens of the Casino in the Pariser Platz.

This took place on a lovely spring evening. We all assembled in the building and then walked out to the gardens to the strains of the overture from "Tannhäuser". The scene which greeted us was like a stage setting for a festival performance of the Nibelungen. Against the sunset the bare branches of the trees wove a strange pattern and between the shrubs and bushes banners fluttered from flagpoles, while the whole garden was illuminated by braziers mounted om high pedestals. About a hundred Brown Shirt youths, like the sons of the ancient German War-God, stood stiffly to attention, their faces hidden in the shadows thrown by the light of the blazing torches. Behind a huge, altar-like table stood Alfred Rosenberg, the Party Director of Education, with a number of other high-ranking Nazis. In contrast to this awe-inspiring gathering, our own party from the Foreign Office, many of them bespectacled and bald-headed, looked slightly ridiculous.

Having given the Nazi salute, which we returned somewhat raggedly, Rosenberg held forth to us for nearly two hours. I was standing between Bargen, who was very soon to become a full member of the Party, and von Bieberstein, who finally joined the Reichswehr as a last resort. Throughout Rosenberg's oration we kept digging each other in the ribs and struggling not to laugh aloud.

At the end of the performance the Horst-Wessel was sung. But since few of us knew the words even that fell flat, and Rosenberg and his Nazi assistants were left to sing alone.

*   *   *

At last, an entirely unforeseen chance gave me the opportunity to escape from Berlin. An elderly, married colleague was at that time Press Attaché of the German delegation to the League of Nations Disarmament Conference. He told me that he was tired of travelling back and forth between Berlin and Geneva and wanted to settle down. I at once said that I would be delighted to take over his post, if the Director of Personnel would agree. So in April I went to Geneva for the first time.

Between the two world wars, this Swiss town on the edge of a lake had a curiously artificial atmosphere. From being a homely, sober place, steeped in puritanical traditions, it suddenly became wildly cosmopolitan, frivolous and a centre of international intrigue. Since it was one of the most beautiful places in Europe, especially in spring, it was not surprising that delegates and diplomats from all over the world crowded to it, so that it took on the atmosphere of a fashionable spa rather than a seat of international affairs. Since everybody's expenses were being paid, they enjoyed themselves without stint. The promenade along the lake teemed with Excellencies and dignitaries of all nations, and their meetings reminded one of a scene from a Viennese comic opera.

"Ah, my dear friend!"

"What a pleasure, Monsieur le Ministre!"

"You are so kind, my illustrious friend......"

"Your Excellency, I am delighted......"

Kind enquiries were made regarding wives, or how the latest slimming cure was progressing; views were exchanged concerning favourite restaurants in Paris or Carlsbad and their specialities; the newest scandals from Cannes or San Sebastian were discussed, while any subject that might cause embarrassment to one party or another was most carefully avoided.

However much they might quarrel around the conference tables, these gentlemen met for an apéritif as the best of friends and shunned any discussion with the utmost delicacy.

But in 1933 the calm and elegance of Geneva was considerably ruffled by the appearance of Doctor Robert Ley and his companions. At that time nearly all the great powers lived in their own chosen hotels in Geneva, and since Stresemann's time we Germans had always stayed at the Carlton Park, on the outskirts of the town, with a charming view of the lake. That spring our Disarmament Delegation, led by the Ambassador, Nadolny, consisted entirely of career diplomats, officials and army officers, all of whom were used to moving in the best circles. The same could not be said for the German representatives sent to deal with other matters.

I heard that the night train was bringing a delegation to attend the session of the International Labour Conference. Its head was that ghastly ruffian, Robert Ley, whose name was already known to the public because he had brought the Trade Unions into line, forming a new organisation known as the "German Labour Front".

For some reason or another I was standing outside the hotel beside our delegation's Mercedes, which I had ordered to take the Ambassador to the Disarmament session, when a stranger appeared in the doorway followed by his entourage. He reminded me of Funk, and so I realised at once that he was a Nazi bigwig of some sort.

Without so much as a glance in my direction, Ley strode up to the car and curtly told the chauffeur to take him to the International Labour Office.

I hurried forward and pointed out that the car was waiting for the Ambassador, who would be appearing at any moment to go to the Disarmament Conference.

I could hardly believe my ears when Ley turned to me and said: "Tell your Ambassador he can kiss my arse!" He then stepped into the car and drove away.

That same morning, Ley denounced the South American delegates to the Labour Conference as "negro apes" because they refused to agree with him.

But not long afterwards a much more sinister figure appeared upon the Geneva scene, who, although less drink-sodden, was also quite unknown to most of us at the time. This was the SS Group-Leader Reinhard Heydrich, the future "Executioner

78

of Prague", who at that time was the Gestapo Chief in Bavaria.

He arrived at Geneva as an expert on para-military affairs, and his business was to explain to the world that the SS and SA movements were just as harmless as the Boy Scouts and other similar youth movements in various countries. Compared with Ley and his uncouth behaviour which were up to a point a source of amusement, Heydrich was a truly sinister and terrifying creature. There had already been a certain amount of scandal about the conditions at Dachau concentration camp of which he was in control, and from the moment he arrived in Geneva there was trouble. As soon as he noticed that we had omitted to hoist the swastika flag outside our hotel he made a scene with the Ambassador, threatening to throw all of us into a concentration camp. So far as possible we avoided him, but in my position as general handy-man to all the notables from Berlin, I had to dance attendance on him.

For some odd reason, he had arrived in Geneva without any luggage and had to buy certain things in the town. As he did not speak a word of French, I had to take him shopping. My instructions were "to take the young barbarian into the town and buy him a clean pair of pants". Thus it was that for the first time in my life I made the acquaintance of a professional murderer.

We set out in the official car, but as it was lovely weather, Heydrich decided to walk, and after making the necessary purchases we strolled back to the hotel together. By way of making conversation I said: "After sitting at an office desk in Munich, this must be a wonderful change for you."

He looked at me coldly. "Nowadays there is no time for pleasure. I have far too many serious things to occupy my mind."

I decided that once again the only thing to do was to appear a half-witted, harmless fool.

"But why not?" I asked. "Everyone has the right to enjoy themselves for a few days."

He gave me a contemptuous look. "You've no idea what happens if I'm not on the spot."

I became curious. "Why?" I asked. "With all the enemies of the State safely locked up in places like Dachau you surely can't have much to worry about?"

Heydrich stared at me archly. "You seem to think that everything's delightfully simple. We have certainly seen to it that some of the most dangerous elements can do no more harm, but there are still far too many running around. Some of them are so cunning that we have to be devilishly careful they don't slip through our net."

I pursued the subject with discretion. "But tell me, what do you intend doing with these people? You can't keep them locked up forever, or the atrocity propaganda will never end. Shouldn't there be a public trial as there was after the Reichstag fire? That would clear the air once and for all."

He stopped dead and glared at me. "You talk like a half-baked idiot," he sneered. "Those swine are not worth trying in a court of law. They can disappear without fuss. We'll fix them all right! We'll either shoot them while they're attempting to escape or polish them off in some other way."

Now, at last, I thought, I had learned from the lips of authority itself what one had always tried not to believe. From now onwards it was impossible for me to associate myself with those Germans who later said: "I never knew what was happening."

Before the autumn session opened at Geneva, I took my annual leave. As I passed through the lovely countryside on my journey south, I brooded on how repulsive Germany had become under the new régime. At that time the Nazis were preparing for their annual rally at Nuremberg, and at every wayside station the platforms were swarming with Brown Shirts, arrogant, swaggering brutes who seemed so utterly alien to their surroundings that they might have been a horde of foreign invaders overrunning my country.

On my holiday I travelled to Venice, Florence, Rome, Naples and Capri. In those beautiful places I met and saw many Fascists, but it was immediately apparent that they were an entirely different breed to those in Germany. One felt that these Italian youths did not take Mussolini's bombast with the bestial seriousness of their German counterparts. Eternal Rome had outlived many "Thousand Year Reichs" in her long history, and I felt instinctively that she would survive this new strutting dictator.

The Geneva Disarmament Conference of 1933 was the occasion for which the German militarists had been impatiently waiting ever since the death of Stresemann. The first step towards rearmament was the building of the first pocket-battle-ship in 1929, and others followed quickly. Brüning, while Chancellor, had boldly included the demand for "equality of military rights" in his programme, and von Papen had adopted it as the central theme of his foreign policy. He also got the Great Powers to agree to the re-appointment of official German Military Attachés in their capitals. Under the Schleicher régime the Powers had finally declared themselves prepared to recognise in principle the German demand for "equality of military rights", and to place this matter on the agenda at the International Conference. As Germany had already begun to re-arm secretly, Hitler was now able to reap the harvest sown by his predecessors.

It was at once obvious that the term "Disarmament" as applied to the proposed negotiations was sheer mockery and that it was in fact a cloak for the legalised re-armament of Germany. Hitler and the German General Staff were determined to re-arm, with or without international sanction. If it were possible, as a result of diplomatic wrangling, to induce the other Powers to reduce their armaments, so much the better. The Allies, however, had no intention of cuting down their armed forces, but were greatly concerned to put certain limits and controls upon German re-armament. If this was not done,

Germany might one day become a serious menace to peace again.

Thus, from the very outset, the Conference was a gigantic game of bluff and counter-bluff. Each side manoeuvred to place the blame on the other should the negotiations fail. Hitler, whose object above all else was to influence the German public in favour of his re-armament plans, announced one "generous peace offer" after another to the world. A standing army of 500,000, 300,000 or even 200,000 men; guns of no more than 30.5, 21 or even 15 millimetres in calibre. He was prepared to accept any and every limitation, provided the Allies would agree to disarm to the same level. Germany was already disarmed, and it cost Hitler nothing to juggle with such figures and hold out his hand in "brotherly understanding". To the Allies, however, who wanted safeguards and security from the eventual threat of a reborn German military machine, such offers were worthless, for they were made without any guarantees.

In such conditions it was scarcely surprising that there was no prospect of agreement being reached, and since neither side wished to be held responsible for the failure of the Conference, the debates degenerated into a slough of argument about trivialities. There were endless discussions as to whether a 15 millimetre howitzer was to be regared as a defensive or an offensive weapon, or when a heavy motor lorry would be classed as a potential of war or merely a peaceful form of transport. Hours were wasted considering whether Youth and Sports Organisations were military or purely civilian. In the midst of this hair-splitting the real problem, disarmament, was completely overlooked.

One day, the ridiculousness of the whole business was under-lined by the Soviet delegate, Litvinov, when in his broken English he declared to the Assembly: "It is all the same to me whether I am going to be stabbed by a knife, clubbed to death, shot with a revolver or blown to pieces by a shell. In any case I shall be dead. In my humble opinion, our task, gentlemen, is to see that none of these things happen, and that we remain alive."

While these negotiations dragged on through the autumn, sensational happenings were taking place in the Carlton Park Hotel. Up till now, the Geneva Conference had been the most important event on the international stage, for it offered the new masters of Germany the opportunity of making a dramatic debut before the world at large. So the most unexpected personalities had turned up in the hope of winning their spurs, and some of them behaved in the most uncouth manner. As I watched them, I could not help thinking that the famous Munich comic paper, *Simplicissimus*, would have paid any money to have reported the "student type" conduct of these beer-swilling, murderous ruffians. Their drunkenness in the bar and schoolboy buffoonery defy description, and sometimes endangered us in international incidents. One evening, for instance, Lord Cecil of Chelwood was forced to endure a revolting serenade under his windows, as a result of which our Ambassador was obliged to apologise officially to the British Delegation.

There was an even more unfortunate encounter which concerned the French. Members of our delegation often visited Mont Salève, just over the French border from Geneva. One evening we received a telegram handed in at the French post office by a party of Nazis. It ran as follows: "......'s body is at the Hotel X here. Please call for it." At first we thought there had been a murder and were about to send for the police when at the last minute the "body" in question turned up very much the worse for drink.

Even Goebbels, whose visit to the "talking shop" was brief, showed himself in a pretty poor light. Although he did not drink as much as some of his companions and was altogether more hardboiled than they were, he behaved like a complete cad. He brought with him about a dozen SS men, who shadowed him wherever he went. On the surface they were smart, dashing youths belonging to the SS-Reiter Sturm No. 13 in Berlin. Unfortunately their good manners were superficial, and in private they behaved even worse than the more usual type of Nazi rowdies. The latter could, at least, hold their drink, but these SS boys were often violently sick over the carpet in the bar after a few drinks.

The largest table in the hotel dining-room was always reserved for Goebbels, and he presided at it every evening and held forth to his admirers. He had brought with him his old friend, Lippert, who had been promoted to the post of Lord Mayor of Berlin. For the most part the conversation round the table consisted of a duologue between the two of them about their early days together. On one occasion I was privileged to listen to it.

"Do you remember that bowler-hatted swine of a Jew in the Kurfürstendamm who always went about with his hands thrust deep in his overcoat pockets?"

"Of course. And you stuck a rubber truncheon under his arm which you pinched from a policeman's belt when he wasn't looking!"

"Yes, neither of the fools noticed what we were up to! And then you ran back and told the policeman that the Jew had stolen his truncheon."

"Do you remember how he went for the Jew! God, it was funny!"

"And that other Jew you punched on the jaw. Remember him? He had the infernal cheek to take us to court!"

"And I got you off!"

"Yes, when you swore you'd slipped on a banana skin and pushed him accidentally......"

"And that ass of a judge believed it!"

"What fun the old days were! Much more fun than they are now when everything goes smoothly for us."

"Yes, life's a bit dull. But, thank God, no bloody Jews would dare to drag us into court nowadays......"

And so it went on......

One evening the club-footed Doctor played a trick on the correspondent of the *Berliner Tageblatt*, which was then not toeing the Nazi Party line and had on its staff one or two journalists who had been regarded as out-and-out Democrats in the days of the Weimar Republic. Amongst these was Herr von Stutterheim, who not only suffered the "fundamental disadvantage" in Nazi eyes of being married to an English-woman, but actually to the sister-in-law of Anthony Eden, the British representative at the League of Nations. Indeed, it was because of this connection that his paper sent him to Geneva. Goebbels had issued invitations to an important press confer-ence at which he intended to explain the significance of the New Germany before an international audience, and he made up his mind to create a sensation.

In an upstairs room in the Carlton Park the interpreters were hard at work translating the Doctor's prepared speech into various languages, since the majority of the correspondents did not understand German. The strictest orders had been issued that its contents were to be kept secret until it was delivered.

On this particular evening we were all sitting in the foyer of the Carlton Park when the hall porter came in with a telegram which had just arrived for His Excellency the Minister.

Goebbels opened it and frowned. "Listen to this, all of you," he shouted. "Here's a real piece of double-crossing!"

One could have heard a pin drop as he read aloud: "Why was not Goebbels's speech published this evening in *Berliner Tage-blatt* submitted to us? Request original official text by return. Press Department, Berlin."

The telegram caused a sensation. Some glared angrily at the quaking Stutterheim; others felt sorry for him as he muttered miserably: "I didn't pass it on. I know nothing about this. I only know it will cost me my job!"

For several minutes Goebbels gloated triumphantly over the wretched Stutterheim. Then he handed the telegram to those

85

sitting with him. We saw that it had not come from Berlin at all, but had been sent off from the Geneva Post Office on Goebbels's instructions. He had simply wanted to give the "damned Democrat, who was Eden's brother-in-law", a nasty fright.

Shortly afterwards, I myself became most unpleasantly involved in the machinations of the Goebbels lying machine. The German Minister of Propaganda's debut before the assembled foreign correspondents in Geneva had been only a very moderate success, and something had to be done about it. To this end, it was decided to make a sound film for general distribution. So the Herr Minister issued an announcement to the Press Room of the Disarmament Conference that he proposed to give a personal film interview to an English, French or American journalist. No-one, however, rose to the occasion. But there seemed to be no situation too awkward for Goebbels to tackle. By hook or by crook he could always find a way out.

Returning one afternoon from the town, I noticed as I neared the entrance to the hotel a whole battery of film camera apparatus set up in the garden. I was wondering what was happening when I was seized by the lapel by the SS leader, Prince Josias zu Waldeck-Pyrmont, who shouted excitedly: "Putlitz, where the devil have you been? We've been looking all over the place for you for the past hour."

Josias, one of Goebbels's chief sycophants, was a notorious bully even as a student in Munich. In 1945, at the end of the war, he was the highly qualified Gauleiter of Buchenwald Concentration Camp.

Now he was in a state of near panic. "For God's sake put your tie straight! You've got to appear in a talkie with the Herr Minister right away. You're to play the part of a foreign correspondent. Here are two versions of the script, one in English and the other in French," he said, handing me a bunch of papers. "You must learn them until you are word perfect.

The Minister will be here in a few minutes, so you haven't much time."

It was not long before Goebbels and his retinue made their appearance, and the show was on. I was seated on a garden chair facing a table, and beside me on a bench were the undersized Goebbels and the hefty Paul Schmidt, who later became Hitler's interpreter when he interviewed ambassadors and Heads of State.

The cameras began to turn.

"Que pensez-vous, Monsieur le Ministre......?" I began to drawl.

Schmidt translated my question into German and Goebbels made his reply which Schmidt repeated to me in French. The same farce was carried through in English.

The film was shown in the Berlin cinemas under the title: "The World Press makes a frenzied rush for interviews with Reichsminister Dr. Goebbels." Friends of mine who saw it were highly surprised to find the World Press solely represented by myself!

The film, incidentally, was also shown in Geneva, where I was to be seen daily in the corridors of the League of Nations Building and was known to everyone as a member of the German Delegation. So the fraud was quickly spotted and gave rise to so many scathing comments that a fortnight later Goebbels himself was forced to disclaim it. It goes without saying that not a word about all this was uttered in Germany, but the foreign press was bluntly assured that the whole affair was a Jewish fake which had been concocted by cunningly devised photomontage.

I must confess that I was delighted that I had contributed in a small way, even if involuntarily, to the exposure of Goebbels's propaganda methods. At the same time I was worried when friends told me that if I returned to Berlin I should probably be thrown into a concentration camp as a scapegoat for the affair.

CHAPTER ELEVEN

THE DISARMAMENT CONFERENCE dragged fruitlessly on. Neither side any longer expected a positive result. Even the Nazis gradually lost interest in the proceedings and top-ranking visitors from Berlin appeared less and less frequently at Geneva. Just as in the old days of the Weimar Republic, the career diplomats found themselves alone in the Carlton Park Hotel. But rumours were rife that Hitler was losing patience and intended to withdraw from the Conference. At that time, we thought that if he did so the Allies would immediately retaliate by re-occupying Germany.

On the morning of October 14th we were at our daily conference in the Ambassador's study when a telegram arrived informing us that Germany had not only withdrawn from the Disarmament Conference but had also resigned from the League of Nations. The telegram instructed us to return to Berlin immediately. This was a far more serious turn of events than anything we had dreamed of, and we were horrified at the news. Even Admiral von Freyberg and the other bigshots from the Bendlerstrasse were furious at such an irresponsible action, which they considered to be nothing more nor less than a gamble with the fate of Germany.

We sat like mourners at a funeral when the Ambassador officially informed the rest of the delegates that Germany was withdrawing. I was deeply moved by the way in which many of my opposite numbers took leave of me. Even in diplomacy there is a certain feeling of comradeship. However much the interests of their countries may be at loggerheads, a fellow-feeling exists, and I was touched by the sympathy shown to me. "Things have taken a serious turn," Sir Arthur Willert, of the British Delegation, said to me as we shook hands. "One can only hope that they will work out in the end and not go from bad to worse. Whatever happens, my wife and I will always be pleased to see you if you happen to be in London."

At dinner that evening with the Ambassador we discussed the events of the day and talked quite frankly about whether Hitler was really insane enough to want war. The Ambassador quoted a remark credited to Jules Cambon in 1914 when he was Ambassador in Berlin. When asked if the Germans wanted war, he replied: "No, they don't want war, but they demand the fruits of victory."

Someone else at the dinner-table remarked prophetically: "The post-war era is over and the pre-war era has begun." All of us were haunted by the certainly that this policy of Hitler's must end in final disaster.

The next day the German Delegation left for Berlin, but I stayed behind in Geneva with two secretaries of the Consulate to clear up the office work. After that, I made a leisurely return journey. It was a lovely autumn and vintage time in South Germany, so I drove slowly through the glorious red and gold countryside, stopping to drink wherever I felt like it. I finally arrived back in Berlin to find that my rôle in the Goebbels film had become the talk of the town. The old *esprit-de-corps* still reigned in the Foreign Office and it was considered most inadvisable for me to return to my former job in the Press Department, where I would come under the vindictive and unpredictable eye of Goebbels himself. Indeed, in the circumstances it seemed risky for me to stay in Berlin at all, so that it was to my great delight when I was appointed to our Embassy in Paris.

At last I had been given the post I had always wanted. Michel, who was now married, let me have his bachelor flat in Passy, and from its windows I could look down over the Seine to the

Eiffel Tower and the dome of the Invalides. I had, too, Pauline, his housekeeper, to look after me, who was an excellent cook. Yet Paris seemed changed. My dream of a Franco-German friendship had been dissipated by Hitler. Now the heavy tread of his marching columns thundering along the highways of the Reich seemed to re-echo down the Paris boulevards.

Michel and I often discussed the European situation. "You Germans have relapsed back into your old barbarism," he said. "You are a menace to the whole of civilisation, and the terrible thing is that while you are growing stronger, we are becoming weaker. I dare not think of the future."

"That's why we must stick together. You should do everything you can to help us to get rid of Hitler," I reasoned.

"I don't want to hurt your feelings, Wolfgang," he said gently, "but I've come to the conclusion that nothing will change Germany. Yet if Hitler were not such a swine, I wouldn't mind taking him off your hands. We need someone like him in France to-day to pull us together."

"You must be out of your mind!" I told him. But, unfortunately, a great many Frenchmen shared Michel's view at that time, especially in the circles in which I moved. There were Fascists who called themselves "Francists", and Schmolz, a Nazi in our Embassy, who was married to Goebbels's private secretary, was in close touch with them, although he admitted that they would never amount to much. Far more powerful were the French reactionaries, particularly the "Croix de Feu", led by a retired Colonel called de la Rocque, which more or less corresponded to Franz Seldte's German Stahlhelm.

Undoubtedly there was much uneasiness in the air in Paris in those days, perhaps akin to that which must have been felt in 1789 on the eve of the storming of the Bastille. There was rioting in the streets and clashes between the "Croix de Feu" and the military. After a while, I began to feel far from happy there, and the situation was not improved by the fact that I did not get on with our Ambassador, Roland Köster. He was not a

Nazi, but a narrow-minded reactionary whose wife had inherited a large fortune from the Liebig Meat Extract Trust.

There was no love lost between us, and he was only too pleased to be rid of me when our Ambassador in London, von Hoesch, offered to take me in exchange for one of Köster's former colleagues.

I left Paris for London in early June, 1934, and on board the Channel boat I ran into my new Chief, Leopold von Hoesch. Prior to von Neurath's departure from London a year before, Hoesch had been Ambassador in Paris for nearly ten years, and still visited his friends there. Since the deaths of Brockdorff-Rantzau and Maltzan, Hoesch was undoubtedly the best man in the German Diplomatic Service. Tall, slim, faultlessly dressed, with an intelligent face and a most kindly manner, he was the complete *homme du monde*.

We lunched together off smoked salmon and caviare for, as he said: "When one had just come from Paris, English food is too depressing."

He was far too much of a diplomat of the old school ever to make a statement which might commit him politically, but from his general attitude it was obvious that he had no patience with the present rulers of Germany. His world was exclusively one of international conferences and diplomatic salons, but in spite of his family background and wealth, he was no bigoted reactionary like his successor in Paris, Köster.

I could scarcely have taken up my new post in more happy circumstances. For a while I stayed with an old friend from Oxford, who lived in Belgrave Square, and later took a flat in Soho Square. As a Nazi diplomat, which I now was, life was altogether easier in London than in Paris. In contrast to France, Germans in general had even become popular in England, where the Nazi régime aroused a certain disgust but, at the same time, was looked upon as a passing phase. My English friends summed it up by saying "it all seems rather silly". Even the news of the Blood Bath of June 30th was treated lightly in

England. I do not think that anyone realised that on that day a deadly blow was delivered to any hope of a "second revolution" in Germany, or that from then on the military party was firmly in the saddle. From that moment the men in the Bendlerstrasse had a free hand to turn the whole country into a vast barracks. No-one could have the slightest doubt that they would plan to avenge the "shame and ignominy of 1918" and, in doing so, change the face of Europe. Even if the officers of the old school privately sneered at the "Bohemian Corporal" and his military qualifications, he was the magician who, after years in the shadows, had cleared the way for the re-establishment of their former glory. When shortly afterwards the Field Marshal died at Neudeck, they swore their allegiance to Hitler without hesitation, and even with enthusiasm. The majority of these opportunists, with their eyes on brilliant future careers, looked discreetly the other way when, on June 30th, Hitler shot two German Generals, Schleicher and Bredow. "Tradition", "Loyalty" and "Military Honour" were fine terms, but no good purpose would be served by protesting because these two men had been shot without even the pretence of a trial.

Captain Roehm and the SA leaders who were murdered with him were undoubtedly a pack of bloodthirsty sadists, and every shepherd boy in Germany was well aware of their morals. But so long as millions of Roehm's supporters, striving after a form of socialism, had a word to say in the policy of the Party, I always felt there was some hope of disrupting the Nazi system. That hope was now dead. The generals were top-dogs, and that fact could only lead to another war.

Over and over again during the months that followed I asked myself what I could do to check this fatal trend? I could, for instance, try to make the British people realise what was happening, for Britain was after all a World Power and, as such, must fear a dictatorship in Germany. It was already painfully obvious that the Western Powers had blundered when they had accepted Hitler's rebuff at the Disarmament

Conference without protest. Now, if this fanatic was not halted, war would be inevitable. But I found that most of my English friends considered Germany had the government which it deserved. "If you try to inflict your Nazism on us," they said, "then we'll give you a rap over the knuckles."

CHAPTER TWELVE

AS SOON AS I got to London I looked up Paul X. Some time ago he had lost his job as correspondent of a German newspaper, for the Nazis were aware of his political views. He now made his living dealing in antiques and pictures, while his wife, Gabrielle, earned her's as a painter. With their youthful son, Hugo, they were then living in a pleasantly unconventional way in a top-floor flat in a house in Kensington. Gabrielle ran the home in true bohemian fashion.

There were no set times for meals, and when anyone wanted something to eat they only had to light the stove in the kitchen and help themselves from the *pot-au-feu* which was constantly replenished with fresh meat and vegetables. How well Gabrielle understood the art of seasoning her dishes! Whatever the ragoût in the casserole might be, it always tasted perfectly delicious. Paul, too, was an excellent cook, and produced wonderful omelettes and pancakes.

As I was an embassy official, it would have been unwise for me to be seen in public with Paul, but I frequently went round to Onslow Gardens. Gabrielle was nearly always busy at her easel, and young Hugo in bed, so Paul and I would sit together chatting on the sofa in a corner of the room.

"Tell me," I asked him one evening, "what are your plans for the future?"

"At present, as you see, I'm just marking time," he answered. "My application for British naturalisation has been granted, as I have lived in this country for over five years. This is not only important for me, but for Hugo."

I asked him if he would not find it hard after so many years of political life to renounce Germany altogether.

"In a way, yes," he said. "But what choice have I when the Germans themselves have kicked me out of my own country? Gabrielle is, of course, French, and Hugo speaks perfect English and two other languages as well. I think we are sufficiently international to get along all right over here."

"And you have no further interest in Germany?"

Paul looked almost shocked at my question. "Of course I have. I shall go on moving heaven and earth to get rid of these damned Nazis!" he said hotly.

"But what can either you or I do? There's not the slightest hope of a revolution. The reign of terror grows daily worse, but no-one over here seems interested in what's happening," I added bitterly.

"The trouble is, Putlitz, that you meet the wrong kind of Englishmen," he said. "There are others who think differently."

"I wish you would introduce me to them!" I said.

"That wouldn't be difficult."

"Whom have you in mind?"

"Who holds the key position in the Foreign Office?"

"Probably the Permanent Under Secretary, Sir Robert Vansittart," I said, "and I can't believe that he approves of what is going on in Germany."

"He doesn't," Paul replied, "and there are many who agree with him. How little you know the British," he added. "You just think they're dull and stupid because they don't shout their opinions from the rooftops as the Germans do. You're wrong, you know."

By now I was convinced that under Hitler's rule disaster must overtake my country and therefore it was justifiable to use every possible means to destroy him. I found moral support for this view in a statement I had read recently in Duff Cooper's life of Talleyrand: "In the history of nations there are moments when an act of treason against a government which is leading the country to catastrophe and ruin is the sacred duty of every patriot."

On the other hand, I was only too well aware that I had no connection with any of the internal German opposition movements. How was one to know who was seriously opposed to the Nazis? So far as my colleagues were concerned, their ranting against Hitler was just empty talk, and the only Communist I had known in Berlin had disappeared without trace.

From now on, however, hardly a fortnight passed that I did not repair to Paul's flat, and there, in the charming and relaxed atmosphere of his family where I felt so perfectly at my ease, I would unburden myself of all the dirty schemes and secrets which I encountered as part of my normal daily routine at the Embassy. By this means I was able to lighten my conscience by the feeling that I was really helping to damage the Nazi cause, for I knew that Paul was in touch with Vansittart, who could use these facts to influence British policy. Though I never met Vansittart privately until 1938, we were often together at official and diplomatic functions, at which I used to make a point of asking to be introduced to him by one of my colleagues. This ritual must have been performed at least a dozen times, but only on one occasion did Vansittart respond with the ghost of a wink.

At the Embassy in Carlton House Terrace I was not directly concerned with questions of Anglo-German relations. I was in charge of the Consular Department, whose offices were in the basement and were known as the "Beer Section". In the latter there was only one really dangerous Nazi, who dealt with passports. The rest of my staff were reasonable enough creatures, and amongst ourselves we never gave the Nazi salute or said "Heil Hitler". In fact, whenever possible, those arrogant portraits of the Führer which were forced upon us were so hung that we saw them as seldom as we could help.

There was plenty of work in the Consular section and, probably more so than with the officials working upstairs, we had a pretty clear insight into the arbitrary workings of the Third Reich. As a result of decisions taken in Berlin, justice was so abused and the fate of individuals treated so capriciously that there were times when our hair stood on end. Most of our visitors were Jews and other refugees for whom a passport was of vital importance. In some cases we were able to help them by turning a blind eye to officialdom, but we had to be careful, for we could have landed ourselves in serious trouble.

Luckily for us, the Chief of the Aliens' Department at the British Home Office, a Mr. H. N. Cooper, was a man with his heart in the right place, and as I was in constant touch with him we soon became friends. Officially it was my duty to see that life in England should be made as difficult as possible for these wretched refugees, while the Nazis who wanted to work there should be given every assistance. "Party Comrade" Bene, a former agent for the hair tonic, "Trylisin", who had risen to the rank of Group Leader, was often in my office dictating harsh instructions or listening to my protests to Cooper which I made sound convincingly Nazi. But since Bene was not particularly bright, he never realised that I was acting, or that Cooper never took any of my protests seriously. We had come to an agreement that I should give him the full details of the various cases privately, and then he could decide what action to take.

At that time I did manage to keep several dangerous Nazis and cleverly disguised spies at a safe distance from England. One instance which resulted in a narrow escape for myself was that of a highly dangerous SS spy, who, like so many of them, went under the code-name of "Ludwig". I had heard that this gentleman would arrive on a certain day by mail-boat at Harwich, and had told Paul to warn the authorities to keep a careful eye on him. Stupidly I thought, the British arrested him before he was able to land, and brought him in custody to London —not, however, before he was able to throw all his compromising papers and a considerable sum of foreign money (in Hungarian *pengoes* of all things) out of the porthole. These, however, were finally fished out of the water, dried and shown me by Paul.

The fact that I now knew every detail of the activities of the sinister Herr Ludwig later proved highly embarrassing to me, as I shall relate presently. In his case the Embassy, contrary to all diplomatic precedent where espionage was concerned, was ordered by Berlin to intervene energetically on his behalf, and do everything in its power to have him liberated as soon as possible. This duty fell to me, of all people, as the head of the Consular Division. I had no option but to hand the case over to a British firm of lawyers with instructions to defend Ludwig in court. To my amazement the case, when it came up, was dismissed, and Ludwig was free to return to Germany quite unscathed. I could not resist a smile as I patted the proud lawyer on the back and congratulated him on his remarkable success. But it was at this moment, too, that I committed one of the most appalling *gaffes* of my career. I asked the lawyer whether it could be possible that Ludwig had spilled valuable information to the British in order to obtain his freedom.

A few days later the Embassy received a furious letter from Gestapo Headquarters in Berlin demanding my presence at a court of enquiry at which Ludwig would accuse me of impugning his honour to the lawyer, who must have reported my words to him. I was terrified and rushed to Paul. Paul in his turn was plunged in gloom. "This is the end of you if you return to Germany," he said. "You'll disappear into a concentration camp before you know where you are. I implore you Putlitz, for God's sake, don't go. Drop the whole dangerous game and take up British citizenship."

But I felt that anything was better for me than to become yet another refugee. There was at least a working chance that I might be able to bluff my way through, and live to continue my fight against Hitler. So I went. The enquiry took place at a Gestapo office in the West End of Berlin, and while it was in progress my brother Walter stood outside on the pavement with my passport in his pocket, in case I should have to make a quick break for it. This enquiry was the more an ordeal for me because I had to remain desperately on the alert to prevent myself revealing facts that could only have come into my possession from the incriminating papers salvaged by the British. Fortunately, however, the affair went better than I could have dared to hope, for, grim and obdurate though Ludwig remaind in face of all attempts at reconciliation, his SS lawyer (whose name was also, curiously enough, Ludwig) seemed increasingly to warm to my personality, so that in the end I really believe that he liked me. In any case, he managed to persuade his client to shake hands, which in the end we did, with assurances of mutual respect for each other's honour.

Another instance of an almost reverse nature was the case of Baillie-Stewart, the "Officer in the Tower". After his release from prison, he almost immediately showed up at the Embassy asking for facilities to move to Germany for good. It was obvious that if these were afforded him he would use them to work against his own country. I passed this information on the same day that I myself interviewed Baillie-Stewart, but it was of no avail. Had the authorities listened to me, and acted quickly on my advice, Lord Haw-Haw would have been deprived during the war of one of his most valuable assistants.

* * *

Inside the Embassy it was easy enough to hoodwink the Nazis; there once again I adopted the attitude of a harmless ass. I remember the case of a young man called Wehrhan. He turned up one day in the Passport Officer's room, handed him some documents and said that the German authorities were after him and he wished to give himself up voluntarily. He was brought to see me. Although he looked ill and down at heel, he did not make a bad impression.

"What have they got against you?" I asked.

"Nothing," he answered. "But someone whom they arrested denounced me, so I ran away."

"And now that you are here you want to go back and be arrested?"

"I don't know what else to do," he told me pathetically. "I haven't eaten for three days and have spent my nights sleeping on benches in Hyde Park. I would cut my throat, but I haven't got a razor. But, anyway, I can't end up here as a suicide because of my family and fiancée."

Nothing I could say would dissuade him from going home.

"All right," I said, "if you insist, I'll give you some money from the Assistance Fund. Then you can go to the German Students' Home where you can get a bed and something to eat. In the meantime, I'll find out when the next German ship sails for Hamburg."

The Passport Officer, wanting to prove his political zeal, immediately got in touch with Bene, who, since there was no German vessel expected in London for ten days, telephoned the Hamburg-Amerika Line and found out that a German-bound ship was calling at Southampton that week-end. It was arranged that the Captain of the ship should personally deliver the wanted man to the Hamburg police.

On the day before he was due to sail, Wehrhan turned up again and asked to see me. I scarcely recognised him. He was shaved, his eyes were bright and his voice steady.

"Hullo, suicide!" I laughed.

"Herr Consul, you must help me!" he pleaded. "The other day I saw no way out. But now I've found someone who will help me. I'm telling you in confidence that I'm not going to Southampton to-morrow. For God's sake give me back my papers!"

"What on earth do you mean?" I blustered. "Are you suggesting that I should take this risk just to help you? I advise you to change your mind. The matter is out of my hands and I can do nothing more about it."

"If I could only have my passport," he begged.

I could not help feeling sorry for him and sent for his papers. Deliberately removing the metal clips, I laid the passport on the top. "I hope you understand once and for all," I said looking at him sternly, "that I cannot act contrary to my instructions. The only thing I can do is to go and get you some more money." I saw that he understood, and when I returned with the money two minutes later, both he and his passport had disappeared. I kicked up a hell of a row and insisted that every corner of the building should be thoroughly searched, but Wehrhan had vanished for ever.

"What young blackguards there are in this world!" I grumbled to my Passport Officer and Bene.

"Yes, Putlitz," the latter remarked pompously, "you're much too trusting and still have a lot to learn."

For a time I enjoyed a far too easy-going reputation amongst the refugees to be regarded with a friendly eye by the Party, so that again and again I had to ask my friend Doctor G., whom I had helped to come to England with his whole family, to spread the rumour among the members of his Jewish Committee that anyone who ran such risks as I did must be under the special protection of the Gestapo. In the end, the suspicion that I was a Gestapo agent resulted in my being treated with greater respect by the Party members, for even they trembled at the thought of secret informers. But leading the life I did, I had to be perpetually on the *qui-vive* to say the least of it, a fact that certainly sharpened my wits but at the same time imposed a desperate strain on my nerves.

CHAPTER THIRTEEN

IN MARCH, 1935, like a bolt from the blue, Hitler announced to the world that he intended to re-introduce conscription in Germany. It was his first act of open defiance against the Versailles Treaty.

This, again, was a moment when the Western Powers should have taken immediate action. Instead, they decided not to answer the Führer's challenge with a categorical veto, although they indulged in threats. At a conference hastily convened at Stresa, they declared unanimously that this was the last breach of the Treaty to be tolerated without swift retaliation, and that any further arbitrary steps would be met by collective military and economic sanctions.

Thus Hitler found himself up against a coalition of the Great Powers. Not only England and France, but also Italy, under his professed friend Mussolini, had formed a united front against him. Indeed, it looked as if the foreign policy of the Third Reich had run into a cul-de-sac.

Like every other responsible member of the Foreign Office, von Hoesch decided that in a crisis of this kind, there was only one practical policy to adopt. There must be no further breach of the Treaty and a resumption of negotiations through the normal channels; in other words, a return to the League of Nations and the rules and traditions of the old diplomacy. It was with this plan in view that he drew up his reports for Berlin.

Hitler snorted with rage and indignation at "the cowardly and decadent" diplomats of the old school who could think of nothing better than to resume such antiquated and irksome methods of procedure. In his opinion, he had an adviser and mentor whose proposals held a far greater appeal. It had long been Herr von Ribbentrop's ambition to make a name for himself in the sphere of the Reich's foreign policy, and he was determined to prove to his Führer that he was the one man capable of achieving objectives which were considered beyond the realm of possibility by the boneheads of the Wilhelmstrasse. He suggested that in order to detach Britain from the Stresa front, a certain proposition should be made to her.

Ribbentrop's summing-up of the situation was more or less as follows: the agreement concluded at Stresa was aimed mainly, or even exclusively, at German re-armament on land. But before all else, Britain was a sea power, and her security did not depend so much on military strength as on remaining mistress of the seas. A great German army, which constituted a serious danger to France, was no direct threat to Britain so long as she possessed a vastly superior fleet.

Why, thought Ribbentrop, should not Britain be prepared to enter into negotiations if she were offered a Pact which would limit the German Fleet to one-third the strength of the British— above all, if she were assured that the West had nothing to fear from the newly created German army, since the Führer only intended to make use of it against Bolshevism in the East? When von Hoesch heard of Ribbentrop's project, he merely exclaimed: "The fool!" He saw what effect such unilateral action on the part of Britain was bound to have on both France and Italy. Moreover, he refused to believe that the British would abandon the united front so recently formed at Stresa in order to protect themselves against some future threat of a German navy, which was at the time non-existent. So far as he, Hoesch, was concerned, this dilletante Ribbentrop could come to London with his fantastic scheme and get snubbed for his pains.

He observed disdainfully the grandiose vanity with which the duly appointed "Emissary Extraordinary of the Führer" comported himself at the Carlton Hotel, surrounded by a staff of nearly a hundred.

For many years Ribbentrop had hated von Hoesch. The former had been an agent of the French champagne firm of Pommery & Grenot, the head of which was an influential member of Paris society, the Comte de Polignac, who was a regular visitor to the German Embassy in Paris while von Hoesch was Ambassador there. But the Ambassador had never invited Polignac's German representative, Joachim von Ribbentrop, to the receptions held in the former house of Hortense de Beauharnais in the rue de Lille. With his falsely assumed "von", the man was regarded as far too undistinguished to be included amongst the carefully chosen guests. As a result, Ribbentrop had long been bent on revenge.

Every member of Ribbentrop's London Delegation was obliged to give his word of honour not to reveal the smallest detail of the negotiations to any of the Foreign Office staff and, above all, to von Hoesch. The only official at our Embassy who was by force of circumstances involved in the secret discussions was the Naval Attaché, Admiral Wassner. He too was sworn to secrecy.

It so happened that the period was particularly suitable for these secret parleys, since they took place during King George V's Jubilee celebrations, and so did not arouse much public interest. At a time when accounts of the daily processions and festivities filled the newspapers, Ribbentrop's presence in London for official conversations passed almost unnoticed.

Even Vansittart did not seem to realise what devastating repercussions this isolated British move would have upon Mussolini and the French Prime Minister, Pierre Laval. The discussions, he said, were confined to mere technical matters which only concerned the naval authorities, who already knew how to keep Hitler within certain bounds. They were, however, conducted in the greatest secrecy.

One day I met Admiral Wassner in the street. "'Ribbentrop is getting away with it," he said. "It is scandalous that I can't talk to Hoesch."

The Admiral was no Nazi, but an officer with the traditional conception of correct conduct. His promise to Ribbentrop worried him, for it seemed to be an act of disloyalty to his legitimate chief. Because of the presence of numerous spies and informers, he could not even risk being seen in conversation with von Hoesch: but together we thought of a way round the problem. We had both been invited to a reception which was being given by Lady Weigall, the widow by a former marriage of the well-known pre-1914 Counsellor of the German Embassy, Baron von Eckardstein, at her house near Ascot. Earlier in the evening, Hoesch was attending the offical banquet at Windsor Castle given by the King and Queen, but told me that he would come on later to Lady Weigall's.

While everyone was dancing, Wassner made his way to the cloakroom. I gave Hoesch the tip to follow him and remained on guard outside the door. By a knock I signalled that the lobby was clear. After a while Hoesch emerged alone. He seemed deep in thought and scarcely noticed me as he returned to the ballroom. So in circumstances that could hardly be called dignified he had been told that the "fool" had proved a shrewder judge of the country to which he, Hoesch, was accredited, than he was himself. Ribbentrop's Naval Treaty was an accomplished fact.

The ceremonial drive of King George V and Queen Mary through the streets of London on His Majesty's birthday, June 14th, was the climax of the Jubilee celebrations. There was no better place from which to watch this spectacle than the broad terrace on the south of the German Embassy, beside the stately flight of steps leading up to Waterloo Place. Below lay the Mall, and from this vantage point we could watch the procession from the moment it left Buckingham Palace until the nodding plumes of the escorting Life Guards disappeared beneath the great Admiralty Arch leading to Whitehall. It was a brilliant summer's day, and the Embassy terrace was crowded with a remarkably mixed collection of people, among them a group of Nazis who made themselves conspicuous by their loud and aggressive behaviour.

I had invited my mother, as I knew how much regal pageantry appealed to her. As we came out on to the terrace, we noticed the Crown Princess of Germany and her sister-in-law, the Duchess of Brunswick, only daughter of the Kaiser, greeting von Ribbentrop. We could scarcely believe our eyes and ears when these two ladies raised their right hands and uttered the words "Heil Hitler!". My mother had been looking forward to meeting the Crown Princess again, but when she saw this exhibition she turned her back on her and said: "I only wish that I had never witnessed this disgrace to the Hohenzollerns!" After that, she deliberately avoided the two Princesses for the rest of the afternoon.

The guests on the terrace gradually drifted into two separate groups. In the left-hand corner, above the steps, stood von Hoesch, the Ambassador and host, surrounded by a throng of people, while on the extreme right Ribbentrop held court among a crowd of his admirers. When the State coach passed and the Royal couple looked up, several of the Nazis present even had the impudence to raise their arms in the Hitler salute. The incident did not receive any publicity at the time, but I can still see the horrified expression on von Hoesch's face as he drew someone's attention to it.

I felt sorry for him. Although he made every effort to appear friendly and at ease, those who knew him could see by his every glance how painful it was to be obliged to tolerate such an undignified situation in his own house. Even my mother remarked: "Why doesn't he retire? He's a wealthy man and not dependent on his salary as an Ambassador."

The results of the Anglo-German Naval Pact were not long in making themselves felt. Hitler had proved that the British Lion was not so dangerous as it appeared to be. Why, then, should

106

Mussolini be afraid of it? In the early summer the latter was bold enough to step hard on the Lion's tail by attacking Abyssinia. Only Britain, who had troops stationed in the Suez Canal Zone and whose fleet controlled the Mediterranean as well as the Red Sea, could have thwarted this move. But Britain now stood alone, since she could no longer count on the support of the other interested powers. France, threatened by the ever-growing strength of the German military machine, considered she had been left in the lurch by Britain and would now certainly avoid anything which might create further difficulties with her Italian neighbour. In fact, Pierre Laval, incensed by the London Naval Pact, even went to Rome to assure Mussolini of his friendship.

In these circumstances, Britain decided not to close the Suez Canal to the Italian Expeditionary Force, and confined herself to invoking the application of economic sanctions against the aggressor through the League of Nations. But Mussolini could regard this step with equanimity. The only commodity vital to the Italian war machine was fuel. In spite of blockade measures formulated on paper, his supply of oil was assured as the great international oil monopolies openly declared that they intended to ignore the ruling of the League. As things turned out, even British oil companies apparently made vast profits out of the Abyssinian campaign, and, furthermore, the shareholders in the Suez Canal found nothing to object to in the mounting dividends reaped from Italian shipping passing through it. So the British Government decided to make the best of a bad job and finally expressed approval of Italian aggression through the so-called Hoare-Laval Pact. They hastily escorted the Emperor Haile-Selassie out of his country and put a house at Bath at his disposal. Apparently he lived there quite humbly, for one of my friends in London, who was in touch with the Abyssinian Court, told me of a somewhat tragi-comic incident. The Emperor, he said, had brought with him a chest from his Treasury in Addis Ababa which contained a gold dinner service alleged to have belonged to the Queen of Sheba. When he found himself short of money, he tried to sell one of the plates, bearing the arms of the Lion of Judah, to a London dealer. To his dismay, he was told that the heavy gold plate was, in fact, made of coated lead!

The unity of the Western Powers, which had been achieved at Stresa with such high hopes for the future, continued to disintegrate. Hitler, in turn, began to adopt a more and more audacious foreign policy. In March, 1936, the Wehrmacht suddenly marched into the Rhineland, demilitarized by the Versailles Treaty. Would the Allies stand this without declaring war?

Not only the Foreign Office but the Ministry of War were apprehensive. But they still overrated the Western Powers' will to resist. Von Hoesch, and even the attachés of the three branches of the Reichswehr in London—military, naval and air force—sent desperate telegrams to the Reich Chancellery with urgent requests that the German troops be ordered to retire if British and French forces entered the zone. Indeed, a secret assurance to that effect was actually secured from Hitler.

The dreaded enemy, however, failed to appear. Mutual trust between Britain and France had already been too badly shaken for the two countries to embark on swift collective action. "You go first" was the attitude, and the only result was a special meeting of the Council of the League of Nations, this time in London.

Ribbentrop had always been alone in his vehement assurances to the Führer that "You can safely tread on the British Lion's tail. He roars, but no longer bites." Whenever the others had counselled caution and discretion, Ribbentrop had been proved right, so that it was now all too obvious that he was the man to act for the Nazis in their relations with the Western Powers.

For the second time within a year a large Ribbentrop delegation arrived at the Carlton Hotel. The only high-ranking official from the Foreign Office amongst its members was

Dieckhoff, later to be an Ambassador, an uncle of Adenauer's future adviser, Herbert Blankenhorn. Although Dieckhoff had strong Nazi sympathies, he was at the same time a man of the old school. The SS and SA men on Ribbentrop's staff being quite inadequate when it came to serious, practical work, he asked the Embassy to lend him a secretary. I was appointed as his assistant, for Hoesch knew quite well that every evening I would give him a detailed report of the day's session.

The meetings of the League Council were held in a mediaeval room in St. James's Palace, where the delegates of the various countries sat round a horseshoe table to discuss whether Germany had been guilty of a breach of the Versailles Treaty. Of course, the answer was obvious to the merest child. When the question was put to the vote the monosyllables "Yes", "Oui" and "Si" were heard all round the table. The resounding "Oui" which came from the tight-lipped mouth of Poland's Foreign Minister, Colonel Beck, remains vividly in my memory to this day.

During the proceedings Ribbentrop sat with arms folded, gazing out of the window with an air of complete indifference. There was no question of any form of sanctions being applied, and, in spite of the verdict, he emerged the undisputed victor.

Only once during the meetings did I see Hoesch, pensive and alone, among the onlookers. Every evening I went to his study and gave him an account of the day's discussions. He possessed very shrewd judgment and gave his opinion on the possible outcome of each move made by the various parties concerned. His distress was quite apparent, for the development of the situation gave rise to acute anxiety. After the final session, which passed without incident, he remarked with a wan smile: "Things may continue to go smoothly for a while, but they can only end in disaster."

The Easter holiday followed and I already had a ticket for Paris in my pocket. As I left my office, I met von Hoesch on the Embassy steps and we walked together a little way towards

Piccadilly. He asked me to give his regards to certain friends in Paris and wished me a pleasant holiday. Then he suddenly broke off and pointed excitedly to the entrance of a travel agency a few yards away.

"Did you see that man they just carried through the door?" he asked. "He suddenly fell down on the pavement. It must have been a stroke. A good way to die," he added, almost to himself.

Actually, I had noticed nothing and wondered whether Hoesch was imagining things.

That same evening I flew to Paris and, on picking up my paper the following morning, saw to my horror the headline: "German Ambassador Dies Suddenly in London".

When his valet brought him his breakfast on Good Friday morning, Hoesch had seemed quite cheerful. But an hour later, the valet found him dead on the bathroom floor. There were endless rumours as to the actual cause of death. Some said Hoesch had always suffered from a weak heart, while others declared he had been murdered by the Gestapo. His valet was inclined to think that he had deliberately taken his own life by swallowing some drug, but there was no evidence in favour of any of these theories.

The British Government paid him the highest honours. With the then Foreign Secretary, Anthony Eden, amongst the mourners, a long funeral cortège set out from the Embassy and proceeded along the Mall, past Buckingham Palace, on its way to Victoria Station, where a special train was waiting to convey the coffin to the coast. There, to the tolling of bells and a salvo of guns, a British destroyer steamed away bearing him across the North Sea on his last journey to Germany.

The German Press paid scant attention to the passing of its country's Ambassador to the Court of St. James'. Only his relations and Herr von Neurath, with a few old friends from the Foreign Office, were present at his burial. The official mourners had been deliberately reduced to the minimum, and even Herr von Ribbentrop saw fit to refrain from paying a final tribute to his rival.

For nearly six months after Hoesch's death no new Ambassador was appointed to London, and during this interim period Prince Otto Bismarck, Counsellor of the Embassy, acted as Chargé d'Affaires, Since I was a child, I had been in contact with the Bismarck family. My father's French governess later looked after the Bismarck children; she often came to see us at Laaske and told us stories about the household at Friedrichsruh. Throughout my life I had run up against Otto, the eldest son, who was three years my senior. Being a Prince, he had enjoyed many advantages over me. In 1916, when I was a cadet training to become a subaltern in the reserve of the 3rd Uhlans of the Guard and sweating on the parade ground at Potsdam, Otto Bismarck stood watching with folded arms. He did not have to start as a humble recruit, but was gazetted straight away a lieutenant in the Garde du Corps. In 1926, when I and others like me were working at our Foreign Office courses, he was appointed without more ado to the rank of Counsellor of Legation, a post which we could only hope to attain after twelve or fifteen years in the Service. At the end of 1932, shortly before Hitler came to power, my brother Gebhard and I spent an afternoon at Friedrichsruh. Prince Otto, who had retired from diplomacy under the Weimar Republic, was living quietly at home where he remained until the advent of the Nazi régime, which promptly re-appointed him to the higher rank of Counsellor of Embassy.

The Prince had certainly become a member of the Nazi Party at the right moment. His wife, a chic, good-looking Swede, spoke German with an accent that apparently reminded fat Hermann Goering of his deceased wife, Karin. For this reason it was said that the Marshal had a tender regard for the Princess Anne-Marie, and it was thanks to him that she became the most charming "publicity agent" in London which the Third Reich ever possessed. Among other things, she caused a good deal

111

of comment at Sandwich by dressing her children in bathing dresses with a swastika embroidered on their left breasts.

The Bismarcks were a couple endowed with all the social graces; they possessed a wide circle of international friends, and the Ribbentrops were quite unable to compete with them. In spite of their recognized propaganda value, this led to the final disappearance of the Bismarcks from the London scene when the Ribbentrop family established themselves in the Embassy in the late autumn.

CHAPTER FOURTEEN

THE BRITISH THRONE also experienced an interim period in the course of the same year. George V., who had celebrated his Jubilee in the spring of 1935, died the following winter, and was succeeded by his eldest son, Edward, Prince of Wales. For several years it had been rumoured that the Heir to the Throne was far from eager to assume the rigid and tedious role of Sovereign, and that he preferred to spend his time in the company of various members of international society on the Continent. His mother, however, had exercised a certain restraint and moral influence over him.

I witnessed an example of this on the occasion of her last Court at Buckingham Palace. Owing to the King's illness she was obliged to receive the homage of his subjects seated on the throne in solitary state. On these occasions, we younger members of the Diplomatic Corps were usually placed behind the Yeomen of the Guard, who stand facing the throne. From here it was possible to watch each and every move of the Monarch and members of the Royal Family.

Erect and dignified as always, Queen Mary sparkled with diamonds and acknowledged with a smile and an inclination of the head all those who made their obeisance before the throne. Around her stood her four sons; on her right, slightly in advance of the others, was the Prince of Wales, on her left, the Duke of York, and in the rear the Dukes of Gloucester and Kent. I noticed that the Prince of Wales fidgetted with his feet and was generally restless. Though the Queen continued to look straight ahead, bowing affably, I saw that something was annoying her. Suddenly diamond bracelets glittered, and almost imperceptibly her hand moved towards the Prince of Wales's arm. A brief but firm touch, a movement of her lips, and the arm was discreetly withdrawn. From that moment on the Prince stood stock still.

The story of his abdication is too well-known to re-tell here. It is sufficient to say that it was deeply regretted by the Nazi Party, who were wrongly convinced that Edward VIII had Fascist sympathies. It is, however, an unfortunate fact that after his abdication he made a long tour through the Third Reich in company with Doctor Ley, for the purpose of studying the social structure of the Nazi régime.

I was not without my own personal worries in the year 1936. Up to that time, Secretary of Legation Brücklmeyer (executed in 1944 for complicity in the plot of July 20th) and I were the only high Embassy officials who were not members of the Nazi Party. The comparatively inoffensive Group-Leader Bene had been recalled and superseded by a far more ruthless type of man, an ex-naval Captain named Karlowa. On Ribbentrop's appointment as Ambassador, the Party Leadership refused to tolerate the old state of affairs any longer, and Brücklmeyer and I were presented with an ultimatum—to agree to join the Party within a week.

This was a bitter and distressing situation. A refusal would have certainly meant the end of our careers. Possibly I would have been allowed to return home and remained unmolested at Laaske, where my father was then suffering from a fatal illness. On the other hand, as Mr. Cooper assured me, I could stay in England as a refugee.

Several times I discussed my predicament with Paul far into the night. Both he and my friend, Doctor G, said that I ought not to relinquish my post. So long as I stayed in the Diplomatic Service there was always the possibility of acting against the Nazi interests. In Laaske, or as a refugee in England, I would be completely isolated. They admitted that my joining the Nazi Party would be a repulsive business, but insisted that Nazi lies and treachery could only be fought with similar tactics. Should I be adversely criticized at a later date, they would be prepared to swear before any tribunal in the world that I was Hitler's enemy, heart and soul.

Needless to say, such duplicity ran counter to my ingrained sense of honour, but I had all my life sought to work for the benefit of my country. Now that I saw clearly that this gang of thugs was leading Germany to catastrophe, I could not possibly throw up the sponge and rest content to let things drift. Moreover, I saw no other field of activity where I could put a spoke in the Nazi wheel.

And so I reported to Karlowa and declared my readiness to become a Party member. In addition to Brücklmeyer and myself, several other members of the German colony were to take the oath of allegiance in the London Nazi headquarters. There were about a dozen of us as we stood before a portrait of Hitler in the presence of a gathering of London Nazis, and repeated after Karlowa the words: "I swear loyalty to my Führer Adolf Hitler". In order to assuage my sense of shame, while I raised my right hand to take the oath, I straightened my left and pointed three fingers to the ground to act as a sort of lightning conductor!

Shortly after this I went to Laaske to see my father, who was dying. During one of his last moments of consciousness he sent for us all to his bedside, and said in a failing voice: "My children, if you allow a single swastika to be flaunted at my funeral or a Heil Hitler to be uttered, I shall risee from my grave and set about you!"

In accordance with tradition, he was laid to rest in the soil of his ancestral home, and we saw to it that his last wish was observed. It was only after his funeral that I confessed to my family what I had done. Even my mother forgave me. She knew how much I loathed the Brown Shirt pest. But only someone who has lived through a similar experience will realise to what a degree I had now lost my zest for life.

I returned to England to marvel again that, in spite of all the reports in the newspapers about the brutalities in the concentration camps, the persecution of the Jews and the arrests of the clergy, the general feeling towards the Third Reich was still not entirely hostile. Indeed, the press seemed inclined to avoid an attitude which the Nazis might regard as provocative.

That summer, the Germans excelled themselves in their brilliant organisation of the Olympic Games. At the same time, tempted by the offer of marks at a dirt-cheap rate of exchange, English tourists were induced by the thousand to spend their holidays in Germany.

Occasionally at official dinner parties I felt acutely embarrassed when an M. P. on my right or an influential journalist on my left remarked: "What Hitler has achieved in Germany is quite amazing. The order and cleanliness...... the punctuality...... the service in the hotels...... really wonderful!"

What sort of reply could I possibly make? As a rule, I merely expressed gratification by saying: "I'm glad you enjoyed your visit to my country." Sometimes I thought I would be provocative: "Take care we Germans don't outstrip you English in a few years!" But it was impossible for me as a diplomat to tell these people what I really thought.

In this same year a society was founded in London under the name of "The Anglo-German Fellowship", whose object was to foster friendship and co-operation with the Third Reich. Many of those who joined it were influential in the world of high finance and commerce, and most of them were deeply sincere in their desire to avoid a recurrence of war. But, in spite of everything, Ribbentrop's arrival was awaited with mixed feelings, not unlike the curiosity aroused by the arrival of the latest strange beast acquired by a zoo. Many of his odd or tactless remarks made during previous visits were going the rounds in London, and even before his appointment as Ambassador he had earned the nickname of "Brickendrop".

When he stepped on to the platform at Victoria Station and held his outstretched arm on high for a full half-minute in acknowledgment of the welcome of the assembled London Nazis, the reporters and photographers just laughed. Then it was the turn of us members of the Embassy staff to accompany him to his new residence. This was not the Embassy in Carlton House Terrace, but a house in Eaton Square of which he had acquired a lease from the owner, no less a person that Neville Chamberlain, the new Prime Minister. The old Embassy, whose dignified and peaceful rooms had, for over a hundred years, been occupied by the representatives of Germany, and before 1870 by a King of Prussia, was not good enough as it stood for Joachim von Ribbentrop. As a result, Hitler, with the utmost generosity, had placed the trifling sum of three million marks—drawn from the financial resources of the German people—at his disposal to modernise the building. At the same time it was to be immensely enlarged by the acquisition of the lease of the adjoining house.

About two hundred German workmen, electricians and plumbers were kept busy on this job for six months. They were lodged in the Embassy attics and meals were provided for them from a field kitchen. The strictest discipline was maintained by an SS-Leader, who issued passes to those who wished to go out. A room was even set aside in which unruly elements were detained: the worst cases were conveyed to Croydon Aerodrome and flown by Lufthansa back to Germany for punishment.

We had to carry on our daily work while our offices were undergoing these alterations. We could often hardly hear ourselves speak above the noise, and frequently went home grey with dust. Actually, the taking over of the house next door was necessary, as Ribbentrop had brought with him so vast a staff that the number employed at the Embassy was increased by one hundred per cent. No-one knew what the duties of many of them were. Most of them spent their time roaming the

117

streets or travelling about the country on supposedly secret assignments. Others were detailed for special jobs or appointed private secretaries or personal adjutants. The Gestapo was represented by two higher police officials called Schulz and Mittelhaus. The new Ambassador had also brought with him a dozen so-called orderlies, some of whom were the usual type of young SS-men, who had imagined that they would be living in grand style in London. Instead, they were put to polishing floors and door-knobs, washing crockery and doing other domestic chores for Frau von Ribbentrop, which made them highly indignant. They, too, were under the strict discipline of an SS sergeant named Scharschewski. Those who were married were obliged to leave their wives behind, and so far as I could discover the only interest von Ribbentrop took in their private lives was to present with a gold watch and chain any of them who announced that his wife had given birth to a son who had been christened "Adolf" or "Joachim".

Fortunately Ribbentrop did not take much notice of me. He considered it beneath his dignity to set foot in my basement offices or show any interest in the Consular Service. He had not the faintest inkling of official routine, and would not have known where to affix the stamp on a affidavit or a sailor's identity papers. He not only left me in peace but even supported me whenever I had to defend myself against the constant attacks made by Karlowa and the Party on the way in which I performed my duties. This mark of favour resulted from a rather singular incident.

When I had last been in Germany, I had called on Raumer at his villa in the Grunewald in Berlin. At dinner we had discussed the peculiarities of my new chief in London.

"I'll give you a talisman which will protect you against anything," the old fox had told me. After dinner, in his study, he had produced a small packet from his writing-table drawer.

"Look at this," he had said, "I bought it the other day in a junk shop in the Friedrichstrasse for three marks."

He had handed me a bronze medallion about the size of a dollar. On the reverse were the arms of the City of Carlsruhe and the date, 1838. On the front was a male head in classical profile, above which were the words: "Pro Meritis de Ribbentrop"—for the services of Ribbentrop.

"I don't know exactly what this Ribbentrop did," Raumer had said, "but he must have played some part in the War of Liberation. He was not a direct ancestor of our Joachim, and from what I've heard, the connection is a distinctly vague one. But that doesn't matter. He was called Ribbentrop and there's "de" before the name. Perhaps this "de" is merely a new form of Latin genitive. But for Joachim it will certainly be taken as proof of noble blood. He'll be everlastingly grateful if you make him a present of it," he had added with a chuckle.

I took the medallion with me to the first dinner party which the Ribbentrops gave to the members of the London Embassy, and before we sat down, walked up to Joachim and said: "Your Excellency, may I be permitted to present you with a medal?"

He looked at me in astonishment. "Have you gone crazy?"

"Not at all, Your Excellency. Here it is." I drew the medal out of my pocket.

Ribbentrop took it and examined it closely. "You wish to give this to me?" he asked smilingly. "It's really most kind of you!" During dinner he raised his glass to me three times, while his Counsellor, Wörmann and the others were accorded this favour only once.

Later, in the drawing-room, he invited me to sit down beside him over coffee. His two adjutants, Spitz and Thörner, stood stiffly by, ready to carry out any order.

"Do you know, Putlitz, whose head that is on the medal?" he asked.

"No, unfortunately, I don't, Your Excellency. But I do notice a certain likeness between yourself and the profile," I flattered.

"This Ribbentrop was historically one of the most influential men of the nineteenth century," he informed me.

119

I remained silent.

"You remember Count Yorck von Wartenberg, who signed the Convention of Tauroggen?"

"Naturally, Your Excellency. I have a fairly good knowledge of Prussian history."

"In that case, you'll agree that the whole course of European history would have turned out very differently during the last hundred years if General Yorck had not made the alliance with the Tzar of Russia. It would have been impossible otherwise to have formed the coalition against Napoleon."

"That, Your Excellency, is highly probable."

"Well, the Ribbentrop on the medal held one of the most important posts on General Yorck's staff. He was Quartermaster-General. So you see you have given me something of exceptional historical interest, and I would like to thank you once again most sincerely."

Then he lapsed into a meditative mood. "Spitz", he said, "remember to send a telegram first thing tomorrow morning to the General Staff in Berlin. So far as I can remember, they have a portrait of this man. It can now be returned to the family."

I never met Ribbentrop on such intimate terms again. But that one conversation bore fruits which lasted for years. Raumer's talisman, bought for three marks, served as a protection against the many perils and pitfalls to which I was exposed during Ribbentrop's term of office.

On taking up his post in a foreign capital, it has always been a traditional custom for an ambassador to address a formal letter to the representatives of other countries in order to establish relations. For several centuries the language employed on such occasions has been French, but the language of the country to which he was accredited was also permissible. Hence, Ribbentrop could have addressed his foreign confrères in London either in French or English. To do so, however, seemed beneath the dignity of the "German Nation's Thousand Year Reich". It

120

was high time that German was recognised as a "world language".

The missives in question were therefore despatched in German. As was only to be expected, the recipients replied in their native tongues. None of us could decipher Japanese, Siamese or Arabic, and so had no idea whether the writer intended to call on Herr von Ribbentrop on Monday morning or, for that matter, at midnght on Friday. So in each case we were obliged to make enquiries by telephone and resort to English or French.

Ribbentrop's preference for the "Deutsche Gruss" or "Heil Hitler" salute was already well-known in London, and it was a matter of amused speculation whether he would indulge his weakness on his first official appearance at Court. Apparently, the King himself was prepared for the worst. The first opportunity for enacting this comedy occurred at a levée held by King George VI at St. James' Palace.

Levées usually take place in the morning and are attended exclusively by men. Neither the Queen nor any other woman is present. On such occasions the King is not seated on a throne, but receives his guests standing on a daïs. To my mind, a levée held in the great mediaeval room of St. James' Palace is a far more romantic and picturesque affair than a Court held in the comparatively modern setting of Buckingham Palace. Members of the foreign Diplomatic Corps assemble in a dark, panelled antichamber, the walls of which are hung with the portraits of long dead Kings and Queens. From this room they walk out in single file, the order of precedence being determined by their seniority and rank.

To Ribbentrop's disgust, fate decided that we were placed between the Ambassador of the U.S.S.R. and the representative of the then Spanish Republic. In England the demands of etiquette are sacrosanct, and there was nothing that could be done about this unfortunate contretemps. So the Ambassador was obliged to enter the Royal presence immediately behind the most junior attaché of the Soviet Embassy.

121

At one time it was customary for an Ambassador to present the members of his staff to the King. Nowadays, however, after making his obeisance, he remains standing at the King's side until his colleagues have passed. By virtue of my official rank I was somewhat in the rear of our lengthy file and could thus watch how von Ribbentrop acquitted himself. His behaviour, however, was normal and correct. Relieved that the dreaded "Heil Hitler" had failed to materialise, the King turned to the next comer, our First Secretary, Wörmann. But at that moment, Ribbentrop, now standing beside the King, suddenly shot up his right arm, almost under the King's nose. George VI, a highly-strung man, was so startled that I feared he would lose his balance. However, he soon regained control of himself and behaved as if the incident had not happened. But everyone present had seen it, and the entire Press regaled their readers with enough stories of Ribbentrop's latest and most brilliant exploit to keep them in a state of laughter or indignation for days.

Many thought that Ribbentrop would realise that he had committed a gross blunder. Personally, I did not think so and never doubted that he would behave in the same scandalous and foolish way again.

A few weeks later there was a diplomatic reception at Buckingham Palace. On this occasion only the Heads of Missions were to be presented together with those who were attending the Court of St. James's for the first time. We old hands remained behind our friends, the Yeomen of the Guard. I was standing next to a Counsellor of the Austrian Legation, a Herr von Blaas, who was a friend of mine.

"Surely your chief won't swing his paw this time?" he whispered to me.

"I'm ready to bet you that he will," I replied, and he accepted my bet of a pound.

Ribbentrop's turn came. He stepped forward before the throne. Promptly his arm shot upwards. Moreover, this time it was fully extended in the true regulation fashion. But the distance between him and the Royal couple was sufficient to arouse only a tolerant smile instead of alarm.

Later, in the magnificient picture gallery where the buffet was installed, Herr von Blaas handed me my easily earned pound note.

When not likely to be overheard by members of his staff, we senior officials of the Foreign Office always referred to Ribbentrop as "the Statesman". We could only listen to his "lectures on politics" with straight faces so long as we never looked at one another. Indeed, at times it was difficult not to laugh out loud. Before he started to speak, he always adopted the same posture of one in a state of deep meditation, not unreminiscent of Julius Caesar before crossing the Rubicon. He liked to make use of pencils, rulers and paper-weights to illustrate his points. A blotting-pad, for example, became the Soviet Union and the pencil pointing towards it from the right represented Japan. A sudden move, and the latter was in Manchuria. The fountain-pen, with the nib aimed at Russia and the other end pointing towards France, was the German Reich. The ruler, which was Italy, reached Abyssinia to the right and Spain to the left. The piece of rubber, England, being well outside this group of powers, was quickly brushed away. France, between the fountain-pen and the ruler, found herself therefore helplessly between pincers. No country on earth could hope to thwart such a colossal strategic superiority!

The problems of international politics could not have been solved in a more naïve yet pretentious manner across the bar of a pub than they were in our "Statesman's" conference room. His ignorance of politics was limitless. When he was busy forming the Berlin—Rome—Tokio Axis, he appointed to his staff a certain Herr Sthamer, later Ambassador in Tokio, as an expert on Japanese affairs. Even Sthamer's knowledge was not overwhelming; nevertheless, he had studied Japanese history to a considerable extent. In a lecture which we all attended he

123

stated that the Peace of Shimonoseki was a decisive turning point in Japan's policy of expansion on the mainland of China. "Please tell me," our "Statesman" interrupted, "who was this Shimonoseki? I cannot remember for the moment."

Sthamer was obliged to inform him as tactfully as possible that Shimonoseki was not a statesman but the name of the place where that questionable Peace Treaty was signed.

One of my colleagues and I often amused ourselves at Ribbentrop's expense. During the reconstruction of the Embassy an electrician had pointed out to me the exact spot in my office behind which a microphone was installed for the use of his Gestapo agents, Schultz and Mittelhaus. In the late afternoon, when they were usually listening, we would sometimes sit near this spot and indulge in a conversation specially intended for their ears.

"Oskar, do you think Ribbentrop is really as great a statesman as Bismarck?" I would ask. And he would answer with conviction: "Do you know, I believe he is probably greater."

These childish pranks were really the result of the uneasy state of mind in which the more serious among us lived from day to day. They were the outlet for our sense of moral cowardice and the fact that there was no escape from our degrading situation.

In 1937 Ribbentrop concentrated most of his energy on the Civil War then raging in Spain, and scarcely missed a single sitting of the Non-Intervention Committee which held its meetings at the British Foreign Office.

The two Fascist dictators, Hitler and Mussolini, were in complete agreement regarding the future of Spain. General Franco was in urgent need of help. His organized plot against the Republic was threatened with failure owing to the fierce resistance of the majority of Spaniards. So he sought allies who could help him materially. To both Hitler and Mussolini this offered a heaven-sent chance to test the efficiency of their latest weapons. Furthermore, they calculated that they could rely on a victorious Franco to support the Axis in any future differences with the Western Powers. Thus, the combined policy of the Axis was to secure a victory for Franco at all costs.

Franco's unofficial envoy in London was the Duke of Alba, descendant of Philip ll's notorious Governor of the Netherlands. Alba was a distinguished figure in English society, a fine shot and a splendid horseman. At the same time, there was a former Ambassador also working for the Franco cause in London who was scarcely less influential than Alba, namely Merry del Val. Both these men were on friendly terms with Ribbentrop, and for hours on end the latter discussed with them ways and means by which the policy of Non-Intervention might be side-tracked. I was not actually involved in these political activities, but did attend one or two secret conferences at which Ribbentrop, Wörmann and others were present. The main object of the Nazis was to see that the Non-Intervention Committee was kept busy investigating alleged Soviet breaches of the Convention. If and when, after weeks of enquiry, the charges proved false or there was lack of evidence to support them, grounds for further indictment were promptly produced. Ribbentrop's accusations concerning the entry of Soviet troops and war material into Spain were, as often as not, pure fabrications.

I remember one instance in which he wanted to announce that 20,000 Russian soldiers had landed in Valencia.

The cautious Wörmann interjected: "That's too many. No-one will believe that!"

Finally, the figure of 2,000 was approved, and a fiery protest immediately delivered. Needless to say, the despatch of German military assistance to Spain was roundly denied. The "Condor Legion" apparently consisted solely of volunteer pilots, and it was beyond the power of the German Government to prevent them making their way secretly to Spain. Nor could it restrain an occasional adventurous youth from stowing away in a collier bound from Hamburg or Bremen and subsequently bobbing up in German uniform on a Spanish battlefield.

It will remain an indelible stigma on the British and French members of the Non-Intervention Committee that they gave the impression of not seeing through this game, and of calmly acquiescing in the deliberate intrigues practised by the Interventionists.

Meanwhile, Ribbentrop's ambition was no longer confined to the post of Ambassador to the Court of St. James's. He lived in a state of perpetual anxiety lest someone might deprive him of his personal influence with the Führer during his absence from Berlin. As a result, he spent as much time as he could in the Reich capital. He had acquired an aeroplane for his private use, which was at his disposal day and night for his frequent journeys between London and Berlin. He would sometimes fly backwards and forwards two or three times a week, always attended by several members of his staff.

One of our women secretaries, Fräulein Fiedler, formerly employed by von Hoesch, was occasionally chosen to accompany him. On returning from her first flight, I asked her if she had had a pleasant trip.

"Good heavens, no!" she exclaimed. "I was shut up in the lavatory most of the time."

"Why, were you air-sick?" I asked.

"No," she laughed," but the men had to change on the way so that they could land at Tempelhof in their SS uniforms. And, as a woman, I was not allowed to see them in their underpants, so I was shut up in the lavatory!"

CHAPTER FIFTEEN

SINCE THE CORONATION of the new King, George VI, was to take place in June 1937, work went on at high pressure in the German Embassy so that the new interior might be ready in time for the receptions and dinner parties which Ribbentrop planned for the occasion. As the walls were not drying quickly enough, great coke ovens were placed immediately beneath my offices and burned night and day for a week, so that the temperature became unbearable. However, all the energy expended was not wasted, and at the opening of the Coronation festivities the last German workman had departed for home.

The dignified and time-honoured interior of the old Embassy was no longer recognizable. In our offices every single stick of furniture had been replaced. We were now supplied with mahogany writing tables, cream coloured telephones and armchairs upholstered in green and red leather.

Upstairs, the drawing-room, enlarged by demolishing intervening walls, was now one hundred feet long, with vast mirrors at either end which added to its sense of spaciousness. It is only fair to say that the planning and decoration, designed by Speer, Hitler's personal architect, left nothing to be desired. Of no particular style, it was completely modern in taste and would have done credit to the Hotel Waldorf-Astoria in New York. Various German museums had been ordered to supply paintings to adorn its walls, but as was only to be expected, their curators had refused to part with their best pictures and sent only second-rate stuff. So most of the pictures were trash, although the head of a horse by Lenbach was worth looking at and also a long-haired Lucrezia by Lucas Cranach, who was about to thrust a dagger into her bare bosom. Ribbentrop often stood before the latter masterpiece blowing his cigar smoke into the lovely suicide's face. The prize picture, however, was a really beautiful and gentle Madonna surrounded by angels and flowers, by Fra Angelico, but this was the personal property of Frau von Ribbentrop and was hung in a room apart.

We had just started work one morning when we were interrupted by the non-stop ringing of an electric bell. Filled with curiosity, we ran out into the corridor, and finally traced the source of the noise to the Angelico Madonna, which was protected from thieves by an electric alarm. One of the SS orderlies had shown too much energy when dusting that morning. But no-one could find the switch to stop it ringing.

* * *

It was wonderful weather during those Coronation days of 1937, and the procession was even more impressive than that of the Jubilee two years before. The Heads of States, princes and potentates had assembled in London in even greater numbers than on the previous occasion, and enlivened the scene with their richly coloured uniforms and robes.

Only the chiefs of the foreign Diplomatic Corps were invited to Westminster Abbey, and so I did not witness the actual scene, although I heard many first-hand accounts of it. The best stories were told me by young Hugo X, who, as a Westminster scholar, was detailed for duty in the Abbey as a page. It was thus that I discovered that even Westminster schoolboys made fun of Ribbentrop, whose son, in fact, was for a short time one of them.

Ambassadors, like the more humble guests, had to be in their seats three hours before the ceremony started. Among the duties of the pages was to attend to those who, during this long period of waiting, were obliged to yield to the calls of nature. They

128

had to come forward whenever a guest raised his hand to signify that he wished to retire. But the boys had come to a secret agreement that if such a gesture were made by Ribbentrop it was to be ignored on the plea that they had mistaken it for the Hitler salute!

During those three hours some of the distinguished guests began to feel the pangs of hunger, a contingency not provided for in the Abbey. According to the etiquette of the British Court, it would have been extremely difficult to bring along anything in the way of nourishment, for any form of pocket in Court robes had always been strictly forbidden. We men, for instance, were not allowed pockets in our knee—breeches, nor the ladies to carry bags. Nevertheless, there were those who found a way out of the difficulty by concealing packets of sandwiches under their coronets.

I attended the Court Ball at Buckingham Palace, which was a scene of fabulous splendour. The magnificence of the jewels and the dresses was beyond description. I think the most striking of all were the Eastern potentates, the Sultans and the Indian Princes. Standing next to me at the buffet at one moment was the youthful, brown-eyed Maharajah of Jaipur, clad in a pink silk robe embroidered with jewels. Beneath his sash hung a gold dagger, studded with rubies and diamonds, and in his turban was an amethyst in the centre of which gleamed the vastest ruby I have ever seen.

I ventured on to the crowded floor for a waltz. My partner and I were at pains to avoid treading on anyone's skirts or patent leather shoes, but, once, when she received a violent blow in the back, I took an involuntary step backwards, and heard a loud, "Ouch!" On turning round, I found myself face to face with young King Farouk of Egypt. But he relieved me of my embarrassment by calling: "Never mind!"

In the course of the Coronation year London season, there was such an endless round of festivities that the Foreign Embassies as a whole confined themselves to the essential minimum of functions. There was no earthly reason, therefore, why the German Embassy should make itself uniquely conspicuous in this respect. But Ribbentrop was quite determined to show that the luxury and magnificence of Nazi Germany could surpass even that of the British Court.

For months he had been making preparations for a reception on a truly grandiose scale, the cost of which was to be no object. In specially chartered aeroplanes he transported chefs and waiters from Horcher, Berlin's best restaurant, together with the very finest its cellars and kitchens could provide. In addition, two Berlin dance bands were brought over, including that of von Gezy from the Esplanade Hotel. As about fifteen hundred guests had been invited, and even the vast interior accommodation would be inadequate, the terrace in front of the house was converted into a large marquee where a sumptuous buffet was installed, with unlimited supplies of lobster, caviare and champagne. The comparatively modest catering at Buckingham Palace could not hold a candle to the lavishness of Ribbentrop's hospitality.

Shortly before this great social occasion was due to take place, the "Statesman" summoned us and his personal staff to his conference room to deliver his final instructions. Looking back on it to-day, we might have been listening not merely to a "Statesman" but to a military commander unfolding his plan of battle.

The members of his staff gathered round him as he assigned to each his special duties.

"Thörner, you will keep in close contact with me and see that I remain in constant touch with my wife."

"Spitz, you will keep an eye on the door and inform me of the arrival of important guests."

"You, Gottfriedsen, will act as liaison between me and the Head Chef."

When they all had been allotted their jobs, it was our turn. Spread out before the "Statesman" were two lists, a long one containing the names of the fifteen hundred guests, and a shorter one which he had marked with a "W". The latter consisted of about two hundred names, and the "W" at the top of the first page stood for "Wichtig", or important. Neville Chamberlain's name headed this list, which closed with that of one of the King's Equerries. Each of us was assigned to three or four of these important guests with strict instructions to see that they lacked nothing during the evening. I was delighted to find that I was to look after Monsieur Yvon Delbos, the French Foreign Minister, the Crown Prince of Saudi Arabia and the Lord Mayor of London.

Ribbentrop went carefully through the list and disposed of each name according to its bearer's rank and importance.

Suddenly he came upon one and paused; it was that of Ormsby-Gore, the British Colonial Secretary. Our "Statesman's" brow puckered and he pondered for a moment.

"He is important," he muttered to himself. "We want our Colonies back." Then, looking up, he said: "Wörmann, you must take charge of him yourself."

Wörmann was the senior among us in rank and Ribbentrop's immediate deputy.

At that moment, unfortunately, I caught the eye of my friend, Oskar. I only just managed to get my handkerchief out in time to simulate a coughing fit. It was obvious that our "Statesman's" tactical plan of operations was doomed to failure.

On the night of the reception it was literally impossible to make any headway through the densely packed, jostling mob of guests. The turmoil and confusion were indescribable, particularly when old Lady Weigall's wheel-chair contrived to get stuck in a doorway. As for my Lord Mayor, I never set eyes on him; probably one glimpse of the seething throng was enough for him. I did manage to procure a chair for Monsieur Yvon Delbos in an anteroom, where Frieda Leider was vainly attempting to drown the babble of voices with one of Schubert's songs. As for the Crown Prince of Saudi Arabia, whom I easily identified by his robes, I conducted him to the marquee on the terrace and gave him a glass of lemonade.

Although everyone was curious to see the "Brickendrop Circus" at close quarters, the majority of the guests beat an early retreat from the dust and din, and by midnight we Germans were left to ourselves. Then the fun really started. I looked about me and marvelled. Everyone seemed smothered in decorations. Many of the London Nazis had been awarded medals for their achievements at the Olympic Games, and Party Leader Krause, from the German Travel Agency, was wearing one of these round his neck like an order. Comrade Himmelmann, boss of the Party canteens, who was slowly becoming a millionaire as the result of his deals in beer and sausages, also wore an order suspended from his neck that should have hung on his left breast.

The food and drink had scarcely been touched by our guests, and there was still plenty of Pommery and Grenot on ice. Now we could indulge ourselves without restraint. But some failed to survive for long. General Milch, of the Luftwaffe, snored blissfully on a sofa with his feet on a silk-embroidered arm-chair. The two studs in his shirt-front had, for some reason, burst open and his hairy chest rose and fell as he slept. Captain Jäger vomited quietly on the carpet. Only Group Leader Karlowa remained his usual brisk self as the last guest departed with the dawn.

The SS orderlies swore for several days on end at the revolting mess they had to clear up in the morning.

CHAPTER SIXTEEN

BRITAIN'S ILL-ADVISED AND pernicious habit of yielding before the increasing arrogance of the Fascist Powers was known as the "Policy of Appeasement". Its leading advocates were the Prime Minister, Neville Chamberlain, Sir Horace Wilson, a very senior member of the Civil Service, and the Foreign Secretary, Lord Halifax.

The Labour Party, as weak-kneed and vacillating as their one time Social Democratic friends in Germany, failed to organize any effective opposition, so that, paradoxically, the champions of Appeasement only met with serious opposition from within the ranks of their own Conservative Party. The leader of this resistance was the redoubtable Churchill, who had been deliberately kept out of office for several years. It was common knowledge that one of Churchill's shrewdest advisers on foreign affairs was Sir Robert Vansittart.

In the autumn of 1937 I felt that at last I had discovered an efficient weapon for a frontal attack on Chamberlain's policy which would have decisive results. Ribbentrop had numerous agents in England, of whom one or more were under the personal supervision of each member of his staff. Money was no object where their activities were concerned. Among the most highly paid and prolific sources of secret information were the reports of a man whom I will call Ivan Petkov, who received £ 100 a month for his services.

Petkov was a Russian by birth, domiciled in London. He was a correspondent to some of the smaller German newspapers, and to certain others in Eastern and South-Eastern Europe. In addition, he was by way of being a social lion, and numbered among his intimate friends Lady Oxford and Asquith and Field-Marshal Chetwode.

Ribbentrop's secret papers were not, of course, intended for my eyes. But the office of Herr Achilles, Head of the Chancellery, happened to be on my floor, and documents destined for Berlin were kept in his safe pending their departure by the next courier. Achilles was not always at hand to put these papers under lock and key the moment they arrived from Ribbentrop's room. Occasionally, they were left lying about on his desk for a good half-hour. One day, I found a twenty-page report from Petkov concerning a visit he had paid the previous weekend to a close relative of Neville Chamberlain at his country house in Scotland. Shortly before, the Prime Minister had been staying there salmon fishing, and one evening had talked quite freely about the problems of his office. His relative had unwittingly repeated his remarks to Petkov.

I managed to memorise this report word for word in the short time at my disposal.

Mr. Chamberlain, it stated, was distressed and disturbed by the fact that his efforts to come to an understanding with the Third Reich were so little appreciated in Germany. Hitler was never satisfied, and was always making fresh and more far-reaching demands. In these circumstances, it would become increasingly difficult to make a policy of appeasement acceptable to British public opinion. Nevertheless, he, Chamberlain, would continue to persevere in the course of action he had adopted because, for good or evil, Hitlerite Germany was the bulwark against Bolshevism which Britain undoubtedly needed. If, on the other hand, German arrogance became still more overbearing, a situation might eventually arise in which even he would be unable to prevent an armed conflict.

The report went on to say that, apart from some unforeseen turn of events, it was now safe for Ribbentrop to assume that so long as Chamberlain remained at the helm, Hitler had nothing

134

to fear from Britain and could continue to twist the Lion's tail. The plan for the annexation of Austria could now be freely discussed, for there was no further reason for concern at the empty threats which appeared at intervals in the British press. The ultimate object of Chamberlain's policy was revealed with the utmost clarity in Petkov's report. "For us, of course," the British Prime Minister was quoted as saying, "the best possible thing would be for those two mad dogs, Hitler and Stalin, to fall out and destroy each other."

That same evening Vansittart was fully informed of this report, and for several days I waited impatiently for the results of my secretly aimed shaft. With such incontrovertible proof of the ineptitude of Chamberlain's policy, I was convinced that Churchill and his supporters could succeed in bringing about the fall of the Prime Minister.

To my intense surprise and dismay, the result was the exact opposite of what I had expected. Chamberlain not only remained where he was, but Vansittart was suddenly relieved of his post as Permanent Under-Secretary and made "Chief Diplomatic Adviser to His Majesty's Government"—in other words, he was given an appointment of no real substance, and one which had hitherto never existed. Subsequently, he was created a Peer and became a Privy Councillor.

What had occurred behind the scenes with regard to my confidential report on Chamberlain's indiscreet utterances, and whether or no this had any effect on Vansittart's change of post, the latter never told me. My sole achievement had been the withdrawal of Petkov's permit to reside in London, and that Ribbentrop lost one of his most useful agents.

Petkov left for Italy, and is said to have moved in Roman society during the Second World War as a "Prince". His name caught my eye again nearly twenty years later when, in 1954 I saw an article by him on the sensational scandal surrounding the murder of Vilma Montesi.

CHAPTER SEVENTEEN

WHEN HITLER ASSUMED power in 1933 he had appealed to the nation: "Give me four years!" The time limit had now almost expired.

The Third Reich already possesed a formidable army equipped with the most modern weapons, and a substantial Air Force. At any moment a highly organized and smooth-running Government machine could set these armed forces in motion by the mere pressing of a button. Everything, therefore, was in readiness for the next move towards the acquisition of the promised "Lebensraum", necessary for the creation of the new world power to be known as "Grossdeutschland".

From our chief's innumerable trips to Berlin in the autumn of 1937 we realised that something was cooking in the Reich capital. Ribbentrop showed less and less interest in the daily round at the Embassy, spent more and more time in Berlin, and after November was no longer seen in London. But we could do no more than guess what was afoot, for there were only two of our colleagues who actually knew what was really happening: Ribbentrop's right-hand man, Counsellor of Legation Erich Kordt, and Hewel, a former landowner in Java, who was the "Statesman's" personal liaison officer with the Reich Chancellery in Berlin. However, from what these two let drop we could gain a fairly clear picture of the situation.

Hitler and his generals in the Bendlerstrasse were agreed that the hour for German conquest had struck. There were, however, differences of opinion as to the direction in which the initial blow should be delivered. The soldiers, mostly of the old school, recalling their experiences in the First World War and wishing to avoid at all costs a war on two fronts, did not want to provoke the Western Powers. They favoured an immediate attack on Poland in order to secure a strategic front for a future onslaught against the Soviet Union. But the Austrian-born Hitler disagreed with this plan. His first objective was the "liberation" of his German brethren on the south-eastern frontier in order to be able to dominate Central Europe.

For such a plan to succeed, as he had once explained to Haevel, he "needed his Colonel Beck": in other words, the friendly support of Poland, the country which the generals, as a preliminary step, proposed to crush. Hitler did not share the apprehension of the Bendlerstrasse in regard to serious inter-ference by the Western Powers. He could rely now on his friend Mussolini since their joint intrigue in Spain. France, in his opinion, would never act alone, and he had Ribbentrop's assurance that the British Lion had lost its pugnacity.

Since the General Staff refused to accept Hitler's arguments, the matter inevitably became a trial of strength. Hitler resorted to his customary methods when faced with opposition, and immediately indulged in slanderous attacks on the moral characters of his adversaries.

Field-Marshal von Blomberg, Minister of War, had recently married for the second time, and had chosen as his wife a "simple girl of the people"—not exactly a desirable match according to old-fashioned standards. But in spite of this disadvantage, Hitler himself had not refused to act as a witness at the wedding. Now, however, the Gestapo unearthed the startling fact that the Führer had been grossly deceived. The so-called "simple girl", it was revealed, had once been a common street-walker. So it was obvious that Blomberg had to go. And go he did.

General von Fritsch was disposed of even more simply. In his case the Gestapo produced a youth who declared on oath that the General had been guilty of homosexual intercourse with him in a house in Schöneberg. So von Fritsch was also banished into the shadows.

Von Blomberg, in spite of his impressive appearance, had always had the reputation of being a spineless nonentity and was nicknamed by the Reichswehr "the india-rubber man". The wrong inflicted upon his young wife did not seem to worry him. Unruffled, and without more ado, he retired on a comfortable pension to the peace and seclusion of Capri.

General von Fritsch, on the other hand, fought desperately for his honour, and a year later succeeded in exposing and gaoling the Gestapo agents responsible for his downfall. He even received a letter of apology from Hitler himself. There was, however, no question of his reinstatement in the Reichswehr.

In January 1938, Baron von Neurath, the Foreign Minister, and several others also received their quietus. The Baron had been among those to point out the danger of the Hitler-Ribbentrop policy leading to a conflict with the West. With Neurath out of the way, Ribbentrop now became the all-powerful chief of the Foreign Office in the Wilhelmstrasse. Hitler's plan for the annexation of Austria was immediately placed on the agenda. The date fixed for carrying it into effect was known as the "Ides of March", by which time everything would be prepared.

In order to allay lingering suspicion and forestall any awkward moves on the part of the British, Ribbentrop returned to London during those fateful days. His sudden re-appearance, he innocently explained, was due to his desire to pay farewell visits to his many English friends. The mere fact that Hitler's Foreign Minister was absent from Berlin had a reassuring effect on opinion in London. No foreign adventure was likely so long as Ribbentrop was there. So, while the Austrian Chancellor, Schuschnigg, was being bullied by Hitler at Berchtesgarten, Ribbentrop was enjoying a quiet cup of tea with Chamberlain and Halifax at 10, Downing Street.

He even played the innocent with us at the Embassy, and

decided to hold a farewell reception at Carlton House Terrace on the very evening when German troops were massing on the Bavarian frontier in readiness for the invasion of Austria. Once again, London society flocked to the German Embassy. But this time the host appointed no-one to act as liaison or deputy, but remained standing in the hall to shake hands with every guest. Impeccably correct, if somewhat pale, even the Austrian Minister, Baron Franckenstein, was present and was rewarded with a particularly, hearty welcome.

In the background, the Press photographers had set up their cameras to record the historic scene. Quite a time was spent on the welcome accorded to Neville Chamberlain. I myself watched Ribbentrop and the British Prime Minister standing together for several minutes beneath the bronze bust of Hitler, looking into each other's eyes, with hands clasped, until the cameras ceased clicking.

The reception lasted until about 8 p.m., when Ribbentrop left hastily to dine with his friend, Lord Londonderry. But owing to the tension in the air, some of us felt disinclined to go home so early and adjourned to the Conference Room, where there was a large wireless set. We were anxious to know what was happening in Austria and switched on to Vienna. Never had I listened to a broadcast so charged with drama. For a long time we heard nothing except the familiar notes of the intermission signal and the repeated announcement that in a few minutes the Austrian Chancellor would speak on his visit to Berchtes-garten. When he did come to the microphone, Schuschnigg's melancholy words left no room for doubt. He was resigning in favour of his Nazi colleague, Seyss-Inquart. Then, for the last time, we heard the Austrian National Anthem. After that, there was no further comment. We listened to gramophone records of the "Unfinished Symphony" magnificently played by the Vienna Philharmonic Orchestra, Mozart's "Kleine Nacht-musik", followed by "The Blue Danube", the overture from "Fledermaus" and other haunting Viennese melodies. At the

139

end of an hour or so the music ended, and Seyss-Inquart came to the microphone. He told his listeners that he himself had asked Hitler to send German troops into Austria to assist his fellow-countrymen to restore law and order. Then, in place of Viennese waltzes, Austrian military music was played, starting with the Radetzky March. One had the strange feeling that every moment the rhythm was becoming more harsh and strident. Shortly after midnight, the strains of the "Horst-Wessel Song" reached our ears. I now knew well enough what would inevitably follow, and strode home through the darkness in the depths of despair.

The next morning, escorted by Wörmann, a select few of us set out for the Austrian Legation in Belgrave Square. We had feared we might meet with a hostile reception, or even be stopped by the police from setting foot in the house. Instead, we were received by Baron Franckenstein with a courteous "Please come in". Without more ado, he handed over the Legation to us, with all its financial resources.

"I think it is only right," he remarked in reference to the latter, "to tell you that I possess a sum of money which does not appear on the books. It was collected from certain charitable quarters for the purpose of helping impoverished artists in Vienna." Then he handed over several more hundred pounds in cash.

I was completely at a loss to understand this display of integrity at such a moment. It subsequently turned out to be due to nothing more than crass stupidity.

As chief of the Consular Division, I was delegated to the task of transforming the Legation into a department of the German Embassy. I even had to sleep there for several nights to ensure that no documents or articles of value were secretely removed.

Wörmann had no idea that by this arrangement he was setting a fox to look after the goose. My friend von Blaas had now to make way for Counsellor of Legation Kunz, with whom, however, I came to an understanding. One of our first moves was to hang a portrait of Hitler in every room; a source of pleasant surprise to Karlowa when he turned up a few hours later.

Compromising documents were disposed of by the Press Attaché, Count Huyn, who was already so hopelessly suspect in the eyes of the Germans that he had to seek, and was granted, the right of asylum in England. Fortunately, nothing of any value from a propaganda point of view fell into the hands of the Nazis. We were obliged, however, to act with the utmost caution, since we were told by Kunz that one of the menservants, Klaffel, was known to be a Nazi spy. Furthermore, we found out that Franckenstein's housekeeper, an elderly spinster called Paula, who had been with him for many years, had been supplied with a special type of camera by Karlowa with which she had been photographing any papers which the Minister left about in his private apartments.

On my first morning in Belgrave Square I was still in bed when Klaffel, the valet, brought me my breakfast.

"Good morning," I murmured, still half asleep.

I soon woke up, however, when, after putting down the tray on the bedtable, he greeted me with: "Heil Hitler!"

Paula, in spite of her photographic activities, merely confined herself to "Good morning".

One of my greatest embarrassments was to prevent Baron Franckenstein from behaving too foolishly. It was quite impossible to talk to him frankly and openly as I did to Kunz and Huyn. Unusually distinguished in appearance, build and manner, he remined me of Wilhelm Furtwängler, the conductor, although the latter's features were not so aristocratic as Franckenstein's. Far above the average in musical knowledge and taste, when it came to politics he was as naïve as a child. In fact, Franckenstein possessed that charming combination of tact and fine feeling with a dull and limited intellect which is the almost exclusive prerogative of the Austrian aristocracy.

Fortunately, I had friends who were able to influence him

more successfully than I: the two famous singers from the Vienna Opera House, Lotte Lehmann and Elisabeth Schumann, who both happened to be in London at that time. Lotte Lehmann was a friend of my childhood. She was born and grew up at Perleberg, our nearest country town; my Uncle Konrad had taken an interest in her and her voice, and had helped her to study to become a singer. She was also a protégée of his brother Joachim, Director of the Stuttgart Opera. As a girl, she had sung to us at Laaske; I was present as a child of twelve when, with long pigtails, and accompanied on the piano by her mother, she had sung before the great Strauss in the Casino at Westerland on the island of Sylt before the First World War. I remember how proud I was that it was through me that she met Strauss, with whose son I had made friends while playing on the sands.

It was only with the help of these two ladies that I managed to prevent Franckenstein from committing an act of utter madness by complying with Ribbentrop's suggestion to pay a personal visit to Hitler in Berlin. Had he done so, there is not a shadow of doubt that he would have disappeared into a concentration camp.

Luckily for him, he had many influential English friends, very quickly became a British subject, and, on being awarded a knighthood, was known ever afterwards as Sir George Franckenstein.

CHAPTER EIGHTEEN

AFTER RIBBENTROP'S DEPARTURE, life in the London Embassy became tolerably normal. The day's work proceeded more smoothly and the number of employees was considerably reduced. The majority of those on his personal staff returned with him to Berlin, including a few of us permanent officials, among them the inoffensive Brücklmeyer, who was pursuaded by Erich Kordt to work for him in Ribbentrop's secretarial office. Six years later, poor Brücklmeyer paid dearly for his simplicity at the hands of the executioner in the Plötzensee Prison.

Finally, the day came when I was the only high official of the pre-Ribbentrop era remaining in the Embassy. Raumer's talisman had certainly protected me in a miraculous manner! Ribbentrop's successor in London was our former Ambassador in Tokyo, Herbert von Dircksen, a heavily built, unimaginative and reactionary bureaucrat. His grandfather had been a peasant landowner in Schöneberg when the latter was still a village on the outskirts of Berlin. Owing to the rise in the value of land as the city grew, Dircksen's forbears had not only become millionaires but had acquired a title. The Ambassador's stepmother now lived in a magnificent house in the Margaretenstrasse, and was the first Berlin hostess to throw open her doors to Hitler and the Nazis.

I had known Dircksen for a long time. Indeed, he had served with me in the Reserve of the 3rd Uhlans of the Guard at Potsdam. In 1932 he was Ambassador in Moscow, where I stayed with him and his wife when on my travels as a courier.

Doctor Theodor Kordt, elder brother of Ribbentrop's personal aide, was appointed to succeed Wörmann as First Secretary in London. Like Dircksen, Kordt also believed in the theory of German expansion in the East and the importance of securing the goodwill of Britain, if not her active help, in this project. Since the Kordt brothers emphatically declared after 1945 that they had played a leading role in the bomb plot of July 20th, 1944, one can, at least, give them the credit of having backed the reactionary generals of the Bendlerstrasse rather than Ribbentrop.

Along with Kordt and a few others I accompanied von Dircksen when he presented his credentials to the King. With us, too, as Chief of Protocol, was Baron Steengracht von Moyland, one of the few members of Ribbentrop's staff still remaining in England. He was a pleasant, easygoing man of the world, as little qualified for his post as a dray-horse for the Derby.

When an ambassador from a foreign country presents his credentials to the Sovereign he is driven to Buckingham Palace in a State Coach. In our silk hats and morning coats we were well on the way to the Palace when Steengracht, thrusting his hand in his pocket, said in a horrified voice: "God! I've left the credentials on my desk!" Needless to say, without these documents our visit to the King would have been meaningless. At the critical moment we managed to attract the attention of the officer in charge of the escort, who immediately brought the cavalcade to a halt in the Mall. We then hailed a passing taxi, which returned in ten minutes with Steengracht and his missing roll of parchment. But, despite all our efforts, we were unable to make up for lost time, and kept King George VI waiting.

That was the last time I set foot in Buckingham Palace. In May, 1938, my term of duty at the London Embassy expired and I was appointed Counsellor of Legation at the Hague.

Hitler had by then overrun Austria without any sign of resistance on the part of the Western Powers, and the probability that further rich morsels would be allowed to fall into the Nazis' mouths filled me with dismay. It was now obvious that the next dish on his menu was to be Czechoslovakia. As early as the beginning of May, reports were received from Berlin that secret troops were concentrating on the Bohemian border. At the same time, Henlein's propaganda in the Sudetenland reached its crescendo. From reliable sources came the news that May 21st had been fixed as the date on which the surprise blow would be delivered. Several military columns were to cross the frontier at dawn and march directly to Prague from different directions. These rumours roused Hitler to issue a categorical denial. The world, however, remained vigilant.

Czechoslovakia hastily sent troops to her frontier and blockaded the main roads. The British and French Embassies in Berlin sent home the families of their staffs. It really looked as if an attack on Czechoslovakia would bring the Western Powers into the lists.

"There will never be another 21st of May!" Hitler shouted in a rage some months later. For the first time, he had been faced with a threat of serious resistance and was forced to climb down. There was, after all, still hope that the West would stand up to him before he was strong enough to unleash a second World War.

Before I left for The Hague, I went to say goodbye to my friends, and amongst them Paul. We were both of us filled with apprehension at the state of Europe, and before I left, he shook my hand and said: "We may meet again sooner than you expect." We did.

I arrived in Holland, however, in a rather more cheerful mood, for the date was May 21st, 1938.

CHAPTER NINETEEN

I HAD BEEN four years in London and had spent day after day at the very centre of world events. The flood of documents and the stream of visitors had never ebbed, and I had grown accustomed to being up to my neck in work. I had had little time for pleasure during those years, and had seldom managed to get away for more than a brief weekend to the country. In retrospect, my life seemed to have been spent in a grey-brown London mist, peopled by hurrying, raincoated figures dodging through the traffic of the crowded streets.

On my arrival in Holland I was immediately struck by the contrast between the two capitals. As I stepped on to the platform of the beautiful railway station at The Hague, the tall red-brick buildings of the Dutch capital rose before me in the sunshine, and behind me, across the railway tracks, was a green meadow in which a herd of black and white cows was peacefully grazing. I decided that this was a place where one could undoubtedly lead a pleasant life.

The hotel where I took a room, the "Oude Doelen", was not only up-to-date but comfortable enough to remind me of home, and well as I had fared in London, from the moment I set foot in Holland I felt at peace.

The two-hundred-year-old Legation, in the centre of The Hague, lay at the end of a long avenue of lime trees and overlooked the lake, in the waters of which were reflected the mediaeval walls of the Parliament House. No Ribbentrop or Speer had committed any act of vandalism here. The rooms in

146

which we worked still breathed an atmosphere of civilisation.

My chief, Count Zech-Burckersroda, who had been German Minister in Holland for over ten years, was a highly educated Saxon country gentleman. His wife was the daughter of the former Imperial Chancellor, von Bethmann-Hollweg, and I had known her brother, Felix, ever since we had been officers together in the 3rd Uhlans. Neither of the Zechs had Nazi sympathies, and we agreed at our first meeting that we must stick together against the Party bosses.

Zech belonged to the same generation as von Hoesch, and, indeed, they had much in common. Both were men of the world in the Diplomatic Service who lived within the exclusive sphere of their profession. But Hoesch was incomparably more shrewd, and had had a more brilliant career. At times Zech's political naïveté reminded me of that of George Franckenstein. Nevertheless, as he was a German, we understood each other better, particularly as we had certain personal connections.

After Zech I was senior in rank at the Legation, and could afford to live comfortably on my salary. On the strength of this, I rented a pleasant villa among the sand-dunes at Scheveningen, three minutes walk from the sea. With my newly acquired car, I was able to be at the Legation and the centre of the town in less than a quarter of an hour.

To look after my house and car I needed someone not only conscientious in his work but whom I could trust implicitly. Among the many who had fled from the Gestapo and from Germany and had come to see me at the Embassy in London, and whom, by devious means, I had supplied with new papers and passports, was a young man called Willi Schneider. At the beginning of the Hitler régime he had served a short term in a concentration camp, and the horrors which he witnessed had made him loathe the Nazis and all their works. For the past year he had returned to his native Cologne, where he had been working as a waiter, and had written to me several times asking if I could find him a job abroad. Instinctively, I felt that Willi was

147

the right man for me, and he was delighted when I sent for him.

Life at the Hague could not have been more pleasant, so far as outward circumstances were concerned. I had a nice house, a car, a post of some importance and as many invitations as I could cope with. At midday I lay in the sun for a couple of hours on the sands at Scheveningen, and in the evenings, if I had nothing better to do, dined in some charming private house. The weekends I spent visiting the museums in Amsterdam, going to places of interest in the country, or on trips to Antwerp, Brussels, Ghent, Ostend or even, occasionally, Paris.

But we were living in the year 1938, and the approaching catastrophe already cast its shadow across the face of Europe.

The political climate in Holland made life far more difficult for Germans like myself, who were engaged in anti-Hitler intrigues, than it was in England. Although the Chamberlain Government permitted the Nazi Party to carry on its activities quite openly, it was not possible for the latter to establish a reign of terror against Germans resident in England. Thus, the power of Karlowa and his henchmen was strictly limited. Even we at the Embassy always retained a certain independence, and if the Nazi bosses went too far, were in a position to see that they received a rebuff from time to time.

Foreign political parties were prohibited in Holland. Thus, no officially recognised Nazi organisation existed, merely a respectable middle-class society which had adopted the innocuous name of "Reichsdeutsche Gemeinschaft"—German Community. Its actual wire-pullers, high Party and SS officials, were found in the Legation under the guise of minor diplomatic functionaries. The local Group-Leader was a Doctor Otto Butting, a pathological fanatic, who had been a nose and throat specialist in Lindau, on Lake Constance. Since he was officially known as an attaché and had all the usual diplomatic privileges, no Dutch official could interfere with him.

This was true, too, as regards the Gestapo agents and members of the naval and military Intelligence directed by

Admiral Canaris. All were officially installed in the Legation as temporary assistants, special correspondents in the Press Department and experts in this, that and the other. Most of them even concealed their true identity under assumed names. They were appointed and controlled by a Dutch-speaking counter-intelligence specialist known by the fictitious name of Schultze-Bernet, although his letters were also addressed to "Jonathan", and sometimes merely to "S-B". He received his immediate instructions from a grey-haired man of distinguished appearance, an unmistakeable senior army officer, who turned up at the Hague at regular intervals without ever revealing his name.

Count Zech had at least seen to it that these dubious characters were not housed in the Legation itself, and they, in their turn, took every precaution against our getting a glimpse of their activities. The domain over which Butting and Schultze-Bernet exercised their authority was a secluded house in the Jan de Witt Laan, which had been bought some time previously for precisely that purpose. There, in an attic, was a secret wireless set by which these agents could send their urgent messages to Berlin undisturbed.

In the early days I was surprised at the number of bags delivered weekly by the couriers from Berlin at such a comparatively minor Legation. Almost all of them were destined for "S-B", or Butting, and it was my duty to forward them intact. I never doubted for one moment that they contained weapons, radio sets and other illegally imported material. When I drew Zech's attention to this, he replied: "We can do nothing about is. Please don't add to my difficulties with these fellows."

Zech could not even prevent Butting's underlings from removing the bronze bust of his father-in-law, Bethmann-Hollweg, from his office to a corridor in his private apartments, and replacing it by a bust of the Führer. He was always complaining to me of the scandalous manner in which he was treated, and it was clear even to him that the Nazis only allowed

149

him to remain because they needed a gentleman as a façade to inspire confidence with the Dutch. For Zech, like von Hoesch, could not bring himself to throw up his professional career.

There were close on a hundred thousand German subjects working and domiciled in Holland at that time, every one of whom was at the tender mercies of Butting and Schultze-Bernet. Since only a very few had joined the Party, the majority of them were in danger of losing their jobs and their permits to remain in the country, and being forced to return to Germany. So membership, or at least some connection with, the so-called "Arbeitsfront" was essential if a man did not wish to expose himself and his relations in Germany to various forms of persecution. There was scarcely a German in Holland whose name was not to be found on Butting's card-index files. No matter in what remote part of the country Schultze-Bernet might want to do a little espionage, he had only to consult this index to find a suitable agent. "We know every square yard of this country," he once proudly informed me.

When, during the summer months, the German armament industry wanted more workers, District Leader Bohle, the Berlin Party Chief responsible for Germans abroad, suddenly withdrew the passports of every German and Austrian domestic servant in Holland. Hundreds of them called daily at the Consulate in a state of deep distress, begging to be allowed to remain at least a few weeks longer. Butting, however, was pitiless, and thousands were forced to return home. It was left to Schultz-Bernet and his assistants to decide where exceptions might be made. Needless to say, these occurred only amongst those who were employed by important officials, or who would be useful for purposes of espionage. It is not surprising that in those days Zech referred to our Legation as "the slave market".

It seemed to me highly improbable that Dutch officialdom was so blind or naïve as not to realise what a dangerous game was being played under its very nose. It took refuge behind the neutrality of Holland, which forbade interference in the affairs of foreign subjects. Although I was on the look-out for confederates, I never once came across a Vansittart or a Mr. Cooper whom I felt I could trust not to betray me to the Nazis if I disclosed where my sympathies lay.

Indeed, the Government at the Hague even turned a blind eye upon the menace of their own Dutch National-Socialists. In England I had never met officials of equal status who expressed their admiration for the spirit of the New Germany in such glowing terms as I did in Holland. Sir Oswald Mosley's British Fascists could hardly claim a single friend in Whitehall, but Mussert's Dutch Nazis found supporters in almost every Ministry, and even in the Queen's own Household.

With my own eyes I saw our Propaganda Attaché, Party Member Husbahn, hand over to one of Mussert's Staff the guilder notes which he received as a monthly subsidy from Berlin. There were certain Prefects of Police who, at a mere hint from Butting, had German refugees escorted across the frontier under cover of darkness and delivered into the hands of the Gestapo.

I never heard that the Dutch Government made any protest against such high-handed action, examples of which were known to us by the score. On the contrary, it was only too willing to give its consent when Butting or Schultze-Bernet suggested that the Dutch law-breakers be awarded Hitler's newly-instituted Order of the German Eagle.

Although I was officially senior to Butting and Schultze-Bernet, in practice they were my superiors. Like Zech, I was also caste for the role of a spurious, symbolic "screen" vis-a-vis the Dutch Government and the aristocratic, austerely convent-ional ruling class. I could appear in morning coat and silk hat, dine with foreign dignitaries, indulge in polite conversation at diplomatic receptions and kiss the Queen's hand at Court. But I had little influence on what actually occurred in the Legation, where matters of real importance were deliberately withheld from me.

Even had I felt inclined to work long hours in my office, I would hardly have had the opportunity. In London I was at least able not only to keep in touch with Vansittart but to sabotage attempts at Nazi scurrility; here in Holland, such things were only possible on the rarest occasions. My sole moral support was the knowledge that I had friends in England with whose assistance I could hope to fight the Nazis when the hour struck.

During the summer months Hitler pressed on with his plans for the destruction of Czechoslovakia. Another international crisis was developing which threatened to be far more serious than any which had preceded it. This time the West would have to stand firm at all costs, for it would probably be the last chance to stop a second World War.

I happened to know that Hitler's re-armament was not yet complete, for Schultze-Bernet himself had confided to me that the construction of the famous West Wall was still only in its initial stages and that the allied forces could cut through it like the proverbial knife through butter. He also told me that the generals in the Bendlerstrasse were still fully determined to restrain Hitler from provoking an armed conflict with the Western Powers.

Immediately I heard this news, I at once got Paul to come over from London so that I could inform him of it. With the co-operation of Willi, I took every possible precaution that the meetings between him and myself should not be observed. To this end, Willi arranged an assignation with a girl friend on a bench in the local park where he could wait for Paul's arrival and bring him to a secret rendezvous.

That evening, I gave Paul a message for Vansittart which concluded: "Stand firm. Do not retreat one step. If you make no concessions, Hitler will be forced to give way."

Paul told me gravely that even Chamberlain was now so exasperated that he had abandoned his policy of appeasement, and I could rest assured that this time Hitler would not get away with it. So, with renewed confidence, I awaited the course of events.

Then came the Munich surrender. Hitler's star rose higher and higher, burning brighter than ever before. Whether one hated or admired him, he had, nevertheless, overcome all opposition, and seemed invincible; a super-Bismarck, against whom no-one dared to raise a hand. Even I was at a loss for words when the jubilant Nazis spoke of their Führer as "the greatest statesman of all time."

CHAPTER TWENTY

THE MUNICH BETRAYAL was a deadly blow to me. I was at my wit's end to know what to do for the best. Many of those who had long hesitated now became ardent supporters of the triumphant Führer. Such a step was unthinkable to me. But could I have any more faith in England after the way she had left us anti-Nazis in the lurch? If I continued my activities, I would only be exposing myself to danger and tilting at windmills.

I was terribly troubled and disturbed, and wanted to vent my anger on the British—in the form, of all people, of poor Paul. When he came to my house next day, Willi had decorated the entire hall with Swastika flags and pictures of Hitler. I received him glaring like a Gauleiter, and flourishing a whip in my hand.

It was a poor joke, but it showed my state of mind

Nevertheless, I could not bring myself to give up the struggle by retiring to Laaske. So I chose a temporary compromise. As a former Army officer, I had for some time been urged to take part in Reserve manoeuvres with the Reichswehr. This I decided to do. After the manoeuvres were over, I could then take a few weeks leave at Laaske, where there was much to be settled following my father's death.

My course with the Reserve was quickly arranged, and at the end of September, only a few weeks after Munich, I reported to my old Guard-Uhlan Regimental Depot at Stahnsdorf, where I had spent that first night on German soil with my brother Gebhard at the end of the First World War.

With Willi Schneider, I drove in my car to a quiet hotel on

the edge of the Wannsee, barely a quarter of an hour's drive from the barracks, and not more than double that distance from the centre of Berlin. My military duties were by no means arduous. Occasionally I put in an appearance at the Officers' Mess, where my Colonel informed me that he considered it of the first importance for officers of the Reserve to have the "good old traditions in the marrow of their bones". In his eyes, apparently, their military efficiency was only of secondary importance.

Things were quiet in my Squadron, which had just returned from the bloodless conquest of the Sudetenland, and was kept busy for several weeks re-fitting vehicles and polishing saddlery. Occasionally I attended lectures on handling a rifle or on "the automatic recoil and forward movement of the machine-gun"— the same old stuff which had bored me to death at Potsdam twenty years before. Nor had the exercises on the barrack square become any less irksome.

An innovation, however, since Kaiser Wilhelm's day was the Hitler Salute during the March Past. The traditional goose-step had always appeared sufficiently comic to me, without adding this arm-raising nonsense!

Apart from a few enthusiastic subalterns, there did not seem to be any Nazis among us. Jazz music from Luxemburg floated from the open barrack windows, for the general verdict was that Goebbels's radio programmes were monotonous and dull. Many of the officers detested the Nazi bosses, and wished for nothing better than to have some petty Brown Shirt leader under them, so that they could "put him through it" as a recruit on the parade ground. Politics were despised, but the general opinion was that, now as ever, the soldier was pre-eminent in the State, and should continue so.

Uncomplimentary remarks, however, were not permitted about Hitler himself, who had now aroused unbounded admiration even among those who had previously poked fun at him as the "Bohemian Corporal".

155

"Not even the great Marshal Moltke," declared my Squadron Leader, Captain von Lüttwitz, "ever conducted a victorious campaign without the loss of a man". In his opinion, the Bohemian defences were so strong that even the most able commander would have been obliged to sacrifice not less than 100,000 men to storm them. Yet Hitler had smashed them without firing a shot.

The captain had, however, been exceedingly annoyed by a recent speech made by the Führer in the presence of Army officers at Eger, when he was alleged to have said: "It is only because I was not yet absolutely certain of the fighting strength of my Wehrmacht that you see me in this paltry hole today, gentlemen, instead of in the ancient castle at Prague."

Not only Lüttwitz but all his fellow officers firmly believed that they would soon be setting out to occupy Prague. Even the date was apparently already fixed, and talk of the "Ides of March" was to be heard everywhere. Even if the vast majority of Army officers had no great liking for the Nazis and their methods, they were only too ready to follow a Leader who could produce a bloodless and victorious march into a neighbouring country every six months.

My course at Stahnsdorf ended on November 9th, and the next day I left for Laaske. The events of the intervening night remain inscribed in the pages of the history of the years of German infamy and dishonour. It was known as the "Crystal Night". About midday on the 10th I was driving through Berlin and, wishing to see something of what had happened, I passed through the Tauentzienstrasse and turned into the Kurfürstendamm, in which were most of the Jewish shops and stores. It was almost impossible to make any headway through the seething mob. As far as the eye could see, crowds were jostling their way along the pavements, gazing at the shattered windows and smashed shutters of the looted shops. Black smoke still issued from the gaping windows of the burnt-out Synagogue in the Fasanenstrasse. Every few minutes closed police vans, their sirens screaming, raced along the streets, and one knew that they were packed with unfortunate Jews on their way to the offices of the Chief of Police.

What impressed me was the strange, almost uncanny silence of those tens of thousands of slowly moving people. To me it was a positive sign that the overwhelming majority of Berliners recoiled with disgust and indignation at this latest outrage of Doctor Goebbels.

Even Laaske was not immune on this dreadful night of organized hooliganism. There was only one Jew, Levi, a watchmaker, in the neighbouring town of Putlitz, who had lived there all his life and married the daughter of the local postmaster, needless to say, a Gentile. Levi was an inoffensive, hard-working little man without an enemy in the world. Since no-one in Putlitz would raise a hand against him, several Nazi rowdies were sent over from Perleberg to wreck his shop, smash up his home and empty pots of jam on to the ripped up feather beds, finally flinging the splintered remains of the furniture into the streets. Levi hung between life and death for several days in a tiny room in which his wife had managed to install what was left of their home.

The following morning my brother Gebhard, passing along the street, saw Frau Levi clearing the debris outside her front door. Looking round to make sure that no one was watching, he casually dropped a fifty mark note into her shovel. That same evening a child called with a note from Frau Levi saying: "You were seen. I was taken to the Police Station and could not deny it. But I said it was only twenty marks."

Gebhard himself was questioned, and a report forwarded to the Gestapo in Perleberg. When the chief of the local Gestapo drove up in person a few days later, we all feared that my brother would be arrested. But not at all. Our caller was affability itself. "I have spent several nights considering your case, Herr Baron," he said, "and have even seen some Government officials in Potsdam in order to settle this unfortunate incident. It would have been terrible to have been obliged to imprison one of the most respected landowners in the district, especially when he is also a member of our oldest noble family. It gives me great pleasure, therefore, to inform you that my visit to Potsdam was not unsuccessful".

We felt infinitely relieved at this news, but more was to follow. "It was, of course, a serious offence. We had expected that you, of all people, would have set an example by having no truck with this Jewish rabble. I must admit that the matter was not disposed of without penalty. We have agreed that you must make a special contribution of five thousand marks to the Winter Assistance Fund here in Putlitz."

Gebhard, of course, decided to pay. Five thousand marks was no trifling sum for such a small town, and the *Putlitzer Nachrichten*, announcing the result of the November collection towards the Winter Assistance Fund, was able proudly to inform its readers in thick, black type that the National-Socialist spirit of sacrifice displayed by the local inhabitants had beaten all previous records.

At the beginning of December I returned to The Hague. My departure was unusually depressing for Gebhard, and I think that we both had the feeling that this was probably the last time that we would be together in our ancestral home.

* * *

During my absence, the bunch of sinister characters employed by the Legation had increased by about a dozen. Since the house in the Jan de Witt Laan was no longer large enough, Zech had put the former Austrian Legation at their disposal, which had been empty for some time. An as yet unknown individual had been installed there as boss: an ex-naval Lieutenant named Besthorn, who spoke Dutch fluently and had only recently returned to Germany after many years in business in Indonesia. Although he had not set foot aboard a warship for close on twenty years, he was at once promoted to the rank of Captain and appointed to The Hague with the official status of Naval Attaché, the better to conceal his true function of espionage.

His actual duties remained wrapped in mystery so far as Zech and I were concerned. There was, in fact, no valid reason for maintaining a Naval Attaché at The Hague. Besthorn was an out-and-out, hard-bitten Nazi. With Butting and Schultze-Bernet, he was from now onwards one of the most influential wire-pullers behind the scenes in Holland.

I was seldom among the first to arrive at the Legation in the mornings, and it was about a fortnight after my return from Germany that I turned up one day shortly before ten o'clock to find my room full of people in a high state of excitement. Butting, Schultze-Bernet and Besthorn were shouting at the office cleaner. In spite of the fact that owing to Zech's absence on leave, I was the temporary Chief of the Legation, my arrival was hardly noticed, for those present were far too deeply engrossed in their momentous deliberations.

It appeared that the charwoman had noticed some glass splinters on the window ledge and had discovered a diminutive lead missile on the carpet. High up to the left in the window pane was a tiny, jagged hole, obviously made by the little projectile. If the marksman had been aiming at anything in the room, it could only have been at the chandelier hanging a foot or so from the high ceiling.

A few weeks previously a Jewish refugee named Grynspan had shot and killed a former youthful colleague of mine, von Rath, in our Embassy in Paris. Goebbels had seized on the murder as a pretext for the organized anti-Semitic outbreak of November 9th, which he had described as the spontaneous, frenzied reaction of the German people. Butting and his companions were now on the track of a second "Jewish assassin", and, determined to exploit the idea, were already busily fabricating sensational announcements to the German press agencies.

159

When I questioned Zech's manservant, who slept at the Legation, he replied in a whisper: "I think it was just some boys in the street. At this time of year the pigeons and sparrows roost on the windowsills. The boys must have been shooting at them with air-guns or catapults. If it had been a firearm, I would certainly have heard the shot."

I mentioned this to Butting. "Don't be frivolous about such a serious matter," he retorted brusquely. "Do you want to give these damned Jews the chance to shoot us all one after another? This time, we must act with the utmost severity as a deterrent against further outrages."

"At least, Doctor Butting," I replied, "be good enough not to drag my name into this affair."

Mercifully, my request was granted. Violent official statements breathing vengeance, concocted by the trio, were now distributed and appeared in Berlin newspapers that same evening under such headlines as: "Another attempted murder by the Jews, this time at the German Legation in Holland."

To forestall any undue anxiety at home, the following morning I put through a telephone call to Laaske to let my mother know that the story was a deliberate invention.

In the meantime, the Dutch Government co-operated gallantly in the deception. At least, it made the outward impression of taking Butting's outcry seriously. Countless photographs were published of the missile in question, which was handed over to the Government Ballistic Laboratory for every known test. Public notices were circulated by the police to aid the search for the unknown assassin, and even armed sentries were posted outside our private residences.

In spite of these stern measures, however, further minute missiles continued to whizz through the air and penetrate not only German but Dutch windows. It was significant that school buildings were the chief sufferers. Even the German school in Amsterdam was obliged to complain of a broken window pane.

Later in the year, when Dutch schoolboys once again spent

their spare moments playing marbles, these "attempts at assassination" became less frequent, and finally ceased altogether.

The Dutch-sponsored investigation undertaken by experts in ballistics was obliged to adjourn without arriving at any definite conclusions.

CHAPTER TWENTY-ONE

AFTER MUNICH HITLER repeatedly declared that he had no further territorial claims to make. The seizure of the Sudetenland was positively his final appropriation of foreign soil. Nothing was further from his mind than to incorporate a single Czech within the frontiers of the Reich. Yet who could possibly believe such declarations when there was ever increasing talk of the "Ides of March" and the inevitable necessity of suppressing the "swarm of bacilli in Prague"? Since I was almost certain that World War would break out in the spring or summer, I realised that if I was to safeguard my future I would have to act quickly.

In January, 1939, I took three days' special leave on the plea that I had to consult my doctor in London. Arrived there, Paul arranged a meeting with Vansittart in the privacy of his top-floor flat. Punctual to the minute, but somewhat out of breath from the effort of climbing five flights of stairs, Vansittart entered and shook me warmly by the hand.

"Well, Putlitz," he said, "I understand you are not too pleased with us. I know Munich was a disgraceful business, but I can assure you that that sort of thing is over and done with. Even our English forbearance has its limits. Next time it will be impossible for Chamberlain to allow himself to be bamboozled by a scrap of paper on which Hitler has scribbled a few words expressing his ardent desire for peace. England is going to put her foot down."

"That is the very reason, Sir Robert, for my anxiety," I I answered. "If you had stood your ground at Munich, you could still have forced Hitler to retreat. But now that you've given way so often and so much, refusal to yield can only mean war."

Vansittart looked thoughtful. "Yes, I too fear that war is now inevitable."

"I suppose you realise that in that case my whole world will collapse?" I asked. "That is why I was so anxious to have a word with you here in private."

"Please speak absolutely frankly," he said. "I came here to listen to what you had to say."

I took a deep breath and then began: "For several years, as you know, Sir Robert, I have tried to convince you people in England by words and actions that it was not in your interests to make the slightest concession to the Nazis. I attached the utmost importance to my friendship with you, and did all that I could to assist you, because I hoped that I might help to prevent England and Germany becoming involved in another murderous war. Now we are agreed that it is too late. So just put yourself in my place and tell me what on earth I ought to do?"

"Whatever happens, Putlitz, we shall always regard you as a friend," he said sincerely.

"But what advantage will that be to me if I am in Germany and you bomb the country and kill thousands of my fellow countrymen?" I questioned. "I shall certainly not fight for Hitler and his gang. I would like to ask you if it would be possible for me to stay in England as a neutral if war should break out? When the Nazis have been destroyed I might, perhaps, be able to contribute something towards establishing a lasting peace and friendship between our two countries."

Vansittart smiled. "I was half expecting that question," he said, "and I have thought it over carefully. I give you my word that at any time, be it war or peace, you can rely upon asylum here in England."

I told him that he had taken a great weight off my mind, but

163

added that before I came to a decision, I needed reassuring on one point.

"What more can you ask after what I have just said?" he enquired.

"You must remember that I'm a German," I insisted, "and that things are therefore more complicated for me than for you. From your point of view, this war will be a national struggle. It won't be just a war against Hitler. For me, on the other hand, Hitler is the only enemy, and to a certain extent this war will be a civil war. In so far as you exterminate Hitler and his Brown Shirts, you can rely on my fullest support. But if it is also your intention to annihilate Germany, then I cannot be on your side."

"Do you imagine that we have learned nothing from Versailles?" Vansittart retorted sharply. "We shall never make a mistake like that again. We know from experience that a discontented Germany constitutes a danger to the whole of Europe. Our aim concerning Germany to-day can be summed up in five words—'Full larders and empty arsenals.' I'm sure you can't find anything to object to in that. You can be certain that this time we will make a reasonable peace, and I daresay you will be able to help us."

"You really mean that?" I asked, almost incredulously.

"You can take my word for it," Vansittart assured me, and held out his hand.

"That sounds almost too good to be true," I said to Paul, after Vansittart had left us.

"I've always told you," he laughed, "that the English are far shrewder and more reasonable than you think."

"It's tragic that they have let things go so far that war is now a foregone conclusion," I said.

I returned to The Hague greatly relieved. Moreover, I had made my decision, and in the circumstances I felt convinced that it was the right one.

A month later, on February 21st, 1939, our military attaché

in Brussels stopped at The Hague on his way back from Berlin, and under a solemn seal of secrecy told Zech and myself that the march on Prague was now definitely fixed for March 15th. The same day Willi sped on his motor-bicycle to Amsterdam and there, from the Central Post Office, rang up Paul in London, telling him that we had decided to take our holiday on March 15th and go to Prague.

"Will you tour the *whole* of Czechoslovakia?" asked an agitated Paul.

"Yes," Willi replied, "we'll tour the entire country."

My warning must have been completely ignored, because a few days before zero hour Sir John Simon, in the House of Commons, remarked in a speech that the horizon of Europe had seldom of late been so quiet and peaceful as at that moment.

And so the Ides of March came and all Czechoslovakia was swallowed up by the Hitlerian Moloch. The German military machine was now the undisputed master of Central Europe. Even the champions of Appeasement in the Western camp could no longer close their eyes to the fact that Nazi Germany, which they themselves had aided and abetted, now constituted a mortal danger. The millions over whom they ruled were impatiently clamouring for an end to interminable surrender.

For the first time an act of Hitlerian aggression met with a markedly hostile reception. The Germans did not venture to set foot in the Czech Embassies in London and Paris, and the diplomatic representatives of the two powers continued to be accredited to the Czech Government in exile.

Furthermore, the British Government took a step which, in contrast to the traditional English policy of caution displayed in recent years, seemed stark madness. It pledged itself to go to the assistance of distant Poland if she were attacked by Nazi Germany. It was obvious, after Hitler's henchman, Colonel Beck, had duly done his duty by safeguarding the Nazis' rear in their attack on Czechoslovakia, that Poland was to be the next victim on Hitler's list. The British guarantee now left us in no doubt that a German onslaught on Poland would automatically bring a declaration of war from Great Britain and France.

The catastrophe which had been threatening for years was drawing near, and might even burst upon the world before the coming summer.

As the tension mounted in Europe, the Nazi bosses developed a remarkable partiality for foreign travel, and during the summer of 1939 Holland was among the countries favoured by distinguished visitors.

A mild sensation was caused in July by a report that "Fat Hermann", then slowly cruising down the Rhine in his luxury yacht, *Karin II*, intended to enter Dutch territorial waters. None of us had received any information of his plans. He had not even deigned to approach the Foreign Office in Berlin, whose duty it would be to fulfill the necessary formalities with the Dutch Government. There was good reason to fear that difficulties would arise with the Dutch officials if Goering unexpectedly turned up in his yacht at the frontier and, with his customary arrogance, demanded the right to enter the country. The Legation at The Hague was therefore instructed to get in touch with him. This was easier said than done, as the *Karin II* was steaming leisurely down the Rhine with no permanent anchorage, and made no reply to our telegrams. Zech therefore bade me set out in person to ascertain the great man's intentions.

Starting my inquiries in Cologne, I learned that the *Karin II* was somewhere between Düsseldorf and the Dutch frontier, so I proceeded to race by car from one landing-stage to another along the entire length of the Lower Rhine. More than once I sighted the shapely craft in the distance with its escort of two police patrol boats, but it was already late in the afternoon when she anchored about a hundred yards out in the stream at Emmerich. The party on board, however, did not disembark and was apparently listening to a discourse from Goering on

166

the West Wall, which, in that part of the world, was only in its early stages. "Fat Hermann", field glasses in hand, was standing at the rail surrounded by a uniformed retinue, when suddenly he turned in my direction. He was clad in white from head to foot. At his neck and shoulders were some braided trimmings, his huge belly was encircled by a gold belt from which dangled a gleaming gold dagger. On his head he wore what appeared to be a combination of a naval, military and rakish sports cap. Lohengrin himself could not have concocted a more remarkable Admiral's uniform!

One of the patrol boats now came over to the landing stage, and out of it stepped a young naval lieutenant, who introduced himself as Goering's nephew. I told him that I was from the Legation at The Hague and wished to know his Uncle's intended route through Holland in order to obtain the formal entry permit from the Dutch Government. Lieutenant Goering returned to the yacht, and I watched him talking to his white-uniformed, pot-bellied uncle. A few minutes later he returned to tell me that the Field-Marshal had been under the impression that he would be able to dispense with the usual formalities. Now, however, he would forego his proposed visit, as he could not spare the time waiting for documents which had to be applied for and approved at The Hague.

Zech breathed more freely next morning when I was able to tell him that the dreaded visitation would not materialise. He had recently suffered much discomfort and annoyance from a visit lasting several days from the Minister of Finance and President of the Reichsbank, Walter Funk, my former bleary-eyed chief at the Wilhelmplatz, in whose honour not only the Legation but the Dutch Government had been obliged to give a sumptuous dinner every evening. The hard-drinking Funk, however, behaved comparatively decently and there were no unfortunate incidents.

Far more disagreeable was the arrival of SS Group—Leader Heydrich, chief of the hated Gestapo Security Service. Ostens-

167

ibly he had come as a member of a team of SS men taking part in a fencing tournament at Zandvoort, near Amsterdam. As I had already met him, Zech thought I was best qualified to play the part of lion-tamer, and on the plea of sudden indisposition left me to represent the Legation at this sporting event.

The tournament took place in a roped-off area on the sands. Heydrich, already in fencing kit, greeted me as "my Geneva innocent from the country". I told him that I knew nothing about swordsmanship, and as it was a warm, sunny day, I spent quite a lot of time sun bathing. During the long intervals between the bouts, he put on his bathing trunks and joined me.

All around us were the summer crowds who had come for the day to Amsterdam's seaside resort of Zandvoort, about which a joke was then going the rounds in Holland: "What is the difference between Zandvoort and Tel-Aviv?" "In Zandvoort there are no Arabs."

Not only Heydrich, I thought, but most of his companions had the life of a Jew on his conscience. Indeed, some of these young Nazis enjoyed impressing me with their luxury cars, which had in all probability once been the property of wealthy Viennese Jews. As we lay on the sands, we were watched by hundreds of Jewish eyes, including no doubt, those of many a German refugee with terrible memories of SS concentration camps. At any moment, I told myself, there might be an attempt on our lives.

As I looked down on Heydrich dozing beside me, I realised how much truth there was in the old saying "It is the spirit which fashions the body." Although his features did not make a bad impression, there was something repulsive about his physique. Not that it was in any way abnormal; in fact, he was built like an athlete. Yet his muscular mass of flesh seemed scarcely human and reminded me of one of those primeval monsters whose pictures had terrified me as a child.

Paul was once again in Holland at that time, and when I had told him that I would be meeting Heydrich at Zandvoort, he could not restrain his curiosity. He wanted a close look at the monster, and I believe that if I had offered to introduce him he would have accepted. It was arranged, therefore, that he would take a stroll along the sands that afternoon but not approach too closely. I had told him that if I had been able to extract any useful information from Heydrich I would scratch the back of my head, so that he could defer his departure for London the next day and come to see me instead.

I now looked up to see Paul passing a few yards away. I scratched the back of my head, and was thoroughly relieved to watch his squat figure disappearing into the distance.

One piece of information I was able to extract from Heydrich in fact made it possible to help save the library of Sigmund Freud which was then in Vienna and, so Heydrich had told me, was destined to be burnt by the Nazis. By the intervention of a Royal personage, an export licence was obtained to have it removed to Paris, where during the war it unfortunately again fell into Nazi hands.

During the time we were together, I had an uneasy feeling that, in spite of his affability, Heydrich was no longer convinced of my rustic simplicity. But I did my best to sustain the illusion by making fatuous conversation and telling silly stories. That same evening he invited me to dine with him and his fellow roughs at his hotel. I guessed at once that his purpose was to get me tight and induce me to make some indiscreet remark. Before each "Prosit", he gave me a keen and unpleasantly searching glance. The longer the dinner lasted, the more unbearable it became, and I found myself wondering how I was to escape from this company with a whole skin. Just before midnight I decided to make a move. It was obvious enough to me that this arch-criminal was fundamentally a typical German petty-bourgeois, so, pulling myself together, I addressed him in the sort of middle-class jargon he could understand.

"Group-Leader, work is work and schnapps is schnapps," I announced pompously. "*You* can lie in bed to-morrow morning, but *I* must be at my office early, and what is more—*sober*. Now I must be off. It is a recognized rule always to leave a party when one is enjoying oneself most. For me, Group-Leader, that moment has come."

He stared at me in surprise, but made no reply.

"I could never forgive myself, however, if I were to leave without drinking your health," I continued. Then, glass in hand, I added formally: "You will permit me, Group-Leader?"

Heydrich, quite overawed by so much politeness, raised his glass.

"You won't object if I remain seated?" he asked.

"Group-Leader, I would regard it as a most exceptional honour if you were to stand up," I told him.

With that, he actually got to his feet, and we clinked glasses. Bowing curtly to the others, I withdrew as quickly and unobtrusively as I could.

Outside, I jumped into my car, and shouted to Willi: "Step on the gas! I hope I never set eyes on that swine again so long as I live!"

CHAPTER TWENTY-TWO

ABOUT TWO MONTHS before the outbreak of war I also had the pleasure of meeting my old acquaintance Doctor Ley again. One afternoon a telephone call from Berlin told us that he had just left at the head of a delegation to attend, the International Trades Union Congress in London. He would be at the Hook of Holland that same evening at about ten o'clock. The caller went on to say that Ley had forgotten to take his expense allowance with him and would be in urgent need of funds. We must, therefore, meet him and let him have an advance on the Legation's account so that he would not arrive in London with empty pockets.

I collected some ready cash from the safe, and even managed to get a few one pound notes from the bank, although it had closed. The remainder I made up in Dutch guilders. Then I telephoned Butting to say that I thought a representative of the Party should also meet Ley, and he appointed his adjutant, Lauffer, to accompany me. The latter was an inoffensive, not overintelligent young schoolmaster, who had conceived an idealistic, blind devotion to the Führer and the Nazi Party.

We were standing together on the platform as the train from Berlin steamed in, and I caught sight at once of a face peering out of the dining-car window which could have belonged to no-one but Ley. A few minutes later he emerged, completely drunk, staring about him with a glazed look in his eyes and obviously not knowing exactly where he was. At his heels were the members of the delegation, who gallantly helped his young, blonde wife down from the train.

"Come along, darling," she said sharply, and thrust her arm under that of her swaying spouse.

Ley had recently married for a second time, after leaving his first wife who was considerably older than himself. Although the present object of his devotion rejoiced in the ingeniously romantic name of Lore, it was only too apparent that I. G. Dye Industries were responsible for her striking golden locks.

With Lauffer beside me, I walked up to the lurching Doctor and informed him that we had come from the Legation at The Hague with the necessary money. "Money" seemed to be one of the few words that he was capable of understanding.

"Money?" he mumbled. "Give it to me!"

I pointed out that I must have a receipt and would be obliged to assess the equivalent value in marks. This was too much for Ley. "Settle all that with my adjutant!" he ordered as he swayed on his way.

The formalities completed, we watched the representatives of the German working class, with the tipsy Ley and his blonde partner, disappear up the lighted gangway, and only then did Lauffer open his mouth.

"He was hopelessly drunk!" he said in a horrified whisper.

"Lauffer, I believe your're right. Do you know, I thought so myself," I told him.

All the way back to The Hague, the simple elementary schoolmaster was quite unable to recover from this appalling revelation.

"But, Lauffer, everyone in Germany knows that Ley drinks," I said.

"But I never believed it until now," he cried.

"Anyway, you would be wiser to say nothing about it," I warned him.

The next day, however, Lauffer could not resist the temptation of telling Butting of the shock which had been inflicted on his faith in the Swastika. That same evening he came to me with his face wreathed in smiles.

"We were both mistaken," he announced. "Doctor Butting knows for a fact that Doctor Ley gave his word of honour to the Führer over a year ago never to touch another drop of alcohol. He would never break a promise like that. What we took for drunkenness was a natural impediment in his speech. Doctor Butting knows all about it. It's not noticeable when he's speaking in public, but Doctor Ley can't always control it in private conversation."

"Well, Lauffer," I said sympathetically, "then everything's all right after all. But remember what I told you yesterday, it would be better not to refer to the matter again..."

*   *   *

Within the course of one year, two sovereign states, Austria and Czechoslovakia, had been incorporated in the Third Reich. Without firing a shot, German militarism had captured the key to the strategic stronghold of Central Europe. However much Mr. Chamberlain might wave his umbrella and shout about the armed intervention of the combined forces of the British Empire, from now on the megalomaniac Hitler would turn a deaf ear.

The next move was to be the ruthless onslaught on Poland. A few days after the announcement of Britain's guarantee, Ribbentrop gave a dinner at the Kaiserhof to his closest colleagues. A friend of mine, Ulrich Doertenbach, who was present, told me that during the evening the "Statesman" remarked with an air of triumph: "I wonder on what pretext the British Lion will retire this time into the undergrowth with his tail between his legs!"

In order to stifle the slightest opposition in the Foreign Office, Ribbentrop circulated a secret warning, signed by the Secretary of State, von Weizsäcker, which contained the following threat: "If anyone working under me expresses himself in a manner likely to cause mischief and thereby undermine confidence, I will summon him to my room and shoot him dead with my own hand. My report on the incident to the Reich Chancellor will read as follows: 'Mein Führer, I have just executed a traitor to his country'."

Our mystery men at The Hague also exuded an air of overbearing cocksureness. In Butting's eyes the Third Reich already had the Continent of Europe in its pocket, and Schultze-Bernet never doubted for one moment that the Polish campaign would be anything more than a "military manoeuvre". According to him, before England had finished rubbing her eyes, her Polish ally would have disappeared from the map. Our naval expert, Besthorn, took it for granted that owing to its outdated obsolescence the British Fleet would refuse combat. The Nazis were no longer afraid of anyone, and there was no doubt that Poland would be devoured at a single gulp; the Western Powers would, of course, protest, but as usual not raise a finger. As for Britain, she seemed half fearful of her own temerity. Chamberlain was making desperate efforts to find an ally to pull the Polish chestnuts out of the fire for him, and had begun to show a hitherto concealed affection for the Soviet Union. At the same time he refrained from making too many rash and headstrong advances, and was careful to leave plenty of back doors open. The delegation he sent to Moscow to find out how the land lay was not led by a Minister or even by His Majesty's principal diplomatic adviser, Vansittart, but by a then little known permanent official of the Foreign Office, Sir William Strang, who did not possess full powers, and could not, therefore, enter into any binding agreements. This mission seemed all the more futile since the Polish Government again emphatically declared that in no circumstances would Soviet troops, even as allies, be permitted to set foot on Polish soil.

In the meantime, Chamberlain himself was calmly engaged in private conversations with Wohltat and other intermediaries who continued to be sent over by Goering, Hess and Ribbentrop.

One morning Butting burst into my room in a state of high

glee and announced that Ribbentrop had just concluded a Non-Aggression Pact with the Soviet Union.

"The Führer is and will remain the greatest statesman of all time!" he shouted.

Above the fireplace behind me hung a portrait of Ribbentrop. I called his attention to it.

"Doctor Butting," I reminded him, "Please don't overlook the *second* greatest statesman of all time."

With the signing of this pact between Germany and Russia, the tables were indeed turned, but not as Chamberlain had intended when he set out on his fishing holiday. Now, in fact, Britain was faced with the prospect of herself entering the lists if the maniac Hitler was to be destroyed.

I was far from being a doctrinaire Marxist, but sheer commonsense told me that for the sake of his own skin Stalin could not have acted otherwise than he did. Neither Hitler nor Chamberlain had ever shown any particular fondness for Moscow. There was no earthly reason why the Soviet Union should come to the assistance of either if one of them found himself in a tight corner.

The sky was a cloudless blue in that month of August, 1939. It seemed almost as if the Almighty desired that Europe should linger a short while longer in the sunlight before the long dark night set in.

Never do I remember such a perfect summer as during those last weeks of peace. Every morning at breakfast my first question to Willi was: "How long can everything remain so peaceful?"

According to secret military information from Berlin the attack on Poland was fixed for August 20th. But that day came and went without incident. Apparently Mussolini had intervened at the last moment and restrained the over-eager Hitler. For a short spell, at least, it was possible to breathe again.

I was filled with a strong desire to see Laaske once more, but it was too far away. Nevertheless, I was determined to spend at least one more day on German soil and breathe the air of my own country. As her estate was at Moyland, near Cleves, and close to the frontier, I telephoned to Frau Steengracht, and she invited me to come over on the following Sunday when her husband, Gustav, would be there on leave from Berlin. She told me that her old father and another mutual friend would be the only other guests.

I took Willi with me as far as the German frontier so that he could go on to Cologne to see his family, and arranged to pick him up at Emmerich Station on my way back.

Moyland was one of the most picturesque castles on the Lower Rhine. Surrounded by a broad moat, it had once been a mediaeval stronghold, but was converted into a residence in the French style in the reign of Louis XIV. A massive drawbridge spanned the moat, and an old archway led into an ivy-clad courtyard, where, it is said, Frederick the Great met Voltaire for the first time.

Gustav Steengracht had been working for nearly a year in the Protocols Department of the Foreign Office in Berlin. As we talked together of old times in London, I reminded him of the embarrassing moment when he had forgotten von Dircksen's credentials, but Gustav had failed to recall it. I could not help noticing that he seemed thoughtful to the point of melancholy and that his old sense of fun had forsaken him.

In the evening the five of us sat on the terrace drinking Moselle. Below lay the moat with its croaking frogs and a lovely wood of ancient trees, beyond which stretched meadows in which rabbits scurried and deer grazed peacefully.

"How much longer shall we be able to enjoy this sort of tranquil life?" I asked, speaking my thoughts out loud.

"It's only a matter of days," Gustav said sadly. "I saw Ribbentrop yesterday. He has gone completely mad. Nothing will stop him pressing on with his criminal gamble."

"But does he imagine for one moment that hostilities will end with the Polish campaign?" I asked. "Does he really believe

176

that Germany can win a war waged against half the world?"

"He is convinced that England will not intervene. He is prepared for anything, and the German Army is actually superior to any other."

Gustav's words had such an effect upon me that I could not sleep that night, my last on German soil, although the summer wind rustled softly in the trees outside my window.

The following evening I left to pick up Willi, but his train was late and I had some time to wait. A strange woman, noticing the Dutch registration plate on my car, came up to me. "Can you take me with you?" she asked. "I want to get away from here."

A man with whom I chatted casually said: "If they dare to let loose that war of theirs, just give us weapons! We'll turn our rifles on 'em and soon put an end to the whole bloody nonsense!"

I spoke to several other people, but came across no war-crazy Nazis. Willi, moreover, told me that his father, for many years a Cologne tram conductor and a former N.C.O., had said to him: "Don't talk a lot of rubbish about war! In the first place, the Führer won't go to war, but if he did, he'd know he was going to win!"

It is only a few miles from Emmerich to the Dutch frontier, and the road runs along a spur of hills overlooking the broad expanse of the Lower Rhine plain. That evening, black clouds were gathering in the West and the whole landscape was bathed in a weird, almost eerie, light. I pulled up the car and looked back towards the horizon and Germany, for I knew we would live through dreadful years before we saw our country again.

When I returned to The Hague, I found the Legation in a state of turmoil. A whole new range of activities had been imposed upon us by Berlin, some of which must have been unique in diplomatic history. Our "Statesman" had conceived a number of remarkable brainwaves, perhaps the strangest of which was an attempt to keep the British Government from declaring war by a wholesale caonvassing of private individuals. A large staff in Berlin had been employed for days toothcombing British directories, telephone and reference books to produce the names and addresses of a polyglot mass of individuals from every stratum of society. There were tens of thousands of them. Another large staff was employed writing their addresses on envelopes to give the appearance of private letters. Inside, the astonished Mr. Smith would find an impassioned appeal to him from an unknown German well-wisher to use his influence to prevent the British Government from going to war with his peace-loving Teutonic blood-brothers.

So that there should be no suspicion of official German propaganda it had been decided that all these letters should be mailed from neutral countries. As a result, there arrived by diplomatic courier a number of bulging washing baskets. The Legation was required to seal the envelopes, stamp them and post them. As this would have constitued too great a strain on our combined saliva, Butting's Fifth Column was mobilised for stamp-licking. In order to allay Dutch suspicions, the letters had to be posted by tens or twenties at the most in single letter-boxes throughout the length and breadth of Holland. Accordingly, nightfall saw the release of a swarm of harassed Party members from The Hague travelling to Rotterdam, Leyden, Harlem, Delft and even as far afield as Leeuwarden, bearing suitcases crammed with letters which were breathlessly dumped at every street corner where a box could be found.

Despite all these precautions, the origin of these letters was unmistakeable, as only two brands of envelopes had been used throughout: pale green and pale blue. I sent a specimen of each to Paul and must plead guilty to Mr. Smith for having deprived him of his last personal message from the Third Reich.

The night before the invasion of Poland started, Paul turned up again at The Hague and telephoned to me under an assumed name. Since I considered it highly dangerous to

178

see him myself, I sent Willi on his motorcycle to the somewhat isolated hotel he had named. It was not long before Willi was back. Vansittart, he reported, wanted to let me know that this time there was going to be no repetition of Munich, and that he, Vansittart, stood by his promise to me. Paul would remain at The Hague in order to keep in contact with me and eventually bring me over to England.

At noon on the following day the British ultimatum to Germany expired. With a few members of the Legation I was sitting in Zech's study listening to the radio, which was tuned in to London. The familiar strokes of Big Ben rang out. Then Chamberlain spoke. His voice sounded solemn and subdued as we listened to the laconic phrase: "We are now at war with Germany".

The Second World War had begun.

CHAPTER TWENTY-THREE

IT WOULD HAVE created a considerable sensation not only in Germany but throughout the world if, on the outbreak of war, a number of German diplomats, whose patriotism was beyond doubt, had unmistakeably rejected Ribbentrop's policy and walked out. Such an action, I told myself, was particularly necessary if one were to take a long-term view of what would be the post-war situation. Anyone who knew the Nazis well was bound to realise that their crimes in time of war would far surpass anything that had been committed to date. The victors, in the fury of their retaliation, would certainly not discriminate between any internal factions in the German war machine, and all would be considered war criminals alike. If, however, responsible Germans remained whose hands were unstained by blood, there was a chance that the true voice of Germany could obtain a hearing. I knew that quite a few of my colleagues were intelligent enough to realise this, and hoped ardently that I would not remain the only one who had already made plans to meet this eventuality.

But at the moment I was caught in a trap, because all communications between Holland and England were closed. I could escape neither by sea nor by air. For the time being at least, all that I could do was to carry on.

Immediately the war had started the "mystery men" attached to the Legation multiplied like rabbits. We already occupied four large houses, but now these were too small to accommodate the many new departments which were being established. A hotel with nearly a hundred rooms was taken over, lock, stock and barrel, to provide offices for the staff employed by Schultze-

Bernet and Besthorn alone. The question of rent was of minor consequence, and the Dutch proprietor was only too willing to accept the terms offered, since it was unlikely that he would welcome any tourists for some time to come.

The Legation itself hummed like a beehive, and I had so much work on my hands that there were times when I scarcely knew whether I was standing on my head or my heels, for, from the moment Germany found herself at war with England and France, Holland had become Hitler's most active Intelligence centre.

Ever since diplomatic relations have existed between nations, it has always been the recognised practice on a declaration of war for the diplomatic representatives of the enemy to be treated with courtesy and afforded every facility to return home. This time-honoured custom, however, was not observed by our "Statesman", Ribbentrop, who would not allow the British and French Ambassadors and their staffs to leave German territory until it was officially confirmed that the former occupants of the German Embassies in London and Paris were no longer on enemy soil. A formal exchange would then take place in neutral Holland.

I was informed of this novel procedure by telephone from Berlin by no less a person than Ribbentrop's tall, red-headed Chief of Protocol, Baron Dörnberg. I had instructions to see that it was carried out according to orders and "with strict impartiality."

The interchange with the French was accomplished fairly quickly and without incident, since the Dutch frontier is practically equidistant from Berlin and Paris and the respective trains arrived in the region of Utrecht almost simultaneously. Unforeseen difficulties, however, arose with the British. There had been some delay before a suitable ship could be chartered at Harwich for the staff of our London Embassy. Ribbentrop, therefore, kept the British Mission stranded for three days in a train somewhere just inside the German frontier. It was only when I was able to inform Dörnberg that the British ship was reported in Dutch territorial waters that the German train with its British occupants received permission to proceed.

On Dörnberg's instructions I was to go to Rotterdam to take charge of the handover, and told Willi to get ready to drive me there. Just as I was about to leave, Schultze-Bernet emerged from the Legation and handed me a sealed package.

"Here are 250,000 guilders in Dutch banknotes urgently required in Berlin to be delivered into trustworthy hands," he said. "Give them to my friend, Herr Z, who will arrive with the others from London. He'll know what to do with them."

I was relieved to know that Schultze-Bernet's faith in my trustworthiness evidently remained unshaken, and with his quarter of a million guilders on my knees, I set out for Rotterdam.

During the drive Willi kept repeating: "This is an act of Providence. Let's go aboard the British ship and hide. With that cash we could live in England for the duration of the war!"

"No, Willi," I said frankly. "If we get out, we'll go with clean hands, and not like thieves."

"The swine are only going to use the dough for some dirty business, anyway," he answered fiercely.

He was certainly right, but I did not give way to his tempting suggestion, and handed the packet to the mysterious Herr Z.

Although I delivered a signed receipt from the latter to Schultze-Bernet, I was later accused by the Nazis of embezzling this money. It may, of course, have vanished when in Herr Z's possession, but certainly not while I was in charge of it.

The train from Germany had not yet arrived when the British ship docked, and our London Germans remained on board or strolled along the quay in the sunshine for nearly an hour. Everyone looked so utterly dejected that they might well have been on their way to a funeral. The Ambassador, von Dircksen, had been recalled to Berlin several weeks earlier, and Theodor Kordt had acted as Chargé d'Affaires in his absence. Kordt and his wife remained in their cabin, so I went in to see them. Both were in a state of acute distress and had tears in their eyes. Kordt told me that he had done his utmost up to the very last to prevent war between England and Germany, and even had lengthy discussions with Vansittart. But nothing would induce the British not to honour their guarantee to Poland. Hitler's foreign policy may, indeed, have been mad, but never at any time had he wanted war with England.

"It was all in vain," Kordt added. "Either way we are finished. If the Nazis win, Germany will become a vast madhouse; if the other side wins, we shall be wiped off the face of the map."

"What do you intend to do?" I asked.

"I really don't know," he said despairingly. "It's impossible for a man with any decency to stay at the Foreign Office and share the responsibility. The right thing would be to join the Reichswehr and be killed honourably."

I did not agree with these views, but could at least sympathise with them. I lost all respect for Kordt, however, when he emerged as Ambassador in Berne three weeks later, and was responsible for the secret Nazi news-service to England. He never once ran foul of the Nazis during the war. But he intrigued with Allan Dulles, Chief of the U.S. Secret Service in Switzerland during the final phase of the struggle, and was subsequently regarded as one of the leading conspirators in the plot of July 20th, 1944. He was appointed Director of the Political Department on the establishment of the West German Foreign Office, and later became Adenauer's Ambassador in Athens.

When I accompanied him to the German train on this occasion at Rotterdam, I did not believe him capable of such lack of character. Followed by his mournful staff, he strode with bowed head past the assembled British from Berlin, who surveyed him with a weary, but hard and hostile expression in their eyes.

In the meantime, Willi had been talking to a waiter in the German dining-car. He told me that the latter had envied him his job in neutral Holland and showed no sign of pleasure at the prospect of returning to Germany. The unfortunate staff of the train had little chance of evading their fate, but not so the diplomats. Yet when I looked carefully through the list of their names in the hope that at least one or two would be missing, I found they were all there. All my colleagues had allowed themselves to be hustled back to the Hitlerian slaughter-house like a flock of sheep.

When Chamberlain declared war on the Third Reich, heavy deliveries of British petrol, copper and other vital war materials were in transit to the Rhineland and the Ruhr. These were now lying in ships and railway trucks in Holland, and one of Butting's and Schultze-Bernet's main objects was to get these valuable supplies through to Germany as quickly as possible. Since the Dutch frontiers were officially closed, this would be no easy matter. Thus some form of illegal means would have to be used, which meant that Dutch collaborators would be needed.

There was no shortage of the latter. Offers of help flowed into the Legation daily and, as I was responsible for the incoming mail, these letters were submitted to me for delivery. My instructions were to forward all such correspondence immediately to Schultze-Bernet. But before doing so, I naturally read them and discovered that some employees of Shell, the Anglo-Dutch Oil Company, displayed a remarkable willingness to offer their services in supplying the needs of Hitler's war machine.

Since I was actively helping to feed the Nazi arsenals by allowing this game to continue, I felt it my duty to do something to sabotage its success. Every drop of oil, every ounce of metal to reach the German armament factories would help to prolong the war.

I therefore decided to make a list of those names which seemed to me particularly influential and dangerous, and see that it came into Paul's hands. I had not hitherto realised what intimate business relations the great international monopolies maintained, even in wartime.

I had no idea to whom Paul would pass this information, but I felt certain he would make good use of it.

It was common knowledge at The Hague that British Intelligence was directed from the Passport Office of the British Consulate at Scheveningen by a certain Captain Stevens. I had never set eyes on the latter and had always avoided meeting any of his associates.

I was completely nonplussed when three days after I had sent Willi to Paul with the list of names, Zech suddenly asked me: "Do you think there is anyone here who is in touch with Captain Stevens?"

I asked what possible reason he could have for even suspecting such a thing.

"Schultze-Bernet has just been here," he replied, "and insists that Stevens is receiving highly secret information from the German Legation".

I began to feel thoroughly alarmed, and that evening sent Willi off again to tell Paul what had occurred. But Paul merely laughed and sent back a message assuring me that my imagination was running riot. However, after luncheon the next day, I found Schultze-Bernet waiting in my ante-room with a face as black as thunder.

"What's the matter?" I asked as casually as I could. "Is anything wrong?"

"Quite a lot," he answered, eyeing me keenly. "Are these names, by any chance, familiar to you?" he asked, mentioning the name of a Rotterdam banker and one or two of the Shell employees who were on the list I had sent to Paul.

"I meet a great many people, Herr Schultze-Bernet," I fenced. "It's quite impossible for me to remember them all. However, I may have met these fellows. What is it you want to know about them?"

185

"They happen to be among those working for me, and they have been denounced to Stevens," he said, glaring at me.

"But how do you know that?" I asked. "Did Stevens tell you? I can't for the life of me see how you could know otherwise!"

"My dear Putlitz," he said pompously, "I would not be Schultze-Bernet if I hadn't an agent with Stevens. I know everything that goes on in his set-up. Where could he have got hold of these names except from here? Answer me that."

"You may, of course, be right. In any case, I can think of nothing to justify your suspicion," I answered firmly.

"Then I must make further enquiries," he said ominously. "I "I can assure you I intend to get to the bottom of this."

Although we shook hands as he left, he was obviously far from convinced. It was vividly clear to me that I was now in the gravest danger and would have to get out of Holland as quickly as possible. I sat down at my desk before the piles of documents and letters, and tried desperately to figure out my position. Every frontier was virtually sealed; no-one could escape to England by the normal routes. Only Vansittart could help me now.

I knew that I would have to send Willi immediately to Paul, but at the same time it was impossible for me to leave my office without arousing suspicion. My telephone would be tapped, and one careless word might cost me my life. Yet I had to get in touch with Willi at all costs. I decided to risk ringing him up.

"Willi, I've got such a lot to do that I shall be working here very late," I told him. "I won't have any dinner, but will be back for high tea between five and six. Have something ready and be there yourself. By the way," I added casually, "I think there is something wrong with the car battery."

Would he or would he not understand that what was wrong was something infinitely more serious? I could only hope and pray that he would.

By now it was two o'clock in the afternoon, and I wondered feverishly how I would be able to stand the strain until five in the afternoon. In order to deaden the awful tension, I tried to concentrate on my work as never before. But the hours dragged by interminably, so that I felt the time would never pass.

Punctually at five I climbed into my car and drove home. Before I had time to produce my key, the front door opened.

"Has anything happened?" Willi asked, his face white with anxiety.

"Yes, something *has* happened," I told him. "If we're not out of here in twenty-four hours, it's all up with us. Whether Paul believes it or not. Schultze-Bernet *has* planted a spy in Stevens' outfit. Get on your bike at once. Paul must get us out of Holland to-night. I'm returning to the Legation very shortly so as not to arouse their suspicion. But I'll be back as soon as I can. By nine o'clock at the latest."

"But what can we do if Paul says he can't help us?" Willi asked. "Shall I go to Hermann?" Hermann was Countess Palland's manservant and a friend of Willi's. "He could hide us for a time, anyway."

"We'll talk about Hermann if everything else fails," I told him. "But you know as well as I do that the Dutch police do exactly as Butting wants. They'd find us and we'd be over the frontier in no time. Go to Paul first. Anything else is hopeless. It's up to the British to get us out".

"I'm scared!" Willi stammered.

I looked at his white face, and tried to laugh. "So am I!" I said, "damned scared!"

I tried to sit down to my coffee and rolls as calmly as I could, and it was with a sense of relief that I heard Willi's motorcycle starting up. I could trust him and knew that he would do nothing foolish. As I ate without relish, I considered our predicament. There was no doubt that we were up against it, just as there was no doubt that Schultze-Bernet was highly suspicious of me. Just how these suspicions had been aroused

I was at a loss to understand. Only after the war did I learn that it was a Dutch policeman, who worked for Stevens and was at the same time in the pay of Schultze-Bernet, who had betrayed me.

When I returned to my office, I found Schultze-Bernet still in the building. He came into my room and behaved as if he had completely forgotten our conversation of the previous afternoon. As usual, we chatted for a few minutes. Then I set to work and cleared my desk of all its papers, after which I returned to my house, where I found Willi and Paul waiting for me.

Utterly exhausted, I threw myself full length on the sofa and told them to sit down.

"Well, is there any hope or are we for it?" I asked Paul. He looked at my calmly. "It hasn't been easy," he said quietly, "but I think it can be managed."

On receiving my message, he had gone straight to Stevens and spoken to Vansittart on the telephone in London. Vansittart had said that if the worst came to the worst he would send a destroyer to Scheveningen to take me off. But it would be better if Stevens could get hold of an aeroplane to fly us out of Holland.

Paul said that Stevens knew a pro-British Dutch pilot who, in spite of the regulations then in force, was allowed to make test flights over Dutch territory. This pilot was, apparently, game for anything. Stevens was in touch with him, and expected a definite answer by ten o'clock that evening.

As Paul was about to leave with Willi, I drew the latter aside.

"For God's sake," I whispered, "don't bring him here again. Whatever you do, come back alone! We can't afford to take these risks."

After they had gone, worn out with the strain of the last hours, I lay down again on the sofa and fell asleep. I was awakened towards midnight by Willi's return.

188

One glance at his deathly pale face told me that something was wrong.

"What's the matter?" I asked, immediately wide awake.

"There's someone in the garden," he answered, his voice trembling. "I'm sure it's Schultze-Bernet. As I passed on the bike, he dodged behind the tree near the gate."

"Then we can only hope to God he wasn't there earlier and saw Paul!" I said. "He wouldn't be suspicious of your coming back late from the town. In fact, he would think you were behaving just as you've always done. Anyway, don't let's think about it. What's Paul fixed up with Stevens and the pilot? That's far more important."

"It's all arranged," Willi said excitedly. "The pilot's Parmentier, the famous long-distance Dutchman, who won the Batavia-Sydney Prize last spring *. He'll be waiting for us at Schiphol with his engines ticking over tomorrow afternoon at two o'clock. Says he can't be there earlier. We're only to take one small suitcase each. There'll be a car ready to take us to Schiphol in a backyard off the Alkemadelaan in The Hague at one o'clock. The best thing is for us go to Hermann at the Villa Palland just before one, and take a taxi from there. I'll leave your car in the garage and bring the suitcases to Hermann's by tram."

"You seem to have everything worked out!" I smiled, rallying a little.

We ceased to bother our heads about the significance of the mysterious stranger in the garden, and took all our letters and papers to the cellar and burned them in the central heating stove. Then we packed our two bags; three suits each, as we reckoned that shirts and shoes were cheaper to replace than suits. Finally, we wrote farewell letters home, so wording them that the Gestapo would believe that our families would be both indignant and horrified at our sudden flight.

We were ready when the dawn broke on September 14th,

---

* He later flew with the R.A.F.

the first dull autumn morning of the year. Willi drove me to the Legation, and on the way I stopped at the Bank to draw the balance of my account. As I entered my office I wondered whether I would be able to hide my anxiety. Zech had called a conference at which I had to preside and at which Butting, Schultze-Bernet and Besthorn were all present. I did not like the look on their faces. Did they know I had been up to something? For one ghastly moment I feared I would have a blackout. Somehow, I managed to keep my head, but throughout the conference I was conscious of those three pairs of eyes watching me.

Later, I had a number of visitors and plenty of work to do. So far as I could tell, no-one had noticed the blood throbbing in my temples or that my hand trembled. Shortly before noon Zech called me to his room, and as I entered he looked up sadly from his desk.

"Have a look at this appeal in aid of the first War Winter Relief Fund which Butting has brought me," he said. "Listen to this first sentence: 'In this war which has been forced upon us......' I can't put my signature to such a blatant lie. You must help me find a formula which will satisfy my conscience and also be acceptable to Butting."

For a long time I had been disgusted by the hypocrisy of this almost universal desire to evade responsibility for every Nazi iniquity, and wanted to have no more to do with it. That morning, for the first time during our long friendship, I felt no sympathy for Zech in his dilemma, and could not resist a sharp retort.

"One can compromise as much as one likes by devising formulas, Count Zech, but no man with any decency can possibly support such a policy."

I left the Legation shortly before one o'clock, telling the porter that I would probably be back late and callers could not expect me before four. As I was walking to Countess Palland's villa I met the Director of K.L.M., the Dutch Air Line, who had placed a free passage to Greece at my disposal the previous spring. "If you only knew that within an hour I shall be making another flight at your company's expense, and, this time, you may even lose the aeroplane!" I thought, as we raised our hats to each other.

Hermann opened the front door to me and lead me to his room, where Willi was waiting with the suitcases. A few minutes later, we were on our way to the house in the Alkemadelaan. There, at the end of a long alleyway was a courtyard, in which a black limousine stood waiting. Beside it stood a man of medium height with a small dark moustache, who turned out to be the famous Captain Stevens. Having introduced himself, he wished us *au revoir* and a successful flight. He added that both the chauffeur of the car and the pilot were completely trustworthy, but it would be wiser for us to talk in English rather than German. After my suspicions of the men working for Stevens, I did not find this suggestion particularly reassuring.

Willi and I were sitting in silence in the back of the car when, to our annoyance, the chauffeur suddenly decided to be chatty. We were forced to answer him, but did so as curtly as possible.

"You speak English with quite a German accent," he remarked.

"Perhaps" I mumbled "that's because I was at school in Germany."

As we approached the aerodrome, he turned to me again and said: "The Offices of the Lufthansa are just round that corner. Herr Frank, the manager, is a good friend of mine. Perhaps you know him?"

"No, I've never met him," I said, as my heart began to beat more violently, for I knew that Frank was one of the key-men in Butting's espionage network.

However, we passed the offices safely and turned into a road running beside the aerodrome. Just beyond the iron fence I saw a passenger plane with its propellors turning slowly. A few yards from it, the car stopped and, seizing our suitcases, Willi and I clambered through the fence and dashed to the plane. Its door was open, and from his covered seat in the cockpit the pilot waved to us to get in. There was not a soul in sight. As we slammed the door, the engines roared to life, and in a matter of seconds we were away.

"So far so good", I muttered to Willi. "Let's hope we're as lucky with Parmentier as we were with the chauffeur. But we must keep a good look-out. If after a while we see land to the left it can only be England, and we're all right. But land to the right may mean that the fellow's taking us back to Germany."

"What then?" Willi asked, scarcely above a whisper.

"Then the only thing to do is to open the door and jump," I told him grimly. "Anything's better than landing up in a concentration camp or being shot."

The great thirty-seater plane seemed uncannily empty with only the two of us aboard it. With one eye on the grey North Sea below, we talked of what had happened that morning. Willi had actually found a Dutchman who had bought his motorcycle. It was at a very low price, but, nevertheless, we had an extra three hundred guilders in our pockets.

Having flown so often from Holland to England, I felt that we were taking an unusually long time.

"We should be able to see land by now," I said to Willi, who was peering out of the window on the right.

"There it is, I can see it quite plainly!" he shouted.

"Good God! It's on the right!" I yelled, and almost started from my seat.

Could that land be Germany? If we wanted to take a chance by jumping into the sea, we had no time to lose.

I looked again and saw white cliffs. It was not Germany! My mind was finally set at rest when I caught a glimpse of land to the left as well; the coast of France, near Boulogne.

An English fighter emerged from the clouds and flew

alongside us. Its sudden appearance gave me a wonderful sense of security, for I felt that it had been sent to meet us. Away in the distance, glimmering in the pale autumn sunlight, I could see the barrage balloons.

The plane now banked steeply, and below the wing-tip I saw an aerodrome. Almost without knowing what we were doing, Willi and I hugged each other and danced up and down.

"We're safe!" I laughed. "We're safe and free!"

A few minutes later, the plane landed. We were on enemy soil. It was a strange experience.

"Willi, my lad," I whooped, "never in our lives shall we have to utter the words 'Heil Hitler' again!"

CHAPTER TWENTY-FOUR

WE LANDED ON a small aerodrome, and some aircraftsmen ran up with a step-ladder which they placed against the open door. As Willi and I climbed down, a young man in civilian clothes came forward to greet us. He introduced himself as Tom Allen (as I will call him), and said that Vansittart had sent him to look after us and take us to London by car.

We had not driven far before I recognised the countryside, for after a few miles we were on to the main Brighton-London road. In the old days I had often driven along it at weekends during the summer when it was seething with traffic. Now it was practically deserted, so that it seemed no time at all before we were in London.

Tom Allen drove us to a block of flats near the British Museum. The flat to which he was taking us, he explained, belonged to his brother and sister-in-law, who shortly before had left for the country with their children because of the expected air raids. There was no reason, he said, why we should not stay there as long as we liked.

When we entered, a housekeeper was already busy preparing supper for us, and on the table in the dining-room were two bottles of champagne on ice. Having unpacked our few belongings, Willi and I settled down in the drawing-room and turned on the radio, for we were desperately anxious to know whether Radio Hilversum would have anything to say about our flight or the disappearance of the K.L.M. plane. At seven o'clock we got the news from Holland, but there was no mention of us. We did, however, pick up a police message saying that they were searching for a D.K.W. motor-cycle, giving the registration number.

Willi let out a yell. "That's my number! The poor devil who bought it this morning thought he'd got a bargain!"

When Tom came up to join us for dinner, we told him what we had heard. He raised his champagne glass and said: "You two just got out in time!"

After dinner, we started talking of our future. "Vansittart and I have been talking about you a lot," he said, "and this morning we came to the conclusion that it would be best if you became a British subject. Germany is certain to lose the war, and things may become awkward for you as a German. But if you have a British passport, you will be free to go where you like over here. You've lived in England for five years. The only snag is that during that time you were a diplomat with extra-territorial rights. But I think we can overcome that in your case. If you want it, we can arrange for you to have British nationality within three months. Think it over until tomorrow and let me know. There's one thing more," he added. "If you wish, we can arrange for you to emigrate to the U.S.A. where you will be on neutral territory."

While I realised that he meant it kindly, I was shocked that apparently the British did not understand in the very least why I had come to their country.

"Tom," I said, "I don't need until tomorrow to think it over. Please don't think for one moment that I'm not very honoured by your offer, because I am. But you've got me wrong. I have come here in order to prove to you people that you have allies amongst us Germans who are ready to fight against the Nazis. In order to do that, it is essential that I should keep my nationality. I would gladly accept your offer if I thought that Hitler was going to win, because then I would be stateless. But since I'm convinced that won't happen, I've come over to England to fight on your side as a German. As for going to America, well, I haven't the slightest desire to retire to a neutral country."

I think that Tom understood how I felt and respected me for it. At any rate, he never brought up the subject again, and I think he must have passed on what I said to Vansittart.

The following morning, I went to call on the latter. He received me with open arms.

"Neither of us had realised how difficult it would be for you to get here," he said laughing. "But 'all's well that ends well' " This last remark he made in German.

He had with him that morning the chief of the Press Department of the Foreign Office, Rex Leeper, whom I had met before. The three of us settled down in armchairs before the fire, and they listened while I told them how, in my opinion, it would be possible to mobilise an internal resistance movement against Hitler.

"At first," I explained, "one must fight in the military sense. I don't believe that enemy propaganda in wartime is worth as much as is generally supposed. I do believe, however, that it is possible to organise a Free German Movement in this country. You've already got Germans of all classes and creeds over here; you've Communists and Social Democrats, former deputies of the Central Liberal Party and even Tories and monarchists like Rauschning and Prince Frederick of Prussia. Get them together on a National Committee of Liberation which can speak with authority over the radio to its own countrymen. Let it tell the German people your peace terms for Germany once Hitler has gone. Then you will get somewhere. The Resistance in Germany has to be told that you are determined to stamp out Nazism totally and ruthlessly, but you do not intend to destroy or subjugate the German nation."

"Very interesting, Putlitz," Leeper said.

"We'll think this over carefully," Vansittart assured me. "But I can tell you here and now that the British Government discriminates most decidedly between the Nazi régime and the German people."

Before I left, Vansittart invited me down to Denham, his beautiful house in the country, whenever I wished, and during the weeks that followed I went there often. He and his wife treated me like one of the family. Indeed, I used their house as if I were at Laaske, shooting rabbits and rooks in the woods, listening to the croaking frogs in the lake and pottering about the kitchen garden, and as I did so I often dreamed of showing the Vansittarts Laaske after the war and introducing them to my family.

Every possible precaution was taken to keep my presence in London a secret so that the Nazis would be in the dark as to what had become of me. But in London, of all places, the news was bound to leak out. Indeed, I had not been there two weeks before I ran into the Counsellor of the Dutch Embassy, Baron van Karnebeek. He was utterly astonished to meet me walking down Piccadilly and immediately began questioning me. I concocted some cock-and-bull story. Then he told me that he was leaving for The Hague the next day for a meeting with the Foreign Minister, van Kleffens. So I said quite frankly: "Kaas, it's no use asking you to keep mum about our meeting. I've been a diplomat and I know that you'll tell van Kleffens, so I may as well ask you to do me a favour. Please ask van Kleffens to look after my personal belongings which I had to leave behind at Scheveningen, to see that they're not stolen by Butting's Gestapo men, and to send them to me here."

Karnebeek promised to do his best, as well as not to tell anyone but his Minister that he had seen me.

About this time Paul returned from Holland, bringing with him Captain Stevens, and we all met again at the former's flat where the winter before I had had that fateful talk with Vansittart. They told me that on the evening of my flight they had had a celebration dinner of oysters and champagne at the famous Restaurant Royale at The Hague. They also told me that the Nazis had spread all sorts of conflicting stories about me. Some said that I had rejoined my regiment at Stahnsdorf, others that I had been killed in a motor accident on the Belgian border. But the story I liked best was that I had run off with all the cash from the Legation and bought a brothel in Rio de Janeiro.

Stevens had other interesting news. "You'll be back in your country sooner than you think," he said. "Hitler is nearly finished."

"Where on earth do you get that idea from!" I laughed. "It doesn't look that way to me. He appears to be winning hands down. He's beaten Poland and the German army in the West is more powerful than ever, but still the Allies do nothing."

"There won't be any need for a military offensive. The Hitler régime is collapsing internally," Stevens insisted with great conviction.

"Go on, tell me more. I'm curious to know," I said cynically.

"I can't tell you everything, for obvious reasons," he explained with an air of mystery. "But you can take it from me that there is a lot hatching in the Wehrmacht which will soon flare up, and that will be the end of Hitler. Some of the top-ranking generals are mixed up in it. I'm in permanent radio contact with them from Holland. As soon as they've got rid of Hitler, they're going to sue for peace."

I asked him the names of the generals. He was very guarded, but in the end mentioned General von Rundstedt. Immediately he did so, I remembered that two years before the Gestapo had used von Runstedt's name as a decoy in abducting the former Reichs Chancellor, Bruening, from a Dutch monastery back to Germany. The plan only failed because Bruening had become suspicious at the last minute.

"Forgive me being sceptical, Stevens," I said, "but you know that I've had some pretty nasty experiences myself with your so-called confidants. I'm afraid they'll lead you up the garden path."

He gave me a rather lofty smile.

"I'm sorry I can't tell you more. But you'll soon see that I'm right".

Some days later van Karnebeek returned from Holland and I went to see him about my belongings. He shifted uncomfortably in his chair, making excuses. Then at last he came out with the truth.

"Van Kleffens didn't consider he could risk quarrelling with the Third Reich over a pair of trousers belonging to Herr von Putlitz!" he said. "Anyhow, your things had all been collected by Butting the day after you left."

The only irreplaceable things that I really regretted were my father's gold watch and chain that my grandfather had bought in 1815 in the rue de la Paix when the Prussians had marched into Paris. The rest of my possessions I wrote off without tears.

In point of fact, I had not really expected any other treatment from the men in power in Holland at that time, for not long before a certain official of the Dutch Foreign Office had remarked to me: "We Dutch are so sincerely neutral that we would like both sides to win."

Not very long afterwards, Captain Stevens, too, had his own taste of Dutch neutrality. By the end of October, General von Runstedt's plot was supposedly so far advanced that only one last personal conference remained to be held. Over the secret radio the anti-Hitler conspirators arranged to meet Stevens in a little café on the German border near Venlo. At an agreed time, Stevens, accompanied by a British colleague, Best, and a Dutch major, went to the rendezvous. But, instead of meeting von Runstedt, they were confronted by a party of Gestapo thugs, who dragged them into Germany under the eyes of the Dutch frontier guards.

For two years Stevens languished in chains in solitary confinement before being sent to a concentration camp, where he had ample time to reflect on his credulity until the end of the war. The Germans made tremendous propaganda out this *coup de main*. They were even more pleased to announce that they now had proof of their claims that it was a member of the British Secret Service who had placed the mysterious bomb which exploded in the beer cellar in Munich on November 9th; a bomb which miraculously failed to kill the Führer, who had left the cellar ten minutes before.

As a result of the Stevens episode, it was quite obvious to me that the Gestapo knew that I was in England.

CHAPTER TWENTY-FIVE

THE "PHONEY WAR", as the British called it, dragged on and, except for the blackout, life was scarcely changed in London. There seemed, almost incredibly, little feeling against the Germans, and Willi and I could talk quite freely in our own language without anyone even turning to look at us.

Frankly, I was appalled at the state of lethargy into which the British people appeared to have sunk and I moved heaven and earth to rouse them. Through Vansittart, I managed to contact members of the Chamberlain Cabinet, and voice my opinions. I saw Sir Samuel Hoare and implored him to form a German Committee of Liberation. But the poise of the old Tory was unruffled by anything I said. He listened to me politely, remarking from time to time: "Very interesting", or "That is worth considering". But, in the end, I came to the conclusion that nothing I could say or do would move these people to action. They would muddle along in their own way until Hitler himself taught them a lesson.

I listened to the Führer screaming over the radio from the Berlin Sportpalast that he would launch such a "blitz" upon the English that they would no longer see or hear. I heard Chamberlain remark soon afterwards that "Hitler had missed the bus".

The way things were going, it looked as if the war would last for ever. In the meantime, it was clear to me that the money I had in the bank would last only for about another twelve months. I had to earn a living.

Fortunately for me, not a stone's throw from Vansittart's house were Denham Studios, where Alexander Korda was making a number of anti-Hitler films. It was not long before I managed to get myself a job there, and a few months later I was engaged by Two Cities Films in an advisory capacity for a film they were making at Shepperton. It concerned a fictitious underground movement in Germany working against the Nazis and was an altogether fantastic story. However, I tried my best to see that at least it appeared fairly authentic. Anthony Asquith was directing the picture, and was very amused at my efforts to teach the extras how to "about turn" and salute in the approved German style. Willi, too, was a great help, for his knowledge of the various Nazi uniforms and insignias of rank was amazing.

While working at Shepperton I earned more money than I had ever done in my entire diplomatic career. Then, in 1940, Hitler invaded Denmark and Norway and the "phoney war" was finished. Overnight the attitude of the British people underwent a change. Now, every German was a suspected agent of Himmler or Canaris. Suddenly it became impossible for me to cross Piccadilly without being stopped and asked for my papers.

I still went every day to the studios. Then, one morning soon after the Nazi occupation of Holland and Belgium, Anthony Asquith took me aside and said: "You must go home. I'm sorry, but my electricians have said that if you show your face in the studio, they'll drop an arc-lamp on your head."

When I arrived back in London that day, the first tired soldiers were just returning from Dunkirk.

I was desperately worried. What else could I do in England? Here I stood, hopeless and helpless, between two fronts. The British, I knew, would fight to the bitter end. But, now, so far as they were concerned, I was nothing but a "hun" who, at best, could count only on their pity. If the Nazis invaded England, I would be one of the first to be liquidated.

That evening I went with Willi to see my friend Doctor G. He told me that he had got his visa for the United States and

202

that he and his family were leaving in a week. All that he could do for us was to give us a prescription for a dose of potassium cyanide large enough to kill us both. With the poison in our pockets we felt an odd sense of reassurance.

I went next to see my old friend Walton Butterworth, whom I had known in Washington, and who was now at the American Embassy. Three years ago I had been able to tell him about a Nazi spy who was working in his London office. At the time he had been most grateful and had said: "Wolfgang, if you're ever in difficulty with your Nazis and want to disappear, I'll break all the rules and regulations to get you a visa."

Now, however, when I appealed to him, reminding him of that promise, he said: "If you still had your diplomatic passport everything would be easy. But for the ordinary immigrant, it's another story."

Vansittart suggested that I should live at Denham, where I would be left in peace. But while I was grateful to him, I explained that I could not sit around living on his charity. I suggested to him that I should go either to the Bahamas or the West Indies, and he agreed with the idea. Through Lord Lloyd, Minister for the Colonies, the Governors of several of the West Indian islands were asked if they were prepared to grant me hospitality. Only Sir Arthur Richards, now Lord Milverton, the Governor of Jamaica, was prepared to do so. On the basis of this assurance, Butterworth was ready to grant me a transit visa to America, limited to ten days, as there was then no other route to Jamaica except via New York.

Vansittart, with his typical kindness, arranged that I could transfer sufficient money to pay my passage from New York to Kingston and still have a few hundred dollars as pocket money. At the last minute I managed to book two passages for Willi and myself on the *Britannic*, sailing from Liverpool.

Six months before, when I had landed on British soil, I had felt a free man. Now, as I stepped aboard the boat train at King's Cross, I was glad to be leaving. A German friend of mine who was living in London came to see us off. Since he could not get away, I gave him the capsules of cyanide which were sufficient for him and his wife. He grinned broadly. "I've never been given such a wonderful present," he thanked me. "Now at least I'm master of my own fate."

Willi and I were the only Germans aboard the *Britannic*, and the rest of the passengers treated us like lepers. Nobody wanted to sit at the same table with us. When we walked around the deck, people muttered that we ought to be thrown overboard and suggested that we were Nazi agents who would certainly whistle up a U-boat to torpedo them. Only Jan Masaryk, the Foreign Minister of the Czechoslovakian Government in exile, befriended us. He had known me from the old days and was also conversant with my story from Vansittart. Every day he took my arm and walked me round the promenade deck. But the hostility of the rest of the passengers never relaxed.

The evening before we landed in New York, we heard over the radio the news of the French capitulation at Compiègne.

The following morning, when the American Immigration Officer came aboard, I showed him my curious stateless identity papers, and my ten-days transit visa. He looked up from his desk and asked: "Haven't I dealt with you before some time?"

"It's possible," I told him.

"I remember now. You were at the German Embassy in Washington," he said.

"You're quite right. But then I had a diplomatic passport and wouldn't have been thrown out of your country in ten days," I ventured.

For some reason, he took pity on me. "It's hard on you," he said. "I know you're a regular guy and won't make trouble. I'll take a chance and extend your visa for four weeks."

So he stamped my passport accordingly. I knew I now had time to look up old friends in Washington who might help me to get a proper entry visa, so Willi and I went ashore in high spirits.

I spent several days in Washington and often paused in front of the familiar red-brick building of my old Embassy, watching the people coming and going. I recognised several of my old colleagues climbing into their cars with a self-assurance that seemed to say that all was right with their world. And as I did so, I wondered whether it was not me who was the fool to struggle against the forces now in power. But I knew in my heart that I would never degrade myself to become a servant of the Nazis again.

So far as my visa was concerned I achieved nothing, and so had no alternative but to continue my journey to Jamaica. I booked the passages for Willi and myself in New York and, according to my instructions from London, informed the British Embassy in Washington of the time of our arrival at Kingston, so that this information could be forwarded to the Governor.

In complete contrast to the grey-green hull of the *Britannic*, the United Fruit Company's *Veragua* lay alongside the quay at Hoboken, gleaming white and freshly painted, ready for her cruise to the sunny Carribean. We sailed at night in a blaze of lights, loaded with passengers, not running away from the Nazi terror but setting out on a pleasure trip and intent upon enjoying themselves. By day we swam in the pool on deck and by night we danced under the stars to the throbbing lilt of a Cuban band.

The night before our arrival we danced until midnight, and then went to bed so as to be fresh for the morning. With the first light of dawn we were woken by men's voices shouting: "The two Germans are to disembark immediately in the Customs cutter!"

We were still only half awake when our steward came with the news that we were to get dressed at once. He explained that the ship had stopped at the entrance to Port Royal and that a British military patrol had come aboard to fetch us.

"Can't we have some breakfast?" I asked.

"No," the steward told me, "the soldiers say you'll have it ashore."

So willy-nilly we dressed and climbed down a rope ladder over the ship's side into a waiting motor launch. As we moved away, I saw the curly dishevelled heads of the two young American girls with whom we had danced the night before watching us with sleepy curiosity. Probably for months afterwards they told their friends about the two dangerous Nazi agents who were so dramatically removed from the ship!

On shore we were met by a party of Canadian soldiers with fixed bayonets.

"Our Guard of Honour!" I said to Willi.

In charge of them was a bearded major, who asked me politely to get into his truck. Next to him at the wheel and behind us sat soldiers armed with revolvers. The party with the rifles followed behind in another vehicle. We set off and wound our way into the mountains, and as we climbed higher and higher I looked down and recognised the big white hotel on the beach where I had stayed ten years before.

After two and a half hours we arrived at Newcastle, the little garrison town perched on a mountain ridge, 5,000 feet above the sea. The major told us that his regiment was the Winnipeg Grenadiers and that, by order of the Governor, he and his men were to stand guard over us. After breakfast he showed us our quarters which consisted of two rooms and a bathroom looking on to a verandah which commanded a wonderful view of Kingston thousands of feet below. At the back, covered by flowering creepers, was a smaller hut in which was a large kitchen, larder and pantry.

Willi and I spent our first day in the officers' mess talking, playing cards and listening to the radio. At ten o'clock that night, full of good Jamaican rum and thoroughly cheerful, we went to bed.

I was still asleep the next morning when Willi burst into my room and, in his broad Rhenish accent, brought me bad news.

"They're building a barbed wire enclosure out there," he said, pointing through the window.

I looked out and, sure enough, saw a dozen sweating, chattering negroes driving fencing posts into the ground around the hut, along which soldiers were unloading rolls of barbed wire.

When the major came to fetch us for breakfast, I asked what all this was about.

"It's only for your protection," he explained rather apologetically. "You mustn't feel you're prisoners. As a matter of fact, you can go where you like so long as you're accompanied by a soldier. Besides, the Governor is inviting you to dinner tomorrow in Kingston and then you can discuss the whole thing with him."

That same morning the order was brought to me that I was to present myself wearing a dinner jacket at Government House. I immediately pointed out that I had been obliged to leave my dinner jacket behind at The Hague for the Gestapo. Later, the reply came that the Governor regretted that since I had no dinner jacket, he would invite me to luncheon two days later.

With my armed guard I arrived on the appointed day at the Governor's residence outside Kingston, which was surrounded by a lovely park. Two dignified black servants in gold-laced uniforms conducted me up the wide staircase under the astonished eyes of my Canadian guards.

Sir Arthur and Lady Richards received me with the greatest kindness and had invited a number of the local dignitaries to meet me, including the Military Commander of the Islands and the Chief of Police of Jamaica. At luncheon I was given the place of honour on the right of my hostess. In peacetime I had attended many such luncheon parties, but now I had to pinch myself to remind myself that I was in fact the chief guest and yet at the same time a helpless prisoner of these people who treated me with such courtesy. Everyone invited me to luncheon and dinner parties to relieve the monotony of my life up at Newcastle. Yet somehow I was never given the opportunity of discussing my problems with the Governor, who was otherwise prepared to make my life as comfortable as possible by providing me with a radio, typewriter and upholstered armchairs. His wife sent me boxes of chocolates and other delicacies, and at least once a month I was invited to luncheon at Government House. I went, too, to other charming houses, but was never allowed to move without my armed guard.

In time, I became very friendly with the Canadians, who were, I think, just as bored with Jamaica as I was. Since Willi was not only an excellent cook, but also a first-rate bartender, he soon became indispensable to life in the camp. The soldiers tumbled over themselves to do guard duties at our quarters in order to enjoy his cooking, and almost every day I presided over a party of fifteen or so soldiers at dinner in our kitchen. In addition to all this, Willi was a shrewd card player, and since the Canadians were a little slow in the uptake, he did pretty well. With his winnings, we paid for most of what we had in the camp, buying fresh vegetables and fruit. But the greater part of them went on the wonderful Jamaica rum which did so much to relieve the dreariness of our existence. Many a night we sat slightly tight on our verandah, fanned by the soft tropical breeze, and looking down on the sea, the thousand lights of Kingston and at the indigo sky brilliant with stars. It seemed strangely unreal at such moments to talk of Germany, the Nazis and the awful war raging across the world.

From a connection in Switzerland, Willi still got news of his family in Cologne, and I received news from Laaske through Lotte Lehmann, then living in California, as well as from a former Swiss governess.

CHAPTER TWENTY-SIX

EVER SINCE WE had arrived in Jamaica we had been paradoxically planning how to escape from our fenced-in paradise.
In the circumstances we decided that the U.S.A. was the only
country in a position to offer us asylum. Moreover, in any
other country we would sooner or later have been stranded
without a penny.

When the Governor provided me with a typewriter, I started
writing my memoirs in the hope of earning some dollars from
articles published in American magazines. As I had no connections with publishers in the United States, I sent my manuscripts
to a former friend in the State Department, asking him to
forward them to some publisher or other. One of my Canadian
guards took the precious parcel of manuscripts to the American
Consul in Kingston, who forwarded it by courier to Washington,
thus avoiding censorship.

I waited for weeks and then months without a reply, and had
almost given up hope when the miracle happened. At a late
hour, when Willi and I had nearly finished our daily bottle of
rum, the Camp Commander appeared on the verandah with the
news that he had had a telephone call from Kingston to say
that an important American would be coming up to see me.
The following day, Willi mixed some of his best cocktails to
put our visitor in a good mood, and in the afternoon a gleaming
Government car stopped in front of our quarters and a man and
woman got out. The former introduced himself as Isaac Don
Levine, from New York, and the lady as his wife. He said that
they were on holiday in Florida and had flown to Jamaica in

their own little plane from Miami. She was an American, but his English quickly betrayed his Polish origin. Both of them were highly indignant at their reception by the British Customs at Kingston Airport. Although the Governor had been notified of their arrival by no less a person than Lord Halifax, the British Ambassador in Washington, they had been practically stripped and searched. Mr. Levine assured me that he was one of the best known and most successful journalists in New York, and, judging by his immaculate white suit and panama hat, I was prepared to believe him. He had recently been responsible for the publication of a sensational book called "Out of the Night", written by a German Communist whose real name was Krebs. In order to hoodwink the Gestapo he had used the pen name of Jan Valtin. According to Levine, Valtin had already made more than one hundred thousand dollars from his book.

"I have read your manuscripts," Levine told me. "They can have an even bigger success than Valtin's, provided, of course, you present them in the American manner."

"Splendid!" I said. "But I don't imagine you're prepared to sit here with me in this golden cage while we collaborate!"

"Quite out of the question. I'm a busy man and you will have to come to New York."

"Mr. Levine, I've been trying for more than a year to do precisely that. But they won't give me a visa," I told him.

He laughed. "Don't worry. I've taken care of that already. If you want to, you can have a visa in a couple of weeks, and then you can start work next month either in my apartment in New York or out at my country place in Connecticut."

Naturally, I agreed. When the Levine's car disappeared round the last bend in the road, Willi and I did a wild dance of joy.

Within a fortnight the promised visas arrived and the British were perfectly willing to let us go. The only difficulty came, most unexpectedly, from the Canadians, who presented us with a bill for £ 58.15.6d. for our rations. I had just sufficient money for the boat tickets with a little left over for our immediate needs in New York. So, if I paid this bill, we would arrive penniless in the States. In the end, the problem was solved by the Governor who, with his habitual kindness, agreed to pay our debt.

The day we left Jamaica, the Colonial Secretary invited us to a farewell dinner party at the Myrtle Bank Hotel, after which we went aboard the *Veregua* once again to find that we had been allotted our old cabin.

After five days at sea we saw the skyline of Manhattan and, passing the Statue of Liberty, sailed once more up the Hudson River. Levine was on the dock to meet us, whisked us through the customs without any trouble and on to his apartment on Fifth Avenue. We agreed that I should drive out with him to Connecticut that same evening, while Willi should stay in New York at some inexpensive hotel.

I spent two days in the country negotiating with Levine about the proposed book. He and I finally failed to see eye to eye as to how it was to be written, and much as I would have liked to have earned hundreds of thousands of dollars, I had to tell him in the end that I could not produce the sort of thing he wanted. Although I was disappointed, I was at least grateful that he had enabled me to escape from behind that barbed wire fence at Newcastle.

In New York I managed to make a little money doing translations and other odd jobs, and I actually sold one article— but only one—for four hundred dollars. In the meantime Willi had found a job in the Pennsylvania Hotel, where he worked at night. So, although we were living together, we saw little of each other. But at least it was something that we were making a living and were independent, even if we only had little to live on.

During those first months in New York, time was heavy on my hands, and if there was nothing better to do I used to stroll up and down Fifth Avenue. Since New York was full of refugees in the same circumstances as myself, I was always running into someone from Europe whom I knew.

One afternoon I was stopped on the pavement by a man who addressed me in a strong Austrian accent. I had not the vaguest idea who he was until he mentioned the names of Gerhard Hauptmann and Hiddensee, and then I remembered that he was an actor from Vienna whom I had met several times in the old days. We stood for a long time by a corner of the Rockefeller Centre, sheltering from the bitter wind and chatting of old times.

Suddenly he looked across the street and said nervously: "Let's move on. I think we're being watched."

I saw across the road a man whom I recognised at once as a German. In 1930, when I was at the Embassy in Washington, he had been a chemistry student. I will call him Schaeffer. While I was watching him, he crossed the street and joined us, greeting me warmly. But as I did not want to desert my actor friend, I asked him for his telephone number and promised to ring him up.

A few days later I kept my promise and Schaeffer invited me to supper. He was living in a charming apartment belonging to an American lady, overlooking Central Park, and the three of us dined in the open air in a roof-garden from which there was a magnificent view of the city. Schaeffer told me that he had a very good job with the great Dupont de Nemours chemical combine. But what astonished me more than anything that evening was how much he knew about myself.

"How is it that you know so much about me?" I questioned.

"I'll be honest with you," he laughed. "Last week I was at our Embassy in Washington and I met Herr von Gienandt. He told me all about you, and, believe it or not, he asked to be remembered to you."

"But, Schaeffer," I said, "Herr von Gienandt has never seen me in his life!"

"Perhaps he's heard about you from other people," he

answered. "Anyway, he said at once that you were a good chap, although he thought you'd behaved rather stupidly. He even said that we couldn't have you running around New York without a job, and that we must find you something. In the meantime, he suggested that you might be glad of a thousand dollars."

According to Schaeffer, Gienandt had been racking his brains to find me a suitable job and thought that he might be able to get me into a gold-mining company in Ecuador. Schaeffer could not praise his efforts to help me highly enough, and was deeply disappointed that I did not immediately jump at the offer.

As I walked home that night, I realised that the Gestapo still looked upon me as a fool, for I knew perfectly well that Gienandt was one of Himmler's spies in the Embassy in Washington and had large secret funds at his disposal.

After that evening, I carefully avoided Schaeffer. But some weeks later I ran into him in the street and he took me to task for not telephoning him. I told him that I had been ill and he insisted that I should walk home with him. So for the second time I found myself sitting in the lovely roof-garden overlooking the park and being lavishly entertained by the charming American lady. After we had had several drinks, Schaeffer came out with the news that Gienandt was joining him for a yachting trip on Long Island Sound and had suggested that I should go with them. The idea was that we should meet on board and spend the day talking things over. Quite possibly Schaeffer and Gienandt might have dumped me overboard, so I said that I could not risk being seen in the company of a member of the Nazi Embassy.

In the end Schaeffer gave up trying to persuade me. As we parted he remarked: "I'm afraid one day you'll regret your stubbornness."

I had another and far more amusing adventure while in New York as a result of meeting my actor friend from Vienna. He

213

asked me quite unexpectedly: "Would you like to meet Herr Hitler to-night?"

Naturally, I thought he was pulling my leg. But he assured me perfectly seriously that he had a date with Hitler in a saloon on Broadway. His Hitler was, however, not Adolf but the Führer's nephew, Patrick, who had long ago arrived in America from England with his mother, Bridget. The latter's husband was Alois Hitler, the eldest brother of Adolf. Alois had emigrated from Austria to England when he was quite a young man and had married an Irish farm girl, Bridget Dowling. Until brother Adolf came into power, Alois had lived with his family in Manchester making a modest living as a waiter, but shortly after, he had deserted his wife and child and returned to Berlin to cash in on his brother's success. But Adolf was no Napoleon ready to give away kingdoms to his brothers. He did, however, present Alois with a bar on the Wittenberg Platz, which he had specially redecorated by his favourite architect, Speer.

For the fun of having our coats taken off by the Führer's brother, I had once dined there with Gebhard. Alois was a polite and thoughtful host, and he wore a little moustache which accentuated the likeness to his brother. After she had been deserted by her husband, Bridget came to see me several times at Carlton House Terrace, always with the same sad story that her pension of £ 30 a month, which she was supposed to receive from Alois or Adolf, had not arrived, so that she was forced to borrow money from us.

The first time she had appeared in my office was in 1935, and I was almost scared when her name was announced. But the moment I saw her I knew she was a sensible woman. She did not make a scene of any kind, but merely spoke quite frankly about her family. By then, not only her husband, but her son as well had run away from her. Apparently, a "Party comrade" called Bene had turned the latter's head, inveigling the seventeen-year-old lad to London, where he had bought him a smart outfit of clothes and sent him to see his uncle at

Berchtesgarten. The story goes that Uncle Adolf had no idea what to do with his nephew from England who could not speak a word of German, so he put him to work as garden boy and did not bother about him further. After a year, Patrick managed to escape and get to Berlin, where Herr Winter, the motorcar king, took him on as a salesman in his showrooms.

At that time I had asked Frau Hitler why she did not go to Germany where she would probably have been better off than she was in England.

"The good Lord preserve us!" she said in her rich Irish brogue. "It's glad I am that there's the width of the ocean between Adolf and me! Even the thirty pounds I accept only because I can't live on air. You must know yourself that as a sister-in-law of Adolf Hitler I can't get a job anywhere. I might as well be related to the devil himself!"

She went on to tell me that in spite of everything she was still better off than her sister-in-law, Paula Raubal, who for years kept house for Hitler, but finally left him because he had driven her seventeen-year-old daughter to suicide. After three years, Patrick had managed to get away from Germany and he and his mother had emigrated to America. For some time the son made a living travelling about the States delivering lectures in which he gave spicily intimate details about his uncle's private life.

Naturally, I was amused at the idea of having a look at the Führer's nephew, and so with my actor friend went along to the bar. The latter, like most of its kind in New York, was practically without chairs so that one had to stand about drinking. The likeness between Patrick and his uncle was astonishing. The former was then about twenty-three and, although a little taller and heavier, he was almost the Führer's double. He cultivated the same lock of hair falling over his forehead and the little moustache. As he spoke very little German, we talked in English, and he told me that now both he and his mother had taken the name of Dowling. I asked him to remember me to Bridget, and as we left the actor raised his glass and gave the toast "Death to Hitler!" in which Patrick joined. So the three of us, a Prussian nobleman, a Jewish actor from Vienna and Herr Hitler, stood together drinking a toast in a New York saloon to the death and downfall of the Führer!

The feeling towards Germans and Germany in America gradually began to deteriorate after the fall of France and Hitler's attack on Russia. Then, in the autumn of 1941, when the Japanese made their sudden attack on Pearl Harbour, the whole situation changed completely. Germans living in the United States became overnight enemy aliens. But of the vast number of us living in America, only about two thousand, including Schaeffer and the declared Nazis, were interned. The rest of us had to register with the police and have our finger-prints taken; otherwise, no-one interfered with us.

Soon after America declared war, a short-wave transmitter was set up for beaming news to Europe. The man in charge of this organisation was Nelson Rockefeller. The German broadcasts were made by fellow countrymen of mine who had emigrated, and I was asked to join them and to put over my own scripts. I agreed to do this on condition that I should decide for myself what I would say. I broadcast twice a week for a quarter of an hour under the title: "A German Patriot Speaks". Since the American attitude towards Germany was even more uncompromising than the British, I could offer the German people little hope from an American victory. Nevertheless, twice a week I shouted to them over the air to end the war before their country was totally destroyed, and urged them to get rid of Hitler.

I do not think that many people in Germany heard my broadcasts, and after a few weeks I was taken off the air. One day I was told that I must keep my broadcasts in line with the "Voice of America". Since this was against my conscience, I declined to do so, a fact that made me distinctly unpopular with a certain section of the American people. Some German refugees even called me a Nazi. The majority of them, including my old friend Doctor G, were applying for American nationality. Many of them hoped to join the American forces and so return to Germany as conquerors.

Although I had many friends in America, the only person who really understood my point of view about the future of Germany was Willi. Once America was at war, there was little I could do to help except by becoming a blood donor. But through a friend of mine I was able to embark on lecture tours, and travelled about the country talking about Hitler, Goebbels and Ribbentrop. Since I had a good market value, the agency which looked after me had no difficulty in selling me. I received between twenty-five and seventy-five dollars an appearance, and after each lecture a cheque was pressed discreetly into my hand. After a tour of two or three weeks I had enough money on which to live comfortably in New York again for a while. When I became short of funds I arranged another tour. But although I met many charming and interesting people on these lecture tours, I was by no means happy. The news from Europe became daily more depressing. In North Africa Rommel had advanced almost to the gates of Cairo. In the Pacific, the Japanese were inflicting heavy losses on the Americans.

Then, suddenly, the tide of the German advance into Russia was stemmed at Stalingrad, and one day I heard on the wireless from Moscow that a National Committee of Free Germany was to be formed. The very next morning I got going. I wrote, in German, a greetings message to the German Committee in Moscow and sent it with a letter to the Soviet Consul in New York, asking that it might be forwarded to Moscow. Shortly afterwards, I found myself in the Soviet Consul's study. From the very outset of our conversation I felt that he not only understood my point of view, but was in sympathy with it. He told me simply: "We shall utterly defeat the Nazis, and after we have done that, we shall help to build up a new Germany. But that task must really be undertaken by the

German people themselves, so we shall be glad to help every sincere anti-Nazi German.

We became so engrossed in the subject that we walked to Central Park and continued our conversation there for another two hours. My hope of being able to go to Moscow did not materialise, but the outcome of that talk was that I made up my mind to return to England.

In the spring of 1943 I wrote to Vansittart asking him to do his best to obtain permission for Willi and myself to return to London. In the following November I received an answer from him; an entry visa had been granted to me, but Willi's return would have to be deferred until later. On the afternoon of Christmas Eve, I received a telegram telling me to be at a certain pier in Hoboken at eleven o'clock on Christmas Day. The night before I left I was invited to a party given by Elizabeth Schumann, who always celebrated Christmas in the traditional German style with such delicacies as carp and roast goose. After dinner, to please me, she sang some of my favourite songs, although she had a cold and was hoarse.

The next morning an icy wind swept the piers. Huddled in overcoats and scarves, some thirty passengers sat, teeth chattering, in the ship's dining saloon, and that day I had my first taste of the real austerity food that the English had been eating for so long.

The ship was a freighter which carried a cargo of frozen meat and did not normally take passengers. So we were all crowded into the few available cabins. In my cabin were four sailors from torpedoed merchant ships on their way home to England, and most of the time they talked about their terrible experiences. One might have expected them to treat me at least coldly, but, in fact, they were extremely cordial.

We sailed in a convoy with about twenty other ships, all of them oil tankers, and my cabin mates told me that if we were attacked by U-boats we would have little chance of survival as the ocean would become a vast sea of flame from the burning fuel carried by those tankers. We zig-zagged our way across the Atlantic, and sometimes for hours on end we lay stopped so that the enemy could not pick up the sound of our propellors on their detecting gear. We passengers were detailed to look-out watches. So it was that on New Year's Day, 1944, I found myself on look-out duty at sunrise. We were somewhere off the Azores, and the sky was clear and the sea calm. I shall never forget how strange I felt as I stood on the wing of the bridge of a British ship, searching the sea through my binoculars, on watch for a periscope through which some German naval officer might be looking at me; an enemy who might well have been my own cousin or school friend. I said a silent prayer that this would be the last New Year's morning that the sun would rise on such a thoroughly unhappy world.

On January 6th, we landed safely at Liverpool, where I was met once again by Tom Allen. He got me through the customs without trouble. But one of the immigration officers gave me a dirty look, murmuring under his breath: "I thought we were at war with the bloody Germans!"

On arrival in London, I was horrified at the devastation that had taken place. Everywhere I looked I saw ruins, and the people seemed utterly weary. After so long in Jamaica and New York I had almost forgotten the meaning of the words "total war". But in spite of everything, I was happy to be back again.

CHAPTER TWENTY-SEVEN

I ARRIVED BACK in England with only a few dollars in my pocket, but fortunately I still had some money in my London banking account which would last me for a while. Since I wanted to keep it for a rainy day, I set out to look for a job.

Tom Allen suggested that I should go to Bletchley Junction, where propaganda broadcasts were being sent out to Germany. I was told that the man in charge of these was none other than the former Berlin correspondent of *The Daily Express*, my old friend, Sefton Delmer. Delmer really knew Germany and spoke German like a native, so I expected better things of him than of the men who had run the "Voice of America" in New York.

Tom had another reason for sending me to Bletchley Junction. He told me that some weeks ago a young SS officer from the staff of Group-Leader Fegelein, Hitler's brother-in-law, had escaped from Sweden to England. He belonged to a secret German resistance movement and was supposed to have collaborated with the Polish Underground, and so had been condemned to death. A few hours before he was due to be shot, friends saved him, and he escaped *via* Scandinavia after some incredible adventures. He was now with Delmer, living under an assumed name. Since he could not speak a word of English and could not be housed with the other refugees, who were mostly Jewish, it had been decided to let him live with someone who knew all about the SS. In Tom's opinion I was the best man for the job.

I confess that I was somewhat sceptical about this man's

story, but since it struck me as interesting, I accepted Tom's invitation. It was arranged that I, too, should assume a false name, so I called myself Gebhard Mansfeld, choosing my brothers' names. For the work I had to do I was given free board and lodging and paid £ 30 a month.

After a few days rest, I was driven down to Woburn, which was the country seat of the Duke of Bedford. We drove through the gates past a lodge into a vast park of splendid trees, beneath which herds of deer were grazing. But just before we came to the lake in front of Woburn Abbey itself, we turned right and stopped in front of a large, rather ugly, nineteenth-century house in which my new companion was living. Through the trees one could see the settlement of huts, and the wireless mast rising high into the sky, which formed Sefton Delmer's mysterious domain.

It was not long before I realised that I was well and truly caught up in the web of the British Secret Service. With few exceptions, everyone at Bletchley Junction worked under fictitious names. The key positions were held by Englishmen, but the rest of the staff of about fifty was composed mostly of Germans and Austrians. Their efforts to disguise themselves were quite absurd, for sooner or later one found out who all of them were. Collectively, Delmer's associates did not comprise the élite of the anti-Fascists, and I am afraid that there were moments when I was seized with the mad desire to shout "Heil Hitler!" at the top of my voice.

Not for nothing Delmer had studied the tricks of Hitler and Goebbels, for his propaganda technique exactly followed the Nazi pattern. All day long the news came rolling in to us from the British Intelligence Service on the Continent; and from this vast supply we picked out those items which suited our particular programmes, edited them and relayed them to Germany. Delmer's policy was, if possible, to break down the last shreds of Nazi morale. We cunningly broadcast announcements of deaths at the front and news items concerning the sufferings of the German people that were likely to spread alarm and despondency.

In one respect Delmer was far superior to his Nazi teachers. His broadcasts, beamed at Germany under such titles as "Gustav Siegfried I", "Soldiers-Sender-Calais" and "Shortwavesender Atlantic", were really amusing, and many of the jokes whispered around the Third Reich were invented by him. For days he chuckled to himself over his brainwave in describing the new architectural style which would rise from the ruins of Germany as "barack"—not baroque. But for the most part his jokes were on the somewhat risky level of students' limericks, and of the "Wirtin an der Lahn" or "Bonifatius Kiesewetter". Many of these were invented by a bearded Austrian chaplain who each Sunday read a solemn sermon over the "Soldiers-Sender-Calais" and spent the rest of the week flirting outrageously with the pretty typists.

My house-mate was, apart from Rudolf Hess, the most mysterious Nazi in England. He, too, was an odd-looking creature with red cheeks, piercing blue eyes and a large bald pate. He looked for all the world like a Prussian N.C.O. and insisted on accentuating the fact by having his head shaved. So far as I can recall, I never saw him open a book.

I was unable to discover how important his resistance group was or what it had achieved. So far as I could make out, he had, under orders from the British Secret Service, sold arms from the arsenals of the SS to the reactionary partisan units of Colonel Borr Komorowski in Poland. The latter were financed by the British, and as a reward for his services he had been given asylum in England. I also had a suspicion that he was in some mysterious way connected with a group of German conspirators with Western sympathies. When the *putsch* of July 20th, 1944 started, he was beside himself with excitement. In those days he used to talk every day on Delmer's radio service. He began all his speeches with the words: "Comrades! All of you listen to me," and finished with a stream of incom-

222

prehensible code words such as "cornflower calls seabird, delphinium wants rhododendron........."

Day after day while I was at Bletchley Junction the swarms of bombers that flew overhead on their way to Germany increased. Occasionally a German V.1 rumbled noisily through the night, red flame streaming from its tail. Now that Hitler occupied the whole of France, I no longer received any mail from Switzerland and was without news of my family. One could only imagine that there could scarcely be a building left standing in Germany, and yet those madmen—Hitler and the rest—kept on fighting.

Tom Allen, the only man who could have helped me to escape from Bletchley Junction, had been transferred to General Eisenhower's Staff somewhere in France. I did not even dare to talk to Vansittart about my activities for fear of being accused of disclosing secrets. So I just had to grin and bear it, and I can remember no time in my life when I was more utterly miserable. But at last the end came. A few weeks before Germany capitulated, the organisation was finally disbanded.

By V-Day I was already back in London. As I had nothing to do, I suggested to the authorities that I should give lectures at the German prisoner-of-war camps around the country. I visited three to five camps a month, but was only once sent to an officers' camp where I met a few intelligent men. But on the whole the atmosphere was distinctly cold, and I soon realised that they had no use for a man who had, in their opinion, broken his oath of allegiance to his country and deserted to the enemy. Even in the soldier's camps I was received with mixed feelings, and in two or three I was shouted down, so that I could not even begin to speak. In those camps where the Commandant told me that the men were particularly well behaved I was always suspicious. But I went on with my lectures in the hope that I should sooner or later meet men from my own part of Germany who might be able to give me news of my family. I was unlucky except in the case of one lad from Pritzwalk who told me that he had seen a warrant for my arrest and my photograph stuck up in the local court. It was later I was to hear the tragic news that my brother Gebhard had been taken away by the Gestapo.

At the end of August a letter arrived for me from Madame Leroy-Beaulieu, the mother of my old Oxford friend, Michel. In it she enclosed a tattered note which she had received from Laaske, brought to her by a French prisoner-of-war. I immediately recognised my sister Armgard's handwriting. She wrote: "Walter missing in Italy. Otherwise we are all alive. Please help us. Greetings with deepest misery."

I went at once to Tom Allen, now a Major at the War Office, and begged him to try to find out whether Walter's name appeared in any of the official lists of prisoners. But there was nothing I could do for my family. Everyone, from Vansittart downwards, told me that it was impossible to contact anyone in the Russian Zone of Germany, in which Putlitz was now situated.

I continued to pester Tom to let me go to Berlin or at least to the Western Zone of Germany so that I could get in touch with my relations. But there was nothing doing. Yet to my complete astonishment my former house-mate suddenly left for Germany in October, having been given an appointment of some kind in the British Zone. To add insult to injury, he proudly showed me the two large cabin trunks he had bought, crammed with clothes made in London.

CHAPTER TWENTY-EIGHT

IN JANUARY, 1946, I was told that the authorities were at last prepared to let me go home. But Tom Allen did his best to dissuade me. Everything in Germany, he said, was in a ghastly state, and he added that I would regret my decision. If I still insisted on going, there could be no question of returning to Berlin. I would be allowed to stay in one of the hotels requisitioned by the Intelligence in the British Zone where I could remain until I found a suitable job. As I stuck to my decision, Tom made the necessary arrangements for me.

On an icy February evening, I waited with my luggage on what once had been the platform of Calais Station but was now a shambles. But I was blissfully happy, for I was at least standing on Continental soil. All around me swarmed generals and other high-ranking and bemedalled officers, waiting for the train. As I was the only civilian, and a German into the bargain, I felt at once small and yet terribly conspicuous, so I sat down on one of my trunks beside my French porter. Mellowed by my English cigarettes, he became quite friendly and boasted about the work he had done for the allies during the occupation. He told me that he had often hidden British agents in his house. "Au fond, ils sont bien bêtes, les Boches," he laughed.

At last the train arrived and I saw that it consisted only of sleeping-cars with a dining car in the middle and luggage vans on the end. I helped the porter put my luggage in the van and then found my sleeper. To my surprise another civilian was already installed in the other berth. He was an inconspicuous little man whom I had overlooked amongst the crowd of brass hats and red tabs on the platform.

The military control officials looked over our papers before the train left.

"Well, Mr. Pierpont," one of them asked my companion, "Where are you going this time?"

"Do you know a place called Belsen?" Mr. Pierpont asked with a suspicion of a smile.

"I see," nodded the official, but he stopped talking when he saw from my papers that I was a non-British subject. As he left the compartment, he turned and said: "Good luck!"

I discovered that my travelling companion was none other than Pierpont, the hangman, and that recently he had travelled back and forth frequently to Germany to carry out his duties. He had already hanged the Commandant and several of the other murderers at the ill-famed concentration camp at Bergen-Belsen. After we had exchanged a few remarks about the weather, we went to bed, the hangman to His Britannic Majesty in the upper berth and myself in the lower.

By dawn we were in Germany and I made my way along the train to the dining-car and sat down at one of the small tables for two. A Polish officer sat opposite me. We settled down to a breakfast such as I had not eaten for years. The waiter brought steaming hot coffee, large pats of butter and a bowl filled to the brim with sugar. I ordered three eggs and bacon. We passed slowly through the ruins of Düsseldorf Station; on the tracks, shoulder to shoulder, stood crowds of people waiting for some train or other. I shuddered as I saw their emaciated faces. They looked like ghosts from the underworld, beating their bare hands against their sides and stamping their feet. Their clothes were in tatters, and some I saw with horror were shoeless, with rags wrapped around their feet.

The Pole stared at them too. "Horrible," he said, " but one can't really pity them. I'm travelling home now, but when I get there I shall find nothing. They burnt my house and killed my whole family."

After breakfast I stood in the corridor staring out of the

226

window. The train wound its way through the Ruhr, but all that I saw in the grey haze were twisted ruins of steel and concrete. An iron bedstead, its mattress disembowelled, hung from the shattered façade of a house. The countryside for miles around seemed littered with burnt-out engines and goods trucks. Wherever I looked I saw ruins and more ruins. The desolate picture of such senseless destruction made me want to weep.

The French conductor came down the corridor and saw me. "On les a bien servis, les Boches," he grinned. "Ils l'ont bien mérité."

Our terminus was Bad Oeynhausen, then the headquarters of the British Military Government. The polite little executioner helped me on with my overcoat. After seven years I climbed out of the train to stand once more on German soil.

A car was waiting to take me to the hotel. I looked for my luggage but it was nowhere to be seen. In fact, the entire luggage van had disappeared. The British R.T.O. shrugged his shoulders regretfully. "Unfortunately this sort of thing often happens," he said. "Usually they turn up, but sometimes they don't."

I filled in a form. But the van with my luggage was never seen again, so everything I had brought from America for my family and all my personal belongings were lost. I arrived at the hotel with only the clothes I stood up in and my little suitcase containing a pair of shoes, pyjamas, a clean shirt and my shaving kit.

The name of the place was Rehlkirchen and the estate belonged to Hans-Georg von Studnitz, whom I had known in the old days when I was a young attaché in Berlin. Studnitz, who was younger than I, had become a journalist and had had a brilliant career under the Nazis. By the end of the war he was Second Chief of Press under Ribbentrop in the Foreign Office. Now he was in a concentration camp. His wife lived in the village in the cottage of one of her husband's tenant farmers,

227

and was not allowed into her own house, now taken over by the British.

Although I felt somewhat embarrassed living as a guest in her comfortable house, I visited Frau von Studnitz, and she was pleased to see me and to hear that her possessions were safe.

As I was not allowed to go to Berlin, I started looking for work in the British Zone, and after a day or two had the good luck to find a distant cousin living in the neighbourhood. She had heard quite by chance that my brother, Walter, had returned from Italy and was now in Holstein. I not only knew that district reasonably well but also spoke its dialect, so I determined to go there. I found out from the British that a certain Doctor Theodor Steltzer had been appointed Minister President of Holstein, and I asked them to give me an introduction to him. Without even having met me, he appointed me First Grade Counsellor to his Chancellery in Kiel. So I set out with my suitcase, breaking the journey to see my brother, who was living on an estate of Prince Philip of Hess near Lütjenburg, some fifteen miles south of Kiel.

Walter was completely dumbfounded when he saw me on the doorstep.

"Wolfgang! We thought you were dead!" he cried.

"And I thought you had been killed in Italy!" I answered him.

For more than six months, Walter told me, he had been hidden by an Italian partisan family and had actually arrived back in Germany without being taken prisoner. He had found his wife and family in Oldenburg where they had fled in April, 1945. By a lucky break, he had managed to get a job as administrator to the Holstein estates of Prince Philip of Hess, a son-in-law of King Victor Emmanuel of Italy and a nephew of the Kaiser, who, as he had been a close friend of Goering and a Gauleiter, was now in prison.

Walter also gave me news of my family. Immediately after my escape, the Gestapo had interrogated them constantly, and repeatedly searched the house. But nobody was arrested. In my absence I was sentenced to death as an enemy of the State, and the two farms which I had owned at Laaske had been confiscated by the Government. However, Gebhard had been allowed to lease them, so nothing had changed much. In the summer of 1944 my mother and Gebhard had been denounced for some reason or other and sent to the Gestapo prison in Potsdam. But my sister Armgard, after appealing in high places, managed to have them released before Christmas. When the Red Army marched into Putlitz in the spring of 1945, Walter's family fled, but the others remained. Gebhard, who was vouched for by Herr Levi and many other victims of Nazi persecution whom he had helped, was accepted by the Communist Party, and after the expropriation of the estates was even allowed to stay on in his own house in Putlitz-Burghof. My sister, who had never owned any property, was given a settlement of thirty acres at Laaske, where she and my mother lived in rooms formerly occupied by our bookkeeper. During the summer of 1945 Armgard made several unsuccessful visits to the British Military Government in Berlin asking them to forward letters to me through Vansittart.

Although I realised that things could not be easy for my family, it was a joy to know that they were still alive and to be in touch with them again. I saw Walter every week and was able to bring him English cigarettes.

The Chancellery of the Minister President of Schleswig-Holstein was in the Town Hall at Kiel. Like every other building in the city it was in ruins, but we managed to fix up offices in one corner of it. Doctor Steltzer received me affably. My work consisted mostly in translating the orders which arrived from the British Military Governor, but I confess that most of the day I sat twiddling my thumbs. I lived in a relatively comfortable room in a schoolteacher's house, where at least one window still had glass in it and the rain did not come through the roof. My hostess did her best to look after me, but since the gas was only turned on for a couple of hours a day at dinner time, I lived chiefly on boiled potatoes which I ate cold for my supper. From time to time she managed to get me candles so that I did not have to sit in darkness. But since neither she nor her husband had good connections with the Black Market, we had to live on the meagre rations allocated to us. We got five slices of bread besides a little meat, sugar and margarine. But I think I would have starved had not Walter provided me with extra potatoes.

After the loss of my luggage I had ordered shirts and suits through various friends in England and America. But as it took an eternity for these parcels to arrive, I enquired about certain relief organisations which supplied clothes to the victims of Nazism. I found a clerk in the basement of the Town Hall who dealt with such matters and told him my story.

"If you were at the London Embassy before the war you probably knew Herr Mittelhaus," he remarked.

"Yes," I told him—but did not add that Mittelhaus had been second Gestapo Chief under Ribbentrop.

Two days later there was a knock on my door and there was Mittelhaus.

"What a surprise!" he laughed, throwing his arms around me. "When I heard this morning that Herr von Putlitz was here, I felt that I must see him!" He settled himself on the edge of the table in my little room. He looked remarkably well and was wearing a smart grey suit. From his hip pocket he produced a handsome silver case and offered me a cigarette. It was a Gold Flake, which on the Black Market were worth twenty marks apiece. He saw that I was staring at his case.

"Yes," he said, passing it to me. "This is a souvenir from London—a farewell present from one of my friends at Scotland Yard. He gave it to me when I left in 1938." Then he came to the point. "Tell me, Putlitz, what are you doing in Kiel? Naturally, I have given you the very best references at the Town Hall for it's obvious that you never became a Nazi."

"How do you know that?" I asked. "When you and your pal Schultze were around I always gave the correct salute and said 'Heil Hitler'."

He grinned broadly. "Of course we noticed that!"

Then my curiosity got the better of me.

"Mittelhaus, my presence here is far less surprising than yours. After all, the English must know who you are."

"But that's why I'm here," he explained. "Up till the end of the war I was on the staff of Admiral Doenitz and there was nothing I didn't know about Kiel. Why, the very day the British arrived I handed them fifteen Werewolf members on a plate! You have no idea what the British are like; they would be in a hopeless mess without me. By the way," he added casually. "if you want to see Schultze again, just go over to Schleswig. He is the Chief of Police there."

Shortly after this meeting with Mittelhaus, I ran across a young English captain whom I knew in the British Military Government.

"I bet you were surprised to meet your old friend here!" he laughed.

"I was indeed," I answered coldly.

"I'll explain everything," he said. "It's like this. We need efficient German police officers, and both Mittelhaus and Schultze are extraordinarily capable. We know all about them and they know that we have enough evidence against them to hang them whenever we like. But they're much too clever to try any funny business, and for that very reason we can rely on them."

At least I admired the young man's honesty!

Before I could be officially appointed to my post I had to be cleared by the De-Nazification Tribunal. The secretary of the committee was a former official at the consulate and an executive of the NSDAP at the German Embassy in Sofia, who had been de-nazified six months previously.

In the offices of the Tribunal I met a certain Herr Kurtzbein, a tall bearded man in his forties. I became quite friendly with him and he often talked to me about a friend of his who had taken part in the 20th July plot in Berlin and who had had a miraculous escape. This friend often brought Kurtzbein food, and as often as he did so I was given some sausage or smoked eel. I was therefore very sorry when my benefactor suddenly disappeared. They told me that his name was not Kurtzbein at all and that he was a well-known SS leader from Potsdam. I found myself wondering whether it was not he and his friend who had arrested my mother and Gebhard.

The winter of 1946—47 was bitterly cold and there was no coal to be had. Now and again Walter managed to get me a few bags of firewood. But even in my featherbed, sleeping in my clothes and my winter overcoat, I could never really get warm.

As soon as my brother Gebhard learned that I was in Kiel, he set out to see me. Since he would have had to wait weeks for an interzone pass and might never have been granted one, he crossed the border "black". He knew the wooded country around Lake Ratzeburg, now a no-man's-land between the Soviet and British control posts, like the back of his hand. Passing through it like a deer stalker, he eventually arrived in Hamburg and sent me a telegram. I met him at the ruined Central Station at Kiel, and although the platform was swarming with people, I recognised him at once. He stooped slightly beneath the weight of the huge rucksack he was carrying, and his first words were: "I'm sure you haven't got enough to eat here." He had brought with him pounds and pounds of butter, sausage and bacon, and even home-made bread from Putlitz which I had not tasted for years.

That night we sat up talking for hours, for a whole world had disappeared since we had last seen each other.

"Everything has turned out worse than we could have dreamed," he said.

I begged him for news of Putlitz.

"Considering everything, things are not too bad. As I know every mill and dairy in the neighbourhood, we have enough to eat. Now, if I wish, I can sleep every morning until nine o'clock. It's the future that worries me," he added sadly.

"What will you do?" I asked him.

"What can I do? So long as I stay in Putlitz, I can manage. But if I come West, I don't know what I could do; I'm not trained for anything, and I have to think of the children. The boy is three now."

"Gebhard," I said almost desperately, "do you think it would help at all if I tried to come over and join you?"

He shook his head. "'That would be sheer suicide for you. All one can do is to sit and wait, and see what happens."

After that first visit, Gebhard came to see me two or three times in the course of the next year, staying either with me or with Walter. Then, at last, in the late autumn, I succeeded in obtaining a travel permit to Berlin from the British authorities. My family had arrived the day before me and were staying with a friend who still happened to have a large flat in the Kaiser-allee.

I found my mother terribly thin and very weak on her legs, but my sister looked much the same. Armgard and I went for long walks together through Berlin. The Kurfürstendamm was now a desert of ruined houses. The Tauentzienstrasse was laid flat, and around the Luetzow Platz scarcely a house was standing. The streets across the Landwehr Canal reminded one of some ghostly town of death. We found the Markgraf of Brandenburg in the Siegesallee, and behind him the statue of old Johannes zu Putlitz still stood in his armour holding the model of Stepenitz Cathedral in his hand. Our ancestor looked shabby, but except that the tip of his nose was missing, he was quite undamaged.

At the Brandenburger Tor, which now marked the border of the Soviet Zone, I asked Armgard if I could dare risk crossing to have a look at the Foreign Office.

233

"It's dangerous," she said, "but if we're quick and turn back by the Potsdamer Platz we might get away with it."

The whole of the Wilhelmstrasse was a heap of ruins, and only the two sphinxes just appearing above the rubble showed the spot where the main entrance had once been. We wandered through what was left of Hitler's Reichs Chancellery and its splendid marble halls, and as we did so I had the strange feeling that I was amongst the ruined walls of Knossos or Mycenae.

In Berlin I met my old friend, Donald Heath, who was there as a representative of the American State Department. In 1931 he had been head of the American Consulate in Haiti when I was there as chargé d'affaires. Having left his wife and children in London, he was a grass-widower.

"Wolfgang, you've turned up just at the right moment," he said. "I'm looking for a one-time German diplomat who will be acceptable to the four Allied Powers. You see, we are thinking of starting a German Consular Office in Berlin. Nadolny's name has been suggested as chief, but he will need assistants. I had thought of putting your name on the list as I'm certain neither the British nor the French will have anything against you, and probably the Russians won't object either. But I had no idea how to contact you."

"Donald, you could have put my name on the list without asking me. I'm simply longing to work on anything that may help to bring about a united Germany," I said.

"How can we keep in touch?" he asked.

It was then that I had a brainwave.

"I'll try to get back to London, then you can reach me through your wife," I told him.

My family agreed that my plan was a good one, for what better could I hope for than to hold a position in the Berlin office which would surely become the nucleus of a new United German Foreign Office? Moreover, my present job at Kiel was a mere sinecure.

The day after my meeting with Heath, I wrote to the War Office in London asking that I might be taken on again to lecture to German prisoners-of-war. I felt that this would give me a good enough reason to ask for a visa to England and at the same time apply for leave from Kiel.

It was two mounths before I heard from London, and I then asked Steltzer for indefinite leave, which he granted me without making any objections. Before I left he handed me an impressive looking document bearing the crested seal of Schleswig-Holstein that stated that Oberregierungsrat Wolfgang Gans Edler Herr zu Putlitz was appointed a civil servant for his lifetime.

CHAPTER TWENTY-NINE

BACK IN LONDON I stayed with Collie Barclay and twice a week went down to Wilton to give lectures to German prisoners on the horrors of Nazism. It was not a particularly onerous job and I rather enjoyed it. When I told my audience about the existing conditions at home, I did not beat about the bush.

Of course, I immediately contacted Louise Heath, who talked to her husband every day on the telephone. She told me that the interallied negotiations for a United German Consulate were making little progress. Then one day she broke the news to me that they had collapsed altogether, so I was faced with the prospect of returning to Kiel.

Shortly afterwards, however, I got a letter from Walter saying that he had heard a rumour that the Holstein Government had given me the sack, and since I had had no official confirmation of this, I wrote to Steltzer. In reply I received a formal letter from the Kiel Ministry of the Interior informing me that the Kiel Cabinet had unanimously decided that my status as a German official was incompatible with my dubious conduct. Apparently, this decision had been taken exactly a fortnight after my departure, when Steltzer had handed me the documents appointing me a civil servant for life!

I protested violently against such high-handed treatment but got no satisfaction. So, in the following August, I went over to Kiel. I found that Steltzer, too, had been sacked. He told me that several of my former colleagues from the Foreign Office, now released from internment camps, had told the Kiel Government certain details about my activities in Holland which had given the impression to the Government of Holstein that I had been placed in the Chancellery as a British spy. When I confronted the Kiel Government and the Home Office with this, they made endless excuses and finally said there had been a misunderstanding. I was offered my old job back but refused to accept it. In the end, we compromised. I handed in my resignation and received my salary, which had accumulated during my absence, paid up to date. So I left with several thousand marks in my pocket.

While all this was going on, Gebhard arrived in Kiel with my mother who told me that as the former owner of Laaske she had been evicted. He, too, had been told to leave Putlitz. But in Gebhard's case the governor of the district had hinted that there was some chance that the order might be rescinded, so he had put in an application and hoped that he would be allowed to stay.

My mother went to live with Walter, and Gebhard and I moved into rooms in Prince Philip's palace. As there was only one bed, Gebhard slept on the sofa, and as usual we often talked the night away. The heart trouble which had resulted from his imprisonment in Potsdam had grown worse.

"I would rather die in Putlitz than leave it for some place I don't know," he told me one night.

I suggested that he should try to find some agricultural job in the West as Walter had done. But he insisted that with his angina no-one would take him on. "No," he said, "whatever happens I shall try to stay on in Putlitz. But what about you?"

"So far as I'm concerned, it's equally hopeless whether I stay in the West or the East. I'm beginning to think that I shall have to forget Germany altogether and become British," I replied.

Gebhard agreed. If I became a British subject, he said, I could emigrate to Canada or Australia and the family could join me.

"It seems to me that Germany is finished for ever, and that

no wheat will ever grow for us again," he added pathetically.

Before he left, I presented Gebhard with a lovely wine-red pullover which Lady Vansittart had given me.

"It's bound to bring me luck!" he laughed.

As soon as he arrived back in Putlitz he was arrested.

I returned to London and had a heart-to-heart talk with Tom Allen.

"Do you remember when I arrived from Holland at the beginning of the war I told you that I would be glad to become an Englishman if Hitler won the war and I lost Germany for ever?"

Tom nodded.

"Tom, I have lost my fatherland," I told him.

I received my British passport a few weeks later and it seemed a stroke of fate that is should be dated January 13th, 1948, which was Gebhard's forty-seventh birthday. I cannot say that I felt particularly happy about it. I think from the very first I realised that I had taken a wrong step towards the solution of my problems. But at the time I could not see what else I could do.

My first journey with a British passport took me back again to Germany, for I was called to Nuremberg to appear as a witness at the War Crimes Trial which the Americans had instigated against some of the high-ranking officials of the Foreign Office. Besides Herr von Weizsäcker, Wörmann, Steengracht and others, was Gauleiter Bohle. The last, as Chief of the Nazi party organization abroad in the Foreign Office, was held responsible for the activities of some of his subordinates abroad. I was called to give evidence against Doctor Butting.

My first-class return fare was paid by the Americans and, in addition to free board and lodging, I was given a generous daily allowance in dollars. Actually, I travelled third class from London to Nuremberg and saved the difference on the fare, so that I arrived extremely flush. I was billeted in the Grand

Hotel which had been requisitioned by the Americans. Although the weather was bitterly cold, I found the place overheated. But we fed like fighting cocks.

In the Court House in the mornings we saw horrifying films of the German concentration camps, or the film specially made for Hitler, showing the execution of the victims of July 20th, whe were hauled up and down on butchers' hooks until they were strangled to death.

The large staff of assistants to the American prosecutors consisted mostly of German refugees who had suffered at the hands of the Nazis, many of whom I had known in New York during the war. The German witnesses at the trials lived apart from us in a house where some of the bosses of the Third Reich were still held in custody. Among these was the first Chief of the Gestapo, Rudolf Diels, the man who, after the Reichstag fire in 1933, had shown the foreign journalists and myself around the Alexander Platz Prison. He was now a grass widower, for he had divorced his wife, Ilse, who was a niece of Hermann Goering, and gossip had it that he was having an affair with the wife of the multi-millionaire owner of a famous pencil concern. Thanks to her, his bare room in the witness' house was comfortably furnished with good carpets. She even put her car at his disposal so that he could go for drives in the country.

In one of the anterooms of the leading American prosecutor, Doctor Kempner, a former lawyer from Berlin, I saw an old gentleman deeply absorbed in some documents. Since I thought that I recognised him I asked one of the secretaries who he was. I was told that he was the chief law expert at the Foreign Office, Gauss, who had once terrified us young attachés in the days of Stresemann. He had continued to serve Ribbentrop until the bitter end, and it was he who reshaped all the Third Reich's breaches of International Law into "incontestable" legal documents.

In addition to the trial of the Foreign Office officials, there

239

were a number of other cases still being heard at Nuremberg against war criminals, among them some of the great industrialists such as von Krupp, Flick and the bosses of IG-Farben. In one case little Franz von Papen was conducting his father's defence, and handled it so skillfully that the latter was set free.

One day I ran across Fränzschen, as he was called, on the staircase of the Court House. It was an unexpected meeting and he looked me over coldly. But as I was well supplied with American cigarettes, he decided to chat with me for a while. As he left me, I noticed that he dropped the end of his cigarette carelessly on the stone stairs. I always saved mine, as there were plently of people who were grateful for them. When I pointed this out to Fränzschen he stared at me with utter contempt. "We Germans must be careful to preserve our dignity in these small things," he said, and walked away.

One of the leading German newspapermen at the Nuremberg Trials was Hans-Georg von Studnitz, in whose house I had stayed at Rehkirchen. After a year in a concentration camp, he was now back in his old job and when he came to report my evidence, he did so with great fairness. My actual interrogation lasted less than half an hour. I stood in the witness box to the right of the judges' bench; opposite me, in the dock, were my former colleagues and seniors. The former Secretary of State, von Weizsäcker, stared blankly in front of him, and Ambassador Wörmann sat brooding gloomily. Most of them avoided looking at me. But Steengracht gave me a friendly wave which I returned. I remembered how, at the beginning of the war, on the terrace of his castle in Moyland, he had predicted the whole catastrophe. Yet he had stayed on in the Foreign Office to become Secretary of State under Ribbentrop. He had done so to please his pretty young wife who was now in Switzerland and had served divorce papers on him while he was still in his prison cell.

I was interrogated by a lawyer from Chicago who did not understand German, so I made my statement in English. But I was cross-examined by the counsel for the defence in German. He did not even attempt to refute any of the points in my statement, but devoted himself to discrediting me as someone whose word could not be believed.

"Why did you escape from Holland?" he fired at me.

"Because I thought I could serve my country better once the Nazis were beaten if my hands were not soiled with the blood of their crimes. If my former colleagues in the dock had done as I did, Germany would not be in the position that she is in to-day," I answered him.

"If you had not run away, you would perhaps be sitting with the prisoners in the dock at this very moment?"

"It is because I foresaw exactly that possibility that I was able to avoid it."

"Did you collaborate with the British?"

"I collaborated with the British just as long as I could do so as a loyal German. My purpose was to prevent the German people from finding themselves in the humiliating position in which they are now."

The battle of wits went on for quite a while, but the counsel for the defence did not get the better of me.

During my cross-examination I had to look for a paper which was in a briefcase which Lady Vansittart had given me for Christmas in 1939. She had gone to a lot of trouble to find a German Baron's crown in gold which was set above my initial. As I left the Nuremberg courtroom I noticed that this crown had fallen off. I did not bother to search the witness box for it, and so it was probably swept into the rubbish heap to share the fate of all this "thousand-year trash!"

* * *

Although I had only a small amount of money in dollars when I left Nuremberg. I did have several thousand American cigarettes which were then worth twenty marks each, so by German standards I was rich, and was able to buy clothes and other things for my mother and family.

241

With my British passport I was free to travel about Europe. For a while I thought of going to the Dominions, but, quite frankly, I dreaded the idea. While I felt in my heart that Western Europe was finished, I was loath to leave it. Once or twice I wondered whether a new world and a new Germany could be founded in the East, but for the moment, at any rate, I was not free to go there. Instead, I drifted about Europe. For a while I gave English lessons at a boarding school in the French part of Switzerland. Then I moved to Paris where I worked for a firm with the somewhat high falutin' name of "Cosmos", which exported goods of all sorts and kinds. Its directors believed that, with my former business connections in Germany, I could be useful to them, and, indeed, I did succeed in selling quite a lot of Moroccan cork to Hamburg.

In the end, I returned to London and found a job in a ship-broker's office, but I was miserably paid. After that, I went as a German tutor to a family who lived in an old and gloomy castle in Scotland which was, of course, haunted. In one way and another I led a colourful if vagabondish existence.

I decided that I was happiest in Paris. I found a highly romantic attic near the Boulevard St. Michel, from the skylight of which I could look over the roofs of the Latin Quarter and see the towers of Nôtre Dame and the delicate filigree steeple of St. Severin. When none of my rich friends asked me out to dine, I ate in a little bistro off a bare table, where the menu was chalked up on a blackboard hanging from the ceiling. The landlord stood behind the counter and his wife sweated over the sizzling pans, while their son, a successful cyclist in the Tour de France, acted as waiter. When I had nothing better to do, I sat for hours in some café on one of the boulevards aimlessly watching life go by.

But I still longed for Germany, and returned there as often as I could—even though I was now an alien. I went several times to Berlin, where I gradually lost my fear of the Eastern Sector. I began to talk to people and read their literature, until

I felt that, although it was strange to me, life there was virile and honest.

When the mutilated torso of Western Germany, calling itself the Federal German Republic, reopened the old Foreign Office, I went to Bonn. I did not offer my services to this new Republic, but I could see no reason why I should not claim from it my pension as a civil servant; a pension that had now been granted to Herr Diels and the widow of Heydrich.

I stayed at Bad Godesberg with Michel Leroy-Beaulieu's brother who had been appointed the Chief of Administration at the French Military Government's Department of Economics and Finance. I drove up to the Foreign Office with him in his official car. The man who dealt with me was a former colleague of mine, who, as had been proved at the Nuremberg trials, had signed his name to hundreds of documents sending wretched Jews to concentration camps.

He was quite polite but not very helpful. He shook his head and said: "Putlitz, you weren't forced to run away in 1939; you went of your own free will. You are still suspected of high treason, and what is more, you are a British subject. I'm afraid there's nothing we can do for you."

I was furious, and told him that even if they threw the money after me, I would not accept it.

The French High Commissioner, François-Poncet, invited me to dine with him, and drove me from his office to his residence, the little castle of Ernich, about twelve miles south on the road to Remagen. With the tricolour fluttering on the bonnet, we sped along the road behind two armed policemen on motor-cycles, and after about fifteen minutes turned past two red-white-and-blue sentry boxes before which soldiers stood stiffly to attention. François-Poncet and his wife lived in great style, and liveried footmen stood behind each of our chairs at dinner. There were only two of us besides our host and hostess.

During dinner, François-Poncet turned to me and said: "One

243

cannot be surprised that the Nazis are coming back into power if people like yourself don't stick to their guns."

I told him of my recent experience at Kiel and then said something that I do not think he liked at all. "Unfortunately it is my experience that the Allied Powers block us at every turn and leave the doors wide open for the Nazis."

My host looked annoyed when I added: "Whatever one may think of the state of affairs in the Russian Zone, so far as I can see there are no signs of a Nazi revival there."

"It's a pity," he retorted, "that all Germans who are not Nazis seem to have reddish-pink ideas."

Shortly after the Federal Republic had been formed, everyone started talking about the European Defence Union which was then supposed to be the greatest hope for a lasting peace. Within its framework, Western Germany was to be rearmed. A strong voice raised against it was that of Pastor Niemoeller.

At a family dinner party at Denham one night, Lord Vansittart started attacking Niemoeller. I was somewhat surprised, for so far as I knew he was a violent opponent of the German militarists.

"But, Van," I said, "you have always insisted that the Germans should have full larders and empty arsenals. Now you seem to be arguing in favour of rearming Germany."

He looked at me a little uncomfortably. "You're quite right, it sounds fantastic. But Soviet policy forces even people like myself into an absurd position."

Gradually it dawned on me that, in the eyes of some of the British, if I was not a Nazi then I must be a Communist of some kind with leanings towards Russia. I began to feel that I should take the plunge and turn my eyes to the East.

Meanwhile, uncertainty as to Gebhard's fate hung over me like a nightmare. I did everything in my power to discover what had happened to him, but without success. Then I found out in a most unexpected way.

I was staying in Cologne, where I had gone amongst other

things to see Willi's parents. Willi, incidentally, was by now married to an American girl. I was walking one afternoon across the square in front of the Central Station, and stopped to watch the pigeons being fed. As I did so, I noticed a man staring at me rather stupidly. Then he came up to me and said: "Am I dreaming or are you Herr von Putlitz?" Owing to the likeness between us, he had recognised me as a relation of Gebhard. In the waiting-room he told me his story. He had recently been released from an internment camp in the East, where he had shared a dormitory with Gebhard and thirty other prisoners.

"Your brother hardly ever spoke to any of us," he told me. "He spent most of the day lying in his red sweater on his plank bed just staring at the ceiling. We used to say that he was a suicide candidate, and sure enough, one day he took his life. I happened to be there when they carried him out. That is why I had such a shock when I saw you just now."

Quite numb, I wandered about the streets of Cologne and it was hours before I found myself back at my hotel.

In the summer of 1950 I happened to be in Paris, so I went to listen to the UN debates at the Palais de Chaillot. One day while I was there I saw a man whose face was familiar to me sitting with the Soviet delegates. Then I remembered that he was the former consul in New York to whom I had given my message of greeting to the National Committee of Free Germany in Moscow in 1943. I sent him my name and he invited me to luncheon with him at a restaurant in the Champs Elysées.

He was deeply distressed when he heard that I had become a British subject. "How can you possibly help your country if you are English?" he asked. "It's a bad thing to renounce your country; you will never be happy that way."

I suddenly felt ashamed and told him about Gebhard. He listened with sympathy and then said: "I don't like talking about my personal affairs, but I have lost two brothers, both as prisoners of war in Germany. One of them we shall never know

245

about. The other we heard of through a friend who was with him when he died. They were in a prison camp near Stettin, and they had to march two miles to their work and back every day. The work was hard and they were half starved and so many of them were too weak to walk. One day my brother couldn't go any further and on the way home lay down in a ditch. The whole column was halted, and his friends saw one of the German guards draw his revolver and shoot my brother through the head."

I felt my heart pounding as I listened to this story.

The Consul went on: "We can't undo the frightful things that have happened. All that we can do is to see that such things never happen again. We must work for an understanding between nations. If we succeed in promoting a permanent friendship between the Soviet and the German people, we shall have founded a strong alliance for world peace. But you won't be in a position to help now that you are British."

I went away and thought over what he had said, and suddenly I made up my mind to go to the East. I went to Berlin and called at the Ministry of Foreign Affairs of the German Democratic Republic. Everything was against me. They did not trust my intentions, and I could scarcely blame them. But my mind was made up. So, having been turned down by the Germans, I went to the Russians. They, too, refused to help me. But I went back again and again until the Consul at last promised me that he would examine my case. The investigation took months and in the meantime I went back to London.

CHAPTER THIRTY

IN LONDON I ran once again into one of the most controversial characters in the history of modern England—Guy Burgess. I had known him on and off for twenty-five years. We had first met in 1932 at a party at Cambridge, where he was then an undergraduate. I was, I remember, immediately fascinated by him, for he was one of the first young Englishmen of good family I had ever met who seemed really to have made a study of Marxism and who frankly and brilliantly claimed definite left-wing ideals. In the general chatter of trivial conversation, I listened with interest to what he had to say.

Later, between 1934 and 1938, when I was at the German Embassy, I met Guy on various occasions, and, as often as we met, I found him not only amusing but out of the ordinary. It would be an exaggeration to say that our casual acquaintance developed at that time into a close friendship. Indeed, I should think that he looked upon me with a certain amount of suspicion for, as a member of the German Embassy, he probably thought of me as a representative of the Nazi régime which he both hated and despised. He never revealed to me the true depths of his political opinions, and I was quite unable to make out whether his "reddish" views were sincere or whether he voiced them merely to shock his listeners. Nor was I careless enough to let him know that my anti-Nazism was anything more than mere grumbling about Hitler such as could be heard from almost every German in London at that time. In fact, our relations were so vague that I did not even know what was his official position or what he actually did for a living during those pre-war years.

We became closer friends, however, after I returned to London from Holland, when, as a "refugee", there could be no further doubt about my genuine hatred for Hitler and the Nazis. At that time Guy was working with the BBC and, I think, also with the British Intelligence. Like myself, he was appalled by the lethargy and lack of fighting spirit which, during the phoney war, characterised the Chamberlain régime. He was violently pro-Churchill long before the majority of Englishmen appreciated the true qualities of their great war leader. In all such matters Guy and I understood each other extremely well and were in complete agreement. Besides, I owed him a debt of gratitude for the trouble he took on my behalf and the many personal kindnesses he rendered me in order to make life easier at a time when my position as a "friendly enemy alien" was far from comfortable.

In those days we met mostly at the Travellers' or the Reform Club, in Pall Mall, to both of which Guy belonged. I felt he had a genuine regard for me, but was amused when he rather flamboyantly introduced me by saying: "'May I present one of the most courageous men in Europe, who threw away everything he had in the world and came over here with nothing but a suitcase to fight for his ideals.'' *

While I was at Bletchley Junction, Guy invited me on several occasions to spend the weekend with him in London. He then lived in a flat in Lord Rothschild's house near Regent's Park, where several of his friends also had flats. There I got to know him much more intimately.

It is true, as the popular press has never tired of stating, that he consumed an enormous amount of whisky and gin. But I never saw him completely drunk. In fact, the more he drank, the

---

* His recollections of my story must have became somewhat blurred by time—at least as set down by Tom Driberg in his recent book.

wittier his conversation became and the more brilliant his ideas. I sincerely believe that he needed drink to assuage the many conflicts which were waging within him. It is also true that he was wildly untidy and careless about his personal appearance. His fingernails and clothes were never quite clean. Once, when sharing his cupboard, I discovered in it an unforgettable pair of trousers. They were covered in grease spots and had two quite incredible holes in them. It was impossible to tell whether these holes were due to old age, moths, cigarette burns or to some accident. Naturally, I never had the nerve to ask Guy about this truly remarkable pair of trousers.

The last time I saw him must have been in 1949 or 1950, just before he left for America to take up his post at the British Embassy in Washington. He invited me to his farewell party at the flat in which he was then living in Bond Street. He had many friends and was certainly very popular at that time.

I remember that among other guests at that party was the then Minister of State for Foreign Affairs, Hector McNeil, as well as several other high officials of the Foreign Office and members of the Intelligence Service. It was a very gay party, and, to say the least, everyone drank to Guy's success in his new job.

I do not pretend to know what were the ultimate motives which finally made him take his sensational step in 1951. But I do know from the way he talked to me during the war years and later that he felt a deep and sincere admiration for the gallant fight which the Russians had put up against Hitler's invading hordes. I also know that after the war he became more and more disgusted and horrified at his Foreign Office's weak-kneed attitude, which he considered was leading his country into a final and total dependency upon the United States. Such views I myself shared, and they contributed largely to my own decision to go East in 1952. Yet he must have had other and even stronger reasons for doing what he did, for it is certainly a hundred times more difficult to transplant oneself into an entirely strange land than to return, as I did, to my own country. Whatever his incentive may have been, I cannot but admire his courage. He, too, left everything behind him that he loved and possessed in order to follow the ideals in which he believed. He alone has to bear the consequences, and nobody has, in my opinion, the right to judge him.

I only trust that he can maintain the moral strength to master the difficult existence which he has chosen, and that Russian vodka will give him as much pleasure as did his native whisky. I sincerely hope, too, that the day will come when he will be able to set foot again in his beloved England and prove to himself, as well as to his countrymen, that he did everything in his power to serve her well and honestly.

CHAPTER THIRTY-ONE

MY ENTRY VISA for the German Democratic Republic arrived at last.

To cross the frontier and pass behind the "Iron Curtain" I did not have to run any dangerous risks. I merely took a ticket at the Zoo Station and crossed the Spree on the S-Bahn railway, for the Spree between the Lehrter Station and the Friedrich-strasse Station forms the border between the East and West sectors of Berlin.

My destination was Bad Saarow on Lake Scharmützel, where I was to stay with my mother's eighty-year-old sister, my only close relation still living in our ancestral homeland. By marriage she bore the name of "Zieten", famous in Prussian history as that of Frederick the Great's foremost cavalry general in the Seven Years' War, the great-great-uncle of her late husband.

My aunt's husband was a veteran of the war of 1870, and when he died was a colonel on the General Staff in the First World War. Since then she had lived with her daughter, who was a school teacher, in Saarow Spa. Their little house there was all that they had managed to save during the Inflation years. In 1945 there was heavy fighting around the property as a fanatical SS-commander had tried to hold a corner of a wood next to it. The garden walls and the trees were pitted with shell splinters, but the house itself was practically undamaged.

I arrived on a snowy January day in 1952 carrying all that I possessed in the world in two suitcases. My aunt, having seen me from her window, came hobbling down to the front door on

251

her sticks to let me in. Although it was fourteen years since I had last seen her, I felt as if it were only yesterday.

Now my wanderings were over and once more there was a friendly and familiar roof over my head. For the first time for years I filled my lungs with the scent of the pine-woods of the Brandenburg Mark.

I had been at Saarow ten days when, one morning, a car bearing a Berlin number plate drew up outside the little house. Out of it climbed a major of the People's Police. He told me that he had come to bring me my identity card, and I invited him in. My aunt quickly hid the torn bedspread she was mending and we sat down with her at the table. She fished out her fountain pen from her work basket and handed it to me so that I could sign my name on the document. The young major looked on with an amused smile. He had a clean-cut, intelligent face and spoke with a Berlin cockney accent. As he gave me the signed document, he shook me warmly by the hand and welcome me as a new citizen of the German Democratic Republic.

After a good deal of fumbling, my aunt took a key from her bag. It belonged to the large carved linen cupboard where she kept her precious bottles. I drew the cork of one of them and filled three glasses. Then we clinked glasses: the widow of an old colonel of the Emperor's Army, a young officer of the People's Police and I, a former Guard's officer of pre-revolution days, now fifty years old, who, after years of wandering, had at last returned to his own country.

We drank a toast to the reunion of our native land and a better and more peaceful world.